Why Marriage Matters

Why Marriage Matters
Reasons to Believe in Marriage in Postmodern Society

Glenn T. Stanton

P.O. Box 35007, Colorado Springs, Colorado 80935

Library of Congress Catalog Card Number: 97-17776
ISBN 1-57683-018-7

Cover photo: Superstock

Some of the anecdotal illustrations in this book are true to life and are included with the permission of the persons involved. All other illustrations are composites of real situations, and any resemblance to people living or dead is coincidental.

Stanton, Glenn T., 1962-
    Why marriage matters : reasons to believe in marriage in postmodern society / Glenn T. Stanton.
        p.   cm.
    Includes bibliographical references and index.
    ISBN 1-57683-018-7
    1. Marriage—United States. 2. Family—United States.
    3. Sex customs—United States. 4. United States—Social conditions—1980- 5. United State—Moral conditions.
    I. Title.
HQ536.S724   1997
306.85'0973—dc21   97-17776
                                                              CIP

Printed in the United States of America

1 2 3 4 5 6 7 8 9 10 / 99 98 97

TO MY PRECIOUS WIFE,

who makes my life rich. I love you dearly, Jacqueline.

And to my miraculous children: Olivia Glenn, who has shown me how to love in a whole new way; Reed Schaeffer and Sophia Grace, our lovely newborn twins, who fill our lives with much busyness and immense joy.

You have all blessed my life beyond measure and consistently demonstrate the wonder and magic of family.

For this cause a man shall leave his father and his mother, and shall cleave to his wife; and they shall become one flesh.

Genesis 2:24

Contents

Preface

The thesis of this book is simple: *First-time, lifelong, monogamous marriage is the relationship that best provides for the most favorable exercise of human sexuality, the overall well-being of adults, and the proper socialization of children.* Marriage has no close rival. It stands independently above any other option: singleness, cohabitation, divorce, and remarriage. I intend to prove this by drawing from the massive body of empirical social science data collected by researchers over the span of the twentieth century.

However, I also want to be clear about what this book is *not* saying! First, it is not saying that people in other situations cannot enjoy happy, healthy, fulfilling lives and that their children cannot prosper. Single, cohabiting, divorced, and remarried people can, in fact, live well-balanced, highly successful lives. I have observed this among my own friends and acquaintances. Rather, I am saying that those who are not in first-time, lifelong, monogamous marriages *are not as likely* to score as high in measurements of well-being as those who are in their first marriage. This distinction is vitally important as we look at how the healthy relationships fostered by first-time marriage affect large populations.

Second, I am not saying that the other options to marriage are equal in their *inability* to provide good and helpful things to adults, children, and society. The research does show, however, that they all rank below marriage in varying degrees. For example, the data[1] shows that singleness is superior to cohabitation and divorce. In fact, it ranks very close to marriage in many measures, yet, below it in ability to provide for overall welfare.

Third, I am not arguing for a return to some nostalgic "June and Ward Cleaver" picture of family life. This lazy assumption is often made whenever there is a call for a return to strong marriages and families. Men and women simply do not relate to each other the way they did forty years ago, and I'm not necessarily suggesting a return to that era. Rather, I'm calling for a return to the ideal that the marriage commitment be worked at and honored. I'm arguing for a return to the ideal where children can count on their mom and dad being present in the same home, where family members and friends expect us to hang in there and make our marriage relationships work.

Whether this takes place in a traditional home with two parents, 2.3 children, and a dog, or in an extended family with the grandma and grandpa living in the basement bedroom is not significant. What matters is that lifelong marriage is the foundation for family life. As we'll see, the perceived "bondage" of this historic and honorable institution is not as damaging to all involved as is the "freedom" of our present ethos.

Fourth, I am not implying (and it would be wrong to conclude from the data) that people should find a mate quick and rush down the aisle because of marriage's benefits. Instead, we should have a realistic idea of the measurable benefits marriage provides, and this knowledge should inform our appraisal of marriage.

Fifth, I am certainly not saying that people who are in physically or psychologically abusive marriages should stay in them because the option of divorce is troublesome. Of course, the dangers of a truly abusive marriage clearly overshadow the benefits of marriage.

Finally, I am not arguing against individuals but ideas. I am certainly not arguing against unmarried individuals; I want to argue against the idea that marriage is superfluous or merely equal to all other relational options. Perhaps better than arguing against anything, it might be best to conclude that I am arguing *for* the ideal of lifelong marriage. *Most simply put, I present this research to prove that good and compelling reasons exist for our culture once again to esteem first-time, lifelong, monogamous marriage as a more valuable lifestyle option than others.*

Acknowledgments

A series of television commercials recently aired by a soft-drink company shows young men in extreme sporting activities. Some bungee-jump off suspension bridges. Others dive out of airplanes, releasing their parachutes at the last minute. A few ride their mountain bikes at incredibly high speeds over rough terrain. The message is clear: These young men are fully engaged and living life to its fullest. They are involved in what existentialists call "life-authenticating" actions.

However, these young daredevils are only fooling themselves—they've not even approached the envelope of extreme. This level is exclusively the domain of the family man. He alone lives life on the edge, in what Chesterton called, "The Wildness of Domesticity."[2] I like this description by French poet Charles Péguy:

> Family life is the most "engaged" life in the world. There is only one adventurer in the world, as can be seen very clearly in the modern world: the father of a family. Even the most desperate adventurers are nothing compared with him. Everything in the modern world . . . is organized against that fool, that imprudent, daring fool . . . against the man who is daring enough to have a wife and family, against the man who dares to found a family. Everything is against him. Savagely organized against him.[3]

This describes so clearly how I feel about family life, and yet no other life could coax me from it! It is intoxicating, yet sobering.

13

Confining, yet freeing. Demanding, yet rewarding. For the man who wants to make the whole exploit still more interesting, try writing a book in the midst of it all!

The really astonishing thing for me is that I completed this book without taking any significant time away from my family. (However, I did finish the bulk of it just days before our twins arrived—a very good thing!) I was astounded at how much I could accomplish during naptime and late in the evening when everyone else was asleep. And when business took me away from home, I found it imperative to redeem those lonely but quiet nighttime hours at hotels with a few uninterrupted hours of writing. (Therefore, my apologies to friends around the country for all the rejected dinner invitations. And I'll admit here to accepting one invitation to go see a baseball game at historic Tigers Stadium in Michigan. It was well worth the missed work time. Thanks, Larry and Brian.)

However, like most mortal authors, I could not have researched and written this book alone. There is an old proverb that says, "It takes a village to write a book." Therefore, I owe a deep debt to a number of people.

To my wife, Jackie, thank you for tolerating this other passion that dominated so much of our conversation. John Perrodin, this book never would have happened without your encouragement. Thank you, friend. Reed Bell, your faith, ideas, and intellectual stimulation were foundational. It was our conversations on family that developed the direction of this project. To Tim Doyle and Mike Ebert, two good husbands, fathers, and men who listened while I thought out loud and offered a great deal of advice and encouragement. Jeanie Crooks, thanks for continually asking, "How's the book going?" and for providing a helpful review from an important perspective.

I owe an immense debt to David Blankenhorn, who was always willing to answer my many questions. You have provided me with an invaluable education through your writings and our conversations. I have great respect for you and commend you for your keen mind, strong conviction, and generous spirit. To David Popenoe, a firstrate scholar, thank you for introducing me to other thinkers and their work. You had the patience to listen and always seemed to have just the answer I was looking for. You have given me a good education. To Brad Wilcox, thanks for the early introductions to some rich resources. To Chris Check and Bryce Christensen at the Rockford Institute, your prodigious work of collecting and cataloguing research on the family made my work easier and the content of this book more comprehensive. Of course, any shortcomings or oversights are my own.

To Joanne and Toben Heim, who believed in this project and helped a first-time author "come in out of the cold" and find a home for his book, again, thank you. And finally, to my very talented editor, Brad Lewis, thank you for your skill, graciousness, and high degree of professionalism.

Many thanks to Bill Malonee, Bob Dylan, David Byrne, Gene Eugene, Elvis "Everyday I write the book" Costello, and Big Head Todd for keeping me company during long, lonely hours of research and writing. Your contributions made the process much more enjoyable.

God, who comes to us as Father, thank You for the precious gift of marriage and the wonder of family. May You use this book to serve, in some small way, to aid its recovery.

Prologue
The End of Marriage?

☐

Broken words, never meant to be spoken,
Everything is broken.

BOB DYLAN, "EVERYTHING IS BROKEN"

BROKEN HOMES.

Once upon a time, this was the only phrase in our nation's lexicon used to refer to a nontraditional family. Today, however, as families break down at extraordinary rates, and as fewer families bother to form in the first place—at least in the traditional sense of being formed on the foundation of marriage— "broken homes" is not the only pathology plaguing family life at the turn of the twenty-first century. *For the first time in our nation's history, a child living in a single-parent family is just as likely to be living with a never-married parent as with a divorced parent.*[1]

"The family in the Western world has been radically altered—some claim almost destroyed—by events of the last three decades," asserts Nobel Laureate Gary Becker in the first line of his celebrated *A Treatise on the Family.*[2] The face of family life in America has indeed undergone a radical transformation. We have become a nation of family relativists, with no clear and common idea of what family relationships ought to look like. We are willing to accept any configuration that presents itself in sincerity. This leaves us with no common script for family life. We have grown accustomed to allowing the players to cast their own roles and write their own lines according to their personal desires. Radical self-autonomy is now our defining virtue. We owe no one anything except to be true to ourselves.

We have also become a nation of family minimalists. We don't have much of a criterion. Love (we're not quite sure what it is, but we know it when we see it) is the only requirement we have for calling any configuration of people a family. Any ingredient beyond this is superfluous and to insist on one would be "narrow-minded" and make us look unfashionably like moralizers. As a consequence, the idea of marriage is dying, and everything is broken.

Of all the social problems facing American civilization, the decline of marriage and the breakup of the family is unquestionably our most pressing problem. Its impact is widespread and comprehensively destructive, as this book will illustrate in great detail. It is the common denominator driving other social ills. But it is also the one social problem that touches our lives most directly.

Think about the children living in your neighborhood. *What social pathology touches these young lives more directly than the fact that their mothers are no longer, or never were, married to their fathers?*

I live in what most would consider a typical middle-class neighborhood where good people work various shifts in white-collar jobs, seeking to raise their children in the best way they know how. My two-year-old daughter, Olivia, is captivated by the seven or so older preschool girls who live nearby and love to mother our little treasure. Of all these little playmates I watch out of my back door, only one of them lives in a home with a married mother and father present—and this is a family that recently immigrated from Poland. The other girls live either with grandparents, divorced mothers, cohabiting mothers, or never-married mothers. Marriage is not well represented in my suburban neighborhood.

While I was hustling my way through college and graduate school, my wife supported us by working as a kindergarten teacher for five years. Over those years, she taught in a variety of settings—

18

rural, suburban, and urban schools—in what many call the Bible Belt of the United States. Her experience over the years in these demographically diverse schools was that, at best, 33 percent, and at worst, 10 percent of her students in any given year lived with both biological parents. Marriage was not alive and well in any of Jackie's classrooms! Can you name another social problem that reaches into more homes and affects more young lives as directly and as deeply as the demise of marriage? I can't in our neighborhood. Jackie couldn't in her classrooms. What about the families that live on your street?

Granted, while personal experience might lend itself to a stark illustration, it is anecdotal and perhaps not the most dependable reflection of the actual state of the family. However, the U.S. Census Bureau recently released an extensive report offering a historical perspective on the state of marriage in America over the years 1970 through 1994. The Census data does not provide much encouragement over my personal observations.[3] In fact, it offers no good news regarding the health of marriage in America. If you observe all of the positive marriage and family indicators, such as rates of

- first-time marrieds,
- children born to married mothers,
- children living with two parents,
- family size and overall fertility rate,

all the trend lines have been moving in a negative direction over the past three decades.

If you examine all of the negative family indicators, such as the trend toward

- never-marrieds,
- divorce,
- cohabitation,
- children born to and living with unmarried mothers,

all the trend lines are moving in an upward direction. This means the bad news has been mounting slowly but steadily. Most alarming, these developments have failed to move us in any dramatic way.

TABLE 1
Percentage of All People Over 18 Years of Age Who Are Divorced

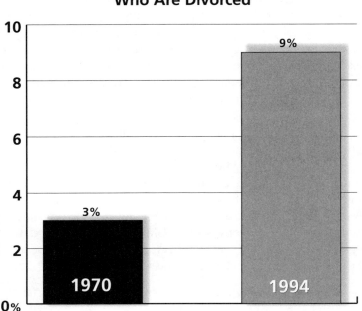

In the past, divorce was the primary engine driving family breakdown, and it still serves as a major cause. The Census Bureau explains, "the fastest growing marital-status category [over this twenty-five-year period] was divorced persons. The number [of] currently divorced adults quadrupled from 4.3 million in 1970 to 17.4 million in 1994."[4] Professor Lawrence Stone, a distinguished family historian from Princeton University, offers an historical perspective on recent divorce trends. He explains: "The scale of marital breakdowns in the West since 1960 has no historical precedent that I know of. There has been nothing like it for the last 2,000 years, and probably longer."[5] Looking at these numbers in light of overall population growth doesn't improve the picture much, as table 1 reveals.[6]

But this high divorce rate represents a group of people who most likely had some appreciation for marriage and its prospects.

While the breakdown of their marriage is tragic, at least they gave it a go. What is more troubling is the rapidly growing proportion of people who have grown cynical of this institution and who are cautious to enter it.

People today are slower and more reluctant to enter marriage than they were in 1970. Table 2 shows that this is true for both men and women.[7]

TABLE 2
Median Age at First Marriage

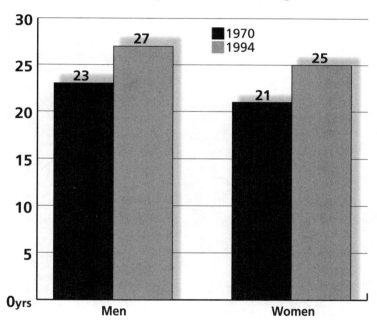

More troubling still is that increasing numbers of people are not even bothering with marriage at all. While 72 percent of all adults were married in 1970, that number had decreased to 61 percent in 1994.[8] Conversely, the number of adults who never married has increased sharply since 1970 (see Table 3 on next page).[9]

The Census Bureau explains that "never marrieds" are "one of the fastest growing segments of the adult population."[10] But this mushrooming "never married" population is not necessarily a result of people having trouble finding a mate. Many people are finding mates and simply setting up house without making that trip down the aisle. What used to be stigmatized and judged as "living in sin" has now gained social respectability and is now called cohabitation. This domestic configuration has also seen a bionic jump (see Table 4).[11]

TABLE 3
Percentage of People Over 18 Years of Age Who Never Married

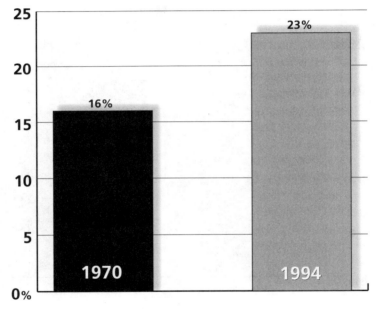

In addition, the number of cohabiting couples with children living in the home has increased nearly 550 percent from 1970 to 1994.[12] Children are present in 40 percent of cohabiting unions,[13] and estimates from the National Survey of Families and Households (NSFH) indicate that 27 percent of all nonmarital births between 1970 and 1984 were to cohabiting couples.[14] This is contrary to the stereotype that cohabitation exists primarily among college students who are in transitional periods of their lives. Instead, it has gained a prominent role on the American domestic stage of family life.

This brings us to another category: How the retreat from marriage affects the living arrangements of children. Table 5 (next page) shows that children are much more likely to be living with one parent today than they were two decades ago.[15]

TABLE 4
Unmarried Cohabitating Couples Per 100 Married Couples

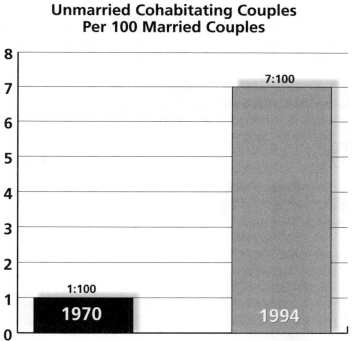

(Incidentally, those single-parent families created through the death of a parent have remained stable and low.)[16]

But again, the surprising story is what kind of single-parent families children find themselves in. Again marriage doesn't fare well. Single-parent families due to separation while the marriage is legally intact have declined over the last twenty-five years. Single-parent families where the marriage has completely died have steadily increased. However, the most dramatic growth is among homes where a marriage never existed in the first place (see Table 6). As distinguished Rutgers University sociologist David Popenoe observes and bemoans, "In the past several decades, the divorce rate has doubled and the percentage of unwed births has quintupled."[17] Larry Bumpass, a noted demographer from the University of Wisconsin–Madison, explains that currently, almost one out of every three children is now born to unmarried mothers.[18] An unprecedented number of parents are seeing no need to secure a marriage certificate before a birth certificate. When the percentages of one-and two-parent families is compared, the Census Bureau data shows that two-parent families have declined by 18 percent and one-parent homes grew by 127 percent since 1970![19]

TABLE 5
Living Arrangements of Children Under 18 Years: All Races

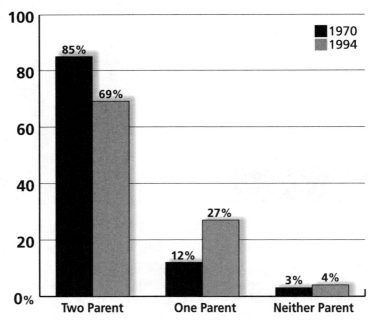

The skyrocketing divorce rates and the rates of births outside of marriage take on new significance when considered along with the overall widowhood rate which has actually *declined* a few percentage points since 1970.[20] *This data hits us squarely in the face with the fact that the end of a marriage and the creation of single-parent families is something we do to ourselves by choice— and it's a choice we're making more and more often.* But it also gives us the hope that we can do something about it . . . if we will only choose to.

TABLE 6
Living Arrangements of Children
In One-Parent Households

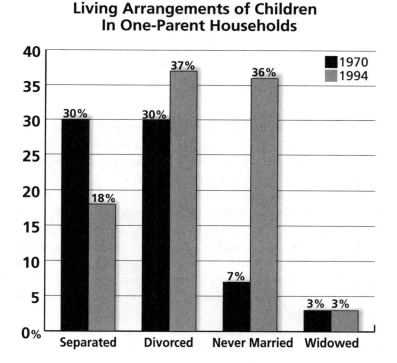

The distinguished demographer Kingsley Davis correctly laments that at "no time in history, with the possible exception of Imperial Rome, has the institution of marriage been more problematic than it is today."[21] Demographers Frances K. Goldscheider and Linda J. Waite conclude that such radical changes in the status of marriage and the family have taken America down a road with only two distinct options: either we will have "new families"

or "no families."[22] Historians Steven Mintz and Susan Kellogg, in their excellent social history of the American family, *Domestic Revolutions*, explain that today "the United States is a society without a clear unitary set of family ideals and values." This development has left "many Americans . . . groping for a new paradigm of American family life, but in the meantime a profound sense of confusion and ambivalence reigns."[23]

Christopher Lasch asserts this spirit of disorientation about the family is not a recent development. "In fact," Lasch explains, "the family has been slowly coming apart for more than a hundred years."[24] The problem is merely becoming more pronounced and impossible to ignore. If left unchecked, it will certainly lead to a disastrous end.

VIRGIL, TEXAS, IS AMERICA

David Byrne, part-time social analyst, cultural philosopher, and former full-time leader of the musical group The Talking Heads, made a film a number of years ago entitled *True Stories*. It is part documentary, part music video, part surrealistic comedy, but largely a clever social commentary about life in postmodern culture. Byrne shows implicitly, but in striking fashion, how American postmodernism has lost some essential ideals: objective truth in life and religion, the sanctity of the home and family, aesthetic objectivity, and a deeper context for the story of our lives. However, one of the overarching themes of the film is how postmodern culture has lost the ideal of marriage.

This is illustrated in the life of the film's main character, Louis Fine (played by John Goodman). Louis is an amiable personality who works by day in the "clean room" at Varicorp, a large computer manufacturer and leading industry in the fictitious town of Virgil, Texas. In stark contrast to his friends and colleagues, Louis's job is not his life. His values and dreams lie elsewhere, someplace deeper, making him a bit of a local oddity. In the introductory interview with Louis, he explains his dream, "I love the women, but I'm not a swinger, not Louis." Commenting further: "I want to settle down and share my life. You see, marriage is a natural thing and I am a natural man. I want someone to share my life." The film's main interest in Louis is his aggressive, but desperately unsuccessful, search for a woman to settle down with and call his wife.

After trying dating services (they set him up with a midget), singles bars (the women aren't serious), some sporty new athletic shoes (in spite of his heftiness, Louis, as he confesses, is "very aware of his appearance"), and a host of other possibilities, Louis has not realized his dream of finding a wife. Everyone he dates is either unable or unwilling to make the kind of commitment marriage requires. No one is interested. The values of these women lie elsewhere. This leads him to take a drastic step.

Despondent in his search, Louis becomes emotionally transparent to the people of Virgil and shares his dream in a cheesy, self-produced television commercial, which he runs on local television. In all his desperation, humility, and vulnerability, he offers this straightforward message:

> Hello. I'm Louis Fine and I am looking for matrimony with a capital "M." I believe in the joys and contentment of matrimony. Now, my chances in this world of printing a new diet book every month may not be that good. I'm looking for someone to accept me for what I am. I'm six foot, three inches tall and maintain a very consistent panda bear shape. I'm pleased with the way God made me; I wouldn't change a thing. I'm willing to share. Won't you please call this number—844-WIFE? Please call! Serious inquiries only.

The movie culminates with a scene of Louis's wedding. He finally finds a wife, but the nuptials are not anything to celebrate. The idea of marriage is so foreign to the citizens of Virgil that Louis must make a major concession in order to find wedded bliss, a compromise he is obviously willing to make. He marries a woman who is very well-off and has a beautiful home complete with a staff of housekeepers. There is one catch though . . . she lives in her bed. Though she is perfectly healthy, she never leaves her bed. As filmmaker Byrne narrates, "Why should she? She has so much money, she doesn't have to." The ceremony is performed in her bed and the happy couple stays right there for their honeymoon. Of course, it's a weird conclusion. But it is also what makes the film fun and helps illustrate an important message that few understand.

Louis represents the values of another age. He is looking for lifelong commitment, an intimate, meaningful, and soulful connection with one woman. His contemporaries are all involved in self-indulgence. Each is so self-absorbed that by comparison, Louis seems a bit freakish. In the end, Louis is forced to make serious compromises to see at least a part of his dreams fulfilled.

Byrne's assessment of postmodern American culture fits with the data we have observed. People today are either skeptical or uninterested in the ideal of marriage. Virgil, Texas, is a microcosm of America. Louis Fine is just as likely to find himself an oddity in your hometown as he is in Virgil. As I've said, this is certainly true in my neighborhood.

But is this development really a loss, or is marriage merely an anachronism? Could it be time to admit that traditional marriage might have run its course? Might social evolution demand we move on to discover a better way of ordering our domestic and sexual lives and the way we raise our children? Does marriage matter? This is the question we will explore.

ORDER OF THE BOOK

Chesterton says that the family is a great mansion with many rooms, all serving diverse but glorious purposes. Sex, explains Chesterton, is the gate leading up to this house. Therefore, it is proper for any discussion of marriage and the family to begin at the gate. Chapter one opens the book with a discussion of the proper expression of sexual intercourse and why people receive more pleasure, and societies are stronger, when sexual expression is regulated and confined to the institution of marriage.

Chapter two examines the consequences of establishing domestic relationships before marriage. Does cohabitation serve as an effective testing ground for marriage? Can it help to ensure that domestic relationships among men and women are safer and more equitable? We shall see that cohabitation, regardless of indicator, has failed as a substitute or preparation for marriage.

Next, we see how marriage benefits adults in *every* measure of well-being. Chapter three details how research demonstrates that people who are married, as a rule, enjoy significantly elevated levels of physical and mental well-being, and how their recoveries from serious illnesses are more successful than people of any other marital status. First-time marrieds also find greater satisfaction in their work, are less likely to miss work, report a higher level of self-defined happiness, and are more likely to have a wide variety and high number of fulfilling relationships.

The next logical step is to explore how children benefit when they live with their married biological parents. In the past few short years, our society has undergone a significant shift in thinking about the nature of family.[25] This is illustrated in a recent *Newsweek* editorial about another successful, high-powered woman who became a mom without the assistance of a husband. The publication, while congratulating the nouveau Madonna with child, refreshingly moralizes that all she needs now is to get married. In this secular sermon, Jonathan Alter explains that marriage is "more than a piece of paper. It's a measure of the commitment necessary to properly shepherd children toward adulthood." He offers a solution for the growing problem of illegitimacy: "a little stigma directed at errant role models wouldn't hurt."[26] *Stigma* certainly wasn't a word fashionably uttered in association with out-of-wedlock child-bearing five years ago. The times they are a-changin'.

Chapter four, then, discusses why children are more likely to excel in all areas of life if they live in a home with a married mother and father. We also find that parents do better as parents if they have the help of a spouse.

Following that, in chapter five we find that it is not just marriage that matters but *first-time marriage* that provides incalculable benefits for adults and children. The most well-respected and authoritative research indicates that divorce is not a victimless event. Rather, the vision of an easy, painless divorce is an illusion. Adults and children suffer long and hard in the wake of a marriage that dies. What's more, the benefits of marriage—especially the benefits the marriage relationship offers for children—cannot be regained through remarriage. Once a first-time marriage dies, so does the possibility of reaping the comprehensive benefits marriage affords. We'll see that sociologists and psychologists are telling us that the stepfamily is the most troubled form of family life.

All of the data presented in this book points to one conclusion: Lifelong, monogamous marriage matters, and matters deeply, in the lives of adults, children, and societies. Given this conclusion, and in light of what we have just seen by way of the demographics on marriage, we are left with one important question: How do we regain a culture of marriage? The epilogue will address this question and explore ideas for developing policies and attitudes that serve to recover a culture that has an appreciation for and a commitment to the invaluable institution of marriage.

One of the first moves in restoring a marriage culture is to assure that as many people as possible hear the message and understand how completely marriage matters. They must understand that losing the idea and institution of marriage in our culture means so much more than fewer people having joyous and grand ceremonies and living "happily ever after" in some magical wedded bliss.

Instead, it means the loss of the most effective mechanism for regulating sexual behavior. It means the loss of the best way of providing for the personal well-being of adults. It means the loss of the only environment to provide for the proper socialization of children.

Just as pre-Socratic atomists Thales, Anaximander, and Anaximenes understood that the physical world must be made of one irreducible element, Aristotle understood that human culture is also made of one irreducible element: the family held together by marriage. In his *Politics* he explains:

> In the first place there must be a union of those who cannot exist without each other; for example, of male and female, that the race may continue. . . . Out of these two relationships, between man and woman, master and slave, the family first arises, and Hesiod is right when he says, "First house and wife and an ox for the plow," . . . The family is the association established by nature for the supply of man's everyday wants, and the members of it are called by Charondas "companions of the cupboard," and by Epimenides the Cretan, "companions of the manger." But when several families are united, and the association aims at something more than the supply of daily needs, then comes into existence the village.[27]

The Milesian philosophers were wrong with the specific basic element but correct with their theory. Aristotle was right on both. What the atom is to the physical environment, marriage is to human culture. It is the one irreducible building block of the *polis*. Without using hyperbole, losing the ideal of marriage means nothing less than the loss of the instrument that provides for the perpetuation of civilization.

David Popenoe explains it this way:

> If the family trends of recent decades are extended into the future, the result will be not only growing uncertainty within marriage, but the gradual elimination of marriage in favor of casual liaisons oriented to adult expressiveness and self-fulfillment. The problem with this scenario is that children will be harmed, adults will probably be no happier, and the social order could collapse.[28]

This book will show, in great and sometimes disturbing detail, how true and troubling Professor Popenoe's forecast is.

ONE

A Time for Every Purpose:

Rediscovering the Need for a Sexual Ethic

□

The monstrosity of sexual intercourse outside of marriage is that those who indulge in it are trying to isolate one kind of union (the sexual) from all the other kinds of union which were intended to go along with it and make up the total union.

C. S. LEWIS, MERE CHRISTIANITY

THE 1960s, THE PERIOD OF AMERICAN HISTORY TYPICALLY referred to as the beginning of the "sexual revolution," ushered in the great divorce between the exercise of sexuality and the institution of marriage. Society seemed to be claiming that the two no longer needed one another.

This new belief manifested itself in all aspects of popular culture. For example, Grossinger's Catskill Mountains resort gave the country its first singles-only getaway weekend in 1962. At the same time, the state of Illinois became the first to decriminalize all forms of consensual private sex between adults. In 1964, the first singles bars opened on New York's Upper East Side. These created the opportunity for adults to participate in a socially approved marketplace of untethered sexuality.

Also in the 1960s, the topless bathing suit was introduced, and waitresses and dancers became unencumbered from the waist up.

The revolutionary Broadway musical *Hair* introduced nudity to the cultured stage, and Woodstock introduced it to the outdoor music festival. Colleges and universities around the country began abolishing curfews and lifting visitation regulations in dormitories.[1]

All of these changes facilitated the formation and maintenance of active sexual relationships outside of marriage. This validation of the sexual revolution gave the revolutionaries high hopes.

The sexual revolution was supposed to set sex and its participants free. Instead, this important dimension of the human relationship called sexuality was seriously impaired in the failed overthrow. As one college student concluded, "The sexual revolution is over and everyone lost."[2]

Reformers proposed that the sexual revolution would relieve the repression that a "Victorian" population was suffering under. Instead, the revolution proved itself oppressive. As a result, the idea of a fulfilling sex life is more elusive to more people than ever before. As we shall see, monogamous individuals committed to one lifetime partner are the most physically and emotionally satisfied people sexually. In addition, societies throughout history that adhere to strict codes of monogamy benefit from the highest levels of social energy. Having lived through the sexual revolution, we've discovered that a consistent code of sexual monogamy is the best ideal for our society, as well as for individuals and families.

However, before we begin to discuss how the sexual revolution and its philosophy of sexual freedom has failed us, it's important to look at recent American history and understand just where and when the sexual revolution got its start.

BEGINNING OF THE SEXUAL REVOLUTION

The American sexual revolution finds its conception long before the tumultuous social upheaval of the 1960s. It started in the closing days of the nineteenth century. *Fin-de-siècle* America was a culture with a new appreciation of and interest in sexuality. As St. Louis *Mirror* editor William Marion Reedy declared as our nation entered the twentieth century, it was "Sex O'Clock in America."[3] One of the most noted historians of this period in America explains that by this time, America had "become obsessed with the subject of sex."[4]

This new ethos manifested itself in a number of ways. "The Flapper," a term coined by H. L. Mencken, was the most evident popular icon of this new revolution in thinking. The Flapper became "The New Woman" of what historian Frederick Allen called the "Revolution in Manners and Morals."[5] Not to be outdone by the male of the species, she displayed a "devil-may-care" attitude marked by unrestrained drinking, smoking, cussing, and petting. She wore dresses that revealed more of her legs, blouses that covered less of what they were supposed to hide, and short-cropped hair. She made up her face in a sexually provocative manner. She was a revolutionary, a pleasure seeker. She was free. University of West Florida Historian James R. McGovern explains the Flapper was marked by "her speech, her interest in thrills and excitement, her dress and hair, her more aggressive sexuality." Further, she "became preoccupied with sex—shocking and simultaneously unshockable."[6] The Flapper revolutionized the way the game between the sexes was played. A Southern Baptist periodical bemoaned "that girls are actually tempting the boys more than the boys do the girls, by their dress and conversation."[7]

But the Flapper was not alone in marking the emergence of a new revolution. A more subtle development was the origination of the social meeting called the "date," which entered the American vocabulary at the turn of the century. Kevin White, in the *First Sexual Revolution*, explains, "As the new century dawned, the middle classes in the cities began to adopt dating as the most convenient mode of courtship for independent young men and women."[8] The earliest detectable entry of the "date" into the American argot came from an 1896 column on working-class culture written by George Ade for the *Chicago Record*. The use of the word, to note intimate social meetings between available men and women, was gaining wider use, even appearing in the works of more notable writers such as Frank Norris, Upton Sinclair, and O. Henry.[9]

For middle-class families living in an ever-growing urban America, it was not practical for a young man to "come calling" on a young woman and visit in her parlor within close proximity of a supervising mother, as was the custom in small-town America. Urban tenement buildings did not offer the luxury of a quiet parlor, and these living quarters were often packed tight with family and extended family. Logistically, courting had to take place away from the home, and the growing urban nightlife, as well as the ensuing innovations of automobiles and drive-in movies, facilitated the move of courtship away from the supervised parlor.[10] Given the revolutionary spirit and influence of the Flapper and the migration of the intimate, courting relationship away from the supervision from the home, it is not surprising that Kinsey would report that among females born before 1900 "less than half as many had had premarital coitus as among females born in any subsequent decade."[11]

But the shape of premarital relationships are not the only change under this new attention to sexuality. There were two types of publications that stimulated and reflected a new interest in sexuality. The first was the rise of the "smut" magazine.

A 1926 *Atlantic Monthly* article, "Sex, Art, Truth, and Magazines," chronicles this print genre's history. First on the scene was the widely popular *True Story*, which sold two million copies monthly and made its publisher a millionaire.[12] It featured such mildly titillating stories as "A Midnight's Memories," which described a couple engaged in a passionate embrace: "Lower and lower the man's face dropped, while the woman waited in suspenseful bliss for the touch of his lips. They brushed hers softly and her being thrilled."[13] The next form moved from the arousing story to the stimulating picture. William Randolph Hearst's 125,000 circulation *Snappy Stories* featured, as early as 1914, attractive, bathing-suit clad women on its cover and, while most of the stories were "not really dirty . . . there [was] usually one story which [went] over the line."[14]

The third was an ingenious, if not devious, way to display a more arousing sort of provocative female image. Some publishers claimed that men were capable of developing an appreciation for art, especially art containing nudes. Therefore, they founded what they called "artist and models" publications that produced and displayed much of this "art." This thinly veiled attempt to make ogling into a high-cultured activity appeared in such publications as *American Art Student* and *Artists and Models*.[15]

However, in the late 1920s, publishers stopped the pretense and went completely modern with what was described as "the out-and-out vulgar group . . . the acme of vulgarity," going by such titles as *Hot Dog, Hi-Jinks, Happy Howls, Paris Nights*, and *Red Pepper*.[16] "These magazines," White explains, "came closest to traversing the delicate line between erotica and pornography."[17]

This new genre was widely popular. Any "Doubting Thomas [was encouraged] to go on a tour of inspection and see for himself." One reporter noted that a jaunt from the Eastern Seaboard to the West Coast revealed that "a lot of these little towns seem literally saturated with sex." In Steubenville, Ohio, for instance "out of 110 publications in a single store, 68 were either out-and-out smut or bordering on the line."[18]

But the other type of publication taking a new interest in sex was of a higher moral and cultural class: the marriage manual. Steven Seidman, in *Romantic Longings: Love in America, 1830–1980*, finds that at the end of the nineteenth century, "marital advice literature reveals a shift in its concerns. . . . Victorian advice writers sought to educate young men and women . . . on the morality of the sex instinct in order to harness its power for personal and social gain."[19] There was a new recognition of sexuality in the marital relationship and a number of authors sought to enhance this aspect of marriage. Perhaps the earliest mention of this was in 1896 by Alice Stockham. She lamented that "marital unhappiness is chiefly caused through ignorance [of] the sexual union."[20] In 1925, the nation's pioneer in marriage counseling (and father of Rutgers sociologist David Popenoe), Paul Popenoe, wrote, "after marriage it is the husband's part to show his aptitude in arousing and maintaining the responsiveness of his wife." This is because "sexual intercourse plays fully as large a part in the life of the average wife as it does that of the average husband."[21]

However, the most popular and explicit of these manuals arrived from Holland in 1926. Theodore Van de Velde's *Ideal Marriage: Its Physiology and Technique* was so popular it went through at least forty-eight reprints, and even today, early editions of this book are easily found in some used bookstores. This early manual, to borrow from the name of a later revolutionary sex manual, could have practically been called, "The Joy of Married Sex," because its discussion of how to enhance the sexual union in marriage was tremendously frank, even by today's standards. Dr. Van de Velde introduced the early editions of his book with an apologetic for why he felt compelled to "transgress the bounds of custom" in what is properly discussed regarding sexuality. But after some years, the publisher dropped the warning, for "there [had] been a complete revolution of thought, largely due to his pioneer work; and what was whispered then is now discussed openly."[22]

Van de Velde believed that every married man "should act the part of Don Juan to his wife" and if he is not an "erotic genius" by nature, "the man needs *explicit knowledge* if he is to be capable of inspiring such desire and imparting such joy" to his wife. In short, Van de Velde explained, the good husband "must know how to make love."[23]

It was this genre of literature, the marriage manual, that concentrated for the first time on richly enhancing the sexual relationship in marriage and making it pleasurable for both husband and wife. Previously, sex was seen as a marital responsibility. Enjoyment, when it happened, was a bonus. It was never an art to be studied, pursued, and mastered. While this pursuit of sexual gratification was a highly praiseworthy goal in that it helped enrich the marital relationship and emphasized the needs of women, its emphasis on pleasure dovetailed with the other cultural developments to create a sweeping "sexual revolution." Taken together, the Flapper, the emergence of dating, the smut magazines, and, to a degree, the explicit marriage manual (by focusing on pleasure as the aim of sexuality) helped our culture view sex as an "autonomous domain of pleasure," making personal satisfaction the highest goal of the sexual act.[24]

By 1950, the relationship between sex, love, and marriage had significantly changed. It was this shift that led the distinguished Harvard sociologist Pitirim Sorokin to write in 1956 about an "odd revolution" in America:

Among the many changes of the last few decades, a peculiar revolution has been taking place in the lives of millions of American men and women. Quite different from the better-known political and economic revolutions, it goes almost unnoticed. Devoid of noisy public explosions, its stormy scenes are confined to the privacy of the bedroom and involve only individuals. Unmarked by dramatic events on a large scale, it is free from civil war, class struggle, and bloodshed. It has no revolutionary army to fight its enemies. It does not try to overthrow governments. It has no great leader: no hero plans it and no politburo directs it. Without plan or organization, it is carried out by millions of individuals, each acting on his own. . . . Its name is the sex revolution.[25]

Sorokin's attention to this "sex revolution" was solely to denounce it. He warned, "Any considerable change in marital behavior, any increase in sexual promiscuity and illicit relations is pregnant with momentous consequences."[26] He contended that a sexual revolution drastically affects the well-being of individuals and the health of their culture. We will now look at how sexual profligacy decreases both.

The Individual Price of Sexual Freedom

A 1971 book entitled *The New Sexual Revolution*, a collection of essays celebrating and seeking to offer direction for this new stage of the sexual revolution (beginning around 1960), contains an essay titled, "Is Monogamy Outdated?"[27] Authors Rustum and Della Roy, a husband-and-wife team of Penn State professors, answer their own rhetorical query with an expected and fashionable 1970s reply: Of course it is! They conclude their essay with the admonition that "For humanists," a group they proudly identify with, "there is no release from the mandate to alter traditional monogamy to make it better serve human needs."[28]

However, as we shall see, contrary to this "progressive" ideal, man was not created as a being who can flourish under the banner of sexual independence. Man and woman were created in such a way that a faithful and lifelong sexual union with one partner is the ideal for both members of the race. When this model for sexual relationships is followed, individuals are healthier and find more enjoyment in sex than those who do not obey this code. The data supporting this truth is clear and distinct.

Sexual Promiscuity and Personal Health

Regarding health of the individual, let's start our discussion with one of the most obvious and direct pathologies of sexual freedom:

sexually transmitted disease. Sexually transmitted diseases (STDs) have plagued the human race for millennia. Historians of epidemiology tell us that Hippocrates (around 460–377 B.C.) was one of the earliest physicians to describe the infection of gonorrhea.[29] But the real concern over STDs in America coincided with the initiation of the sexual revolution at the turn of the century.

As people became more sexually active, syphilis and gonorrhea, the two main venereal diseases of the day, became more prevalent. As historian John C. Burnham explains, toward the end of the nineteenth century "the known prevalence of venereal illnesses increased and a huge fraction of the population appeared to be infected."[30] By the 1890s, the New York City Hospital found the need for six venereal disease wards.[31] In the early stages of such an unprecedented venereal outbreak, physicians attending a 1901 professional conference in New York heard an important paper presented on the urgency of treating and preventing venereal disease. And the Physicians' Club of Chicago called an evening meeting to discuss "The Ravages of Venereal Disease." By 1903, the American Medical Association selected and established a committee dedicated to the prevention of venereal diseases.[32] In 1905, Dr. Prince A. Morrow, a leading social reformer and noted dermatologist (which at that time included the treatment of venereal diseases), founded the American Society for Sanitary and Moral Prophylaxis. Morrow was, as he claimed at a major medical society meeting, motivated by the fact that the principal sufferers of syphilis and gonorrhea were innocent women who contracted the diseases because unfaithful husbands brought them into the home.[33]

However, things became much worse as the sexual revolution got more revolutionary. Until the early 1980s, there were only five classical venereal infections, and until 1972, most of the emphasis from health officials was placed on controlling syphilis. Today, there are more than fifty different organisms and syndromes that are spread through sexual activity.[34] There are an estimated twelve million new STD infections every year, and one out of every five Americans now has an incurable sexually transmitted disease. At current rates, at least one person in every four can be expected to contract an STD in the future.[35]

Specifically, 1 million Americans are infected with human

immunodeficiency virus (HIV), 1.5 million people are chronic car-
riers of the hepatitis B virus, at least 31 million suffer from the gen-
ital herpes virus, and anywhere from 24 to 40 million people are
infected with the human pappillomavirus (HPV), all of which are
incurable.[36] The Alan Guttmacher Institute estimates that the collected public and private costs of STDs totaled approximately $5.4
billion in 1990.[37]

These diseases, by their ubiquity and their destructiveness to
the human body and psyche, serve as a tragic but powerful mega-
phone, loudly proclaiming the failure and end of the sexual revolution. However, this revolution has also failed in another lesser
known yet equally important area.

Sexual Satisfaction
Free sexual expression also serves to limit a person's happiness and
sexual fulfillment. A number of studies show that sex is significantly more emotionally fulfilling and physically satisfying when
shared with one person over the span of a long-term commitment
such as marriage affords. A highly sophisticated study on sexuality
in America, referred to by *U.S. News & World Report* as the "most
authoritative ever,"[38] was conducted by researchers at the University of Chicago and the State University of New York at Stony Brook.
This study, called the National Health and Social Life Survey
(NHSLS), is much more comprehensive than all of the studies on
sexuality that predate it (for example, the Kinsey, Masters, and Johnson, *Redbook*, and *Playboy* studies, or the Hite and Janus reports).[39]
Unlike these earlier studies, the NHSLS study, working through the
National Opinion Research Center (NORC) at the University of
Chicago, employed a staff of 220 interviewers who spent seven
months interviewing 3,432 scientifically selected respondents. *Time*
magazine characterized this work as "probably the first truly scientific survey" of sex in the United States.[40]

The research is presented in two different volumes. The smaller,
Sex in America: A Definitive Survey, is a very readable abstract of the
much larger and academic main presentation, *The Social Organization of Sexuality*.[41] One of the most interesting aspects of the report
is summed up in one fourteen-word sentence: "The public image
of sex in America bears virtually no relationship to the truth."[42]

What these researchers found regarding sexual satisfaction and who finds it is certainly surprising. The popular notion is that married people do have sex, and it can be enjoyable on occasion, but it is usually mediocre at best. The widely believed myth is that it is the unattached single or the newly married who is really having all the fun. These researchers discovered that this fable bears no relationship to the truth because, "in real life, the unheralded, seldom discussed world of married sex is actually the one that satisfies people the most."[43] Of all sexually active people, the group with the highest percentage reporting being "extremely" or "very" satisfied with the amount of physical pleasure and emotional satisfaction they received from their partner are the faithfully married respondents. The numbers are as follows:[44]

Type of Partner	Physical Pleasure	Emotional Satisfaction
Only one:		
Spouse	87.4%	84.8%
Cohabitant	84.4%	75.6%
Neither	78.2%	71.0%
More than one: (in a lifetime)		
Spouse	61.2%	56.7%
Cohabitant	74.5%	57.9%
Neither	77.9%	61.7%

The data also shows that having a spouse as an exclusive sex partner is associated with the highest reported feelings of sex, making the respondents feel "satisfied," "loved," "thrilled," "wanted," and "taken care of." The faithfully married were also least likely to report sex making them feel "sad," "anxious or worried," "scared or afraid," or "guilty."[45]

The highly positive feelings connected with sex within the marriage relationship correspond to the fact that a married woman is least likely to be forced to do something sexual with or to a partner she knows than women in any other category.[46]

Percentage of Respondents
Forced to Perform Sexual Act by . . .

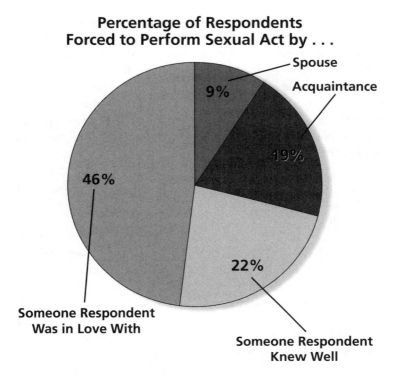

Because sex among married couples is so physically and emotionally satisfying, and they are not likely to be forced to perform unwanted sexual acts, it's not surprising that both married men and women are least likely to report lacking an interest in sex.[47] The data consistently indicates that when any marital category involves more than one partner, each indicator of physical pleasure and emotional satisfaction is significantly diminished. This research team concludes:

> Although popular representations of marriage often portray the dulling of mutual affection over time, the relative security that marriage provides may be a significant source of emotional satisfaction as well as a comfortable context in which to pursue physical pleasure.[48]

This reminds me of a wonderful story I read a few years ago. A mother was contemplating what she would tell her preteen stepdaughter about sex in the age of acquired immune deficiency syndrome (AIDS), especially in light of all the talk about "safe sex." The mother decided to be honest and explicit about these words being "ludicrously contradictory." She told her daughter that sex is many things—dark, mysterious, passionate, wild, gentle, even reassuring—but it is certainly not safe. "If it is safe," she explained, "it's not likely to be very sexy."[49]

This mother has a high view of sexuality. What our culture has come to recognize as "safe sex" is not sex at all, but a cheap and disappointing imitation. It can never be truly safe, and as a consequence, it cannot be sexy.

What is more, there is no condom for the heart. The best sex—wild, passionate, real sex—is reserved for the couple who experiences it exclusively within the safe harbor of a lifelong, monogamous partnership. Only in this relationship are there no dangers, and the married partners can abandon themselves to each other. They don't have to be concerned about disease, they don't have to be afraid of being forced to do something against their will, and through experience they know what brings pleasure to their spouse. This exclusive community—husband and wife—has the emotional security of the marriage bond and is able fully to enjoy the most intimate form of intercourse two people can experience because they know, trust, and find comfort in each other.

The mother's advice to her daughter was wise. Good things do come to those who wait. With this, the mother ignited her daughter's imagination toward a larger, more captivating picture of sexuality, helping her understand that it is easier to forego an immediate, cheaper pleasure when one possesses a vision for something more grand.

This is the message we ought to be sending to our young people, for it is the one that matches reality and lifts them to a higher manner of living.

Sex cannot be successful when it has to be approached with the same caution exhibited in handling toxic waste. The experience will be terribly disappointing.

Our young people's imaginations should be captured by something larger, like this mother sought to do. We should ask, "Do you seek wild, passionate, incredible sex that will blow your mind and your partner's? Well, it's found only in a long-term relationship with one special partner you decide to spend the rest of your life with. Anything else is a cheap imitation. The best is worth waiting for."

A Reason for the Connection between Marriage & Sexual Pleasure
The work of Dr. Winnifred Cutler, a leading authority and researcher from the University of Pennsylvania in the fields of sexuality and the biology of human reproduction, provides another, more detailed reason for the higher level of sexual satisfaction within a long-term monogamous relationship.

In her book, *Love Cycles: The Science of Intimacy*, she discusses her findings collected over fifteen years in the study of human anatomy and biology. Her conclusion: "Regular sex within a loving monogamous relationship is good for you."[50] She explains that her discovery is reflected in the wisdom of Solomon, who wrote that there is a proper time for every purpose, including a "time to embrace." Cutler notes:

> Nothing has changed in the last three thousand years. My research with more than seven hundred women confirms the value of weekly sexual contact, a weekly love cycle. Weekly sex is still good for women, helping to ensure hormonal levels that promote good health, retard aging, and increase fertility. With a period of abstention when the menstrual blood is flowing, regular sex is ideal.[51]

And, Cutler notes, this sexual relationship should be confined to long-term monogamous relationship such as marriage.

> Throughout recent history . . . women were counseled by their mothers and grandmothers to retain their virginity. My results suggest that the old advice was probably good.[52]

Cutler explains her conclusion: "Biology does not seem to condone promiscuity."[53] A regiment of regular sex with a marriage partner enhances personal well-being and sexual gratification because the man and woman produce what Cutler calls a "love cycle." Magically, these two individuals learn—over time—to fit one another. This occurs not just physically, but hormonally, creating a beautiful and glorious "hormonal symphony." Cutler reports that the testosterone level in men tends to reach its highest point simultaneously with their wives' estrogen peaks, leading to what she calls a rhythmic dance of endocrine harmony.[54] Other types of sexual activity, either with multiple partners or individual masturbation, are incapable of producing this type of cyclical harmony. The married couple's minds and motor skills learn to work together for sexual fulfillment by discovering what is pleasurable to one another, but so do their bodies in an intangible way. "The facts are," explains Cutler, "nature discourages human promiscuity and rewards stable sexual behavior."[55]

Premarital Sex and Overall Marital Satisfaction

Beyond increased sexual fulfillment, there are other reasons for confining sexual activity to the bonds of the marital relationship. Research indicates that people involved in premarital sexual activity are likely to be less faithful after marriage. Andrew Greeley, a sociologist at the University of Chicago, has also conducted research on the issue of marital fidelity and its correlation with sexual fulfillment. His findings are found in *Faithful Attraction*, and his data matches the findings of the NHSLS study.[56] Faithfully married people are the most sexually satisfied of any other sexually active group. In addition, Greeley found that "premarital sex with someone other than the intended spouse correlates with marital infidelity." Specifically, only 3 percent of spouses who did not engage in premarital sex with someone other than their present spouse were unfaithful in marriage. For those who engaged in premarital sex with someone other than their spouse "fairly often," 18 percent were unfaithful in marriage. Premarital sex also affects overall marital satisfaction for men. Of those men who engaged in premarital affairs, 79 percent said they would choose to marry the same wife again. For those who didn't engage in premarital affairs, the number was higher, at 89 percent.[57]

So, it's not surprising to find that engagement in premarital sex is connected with a higher risk of divorce. A study conducted by researchers at the University of Maryland and the National Center for Health Statistics, looking at a nationally representative sample of women ages fifteen to forty-four over the years of 1965 to 1985, found that "women who were sexually active prior to marriage faced a considerably higher risk of marital disruption than women who were virgin brides."[58] This is troubling since 43 percent of white women marrying between 1960 and 1965 were virgins while only 14 percent of those who married between 1980 and 1985 were.[59]

The researchers attribute this correlation between nonvirgin status and increased likelihood of divorce to a willingness on the part of the individuals to break traditional norms. In fact, other data indicates that couples who hold nontraditional attitudes report being less satisfied with their marriages than couples who hold more traditional ones.[60]

Also, women show a strong preference for marriage partners who have had no sexual history, while males will tolerate a limited sexual past.[61] The number of sexual partners a person is likely to have is directly associated with the age at which they initiate sexual activity. Women who become sexually active in their teens report two to three times as many partners as women who have initiated sex in their twenties.[62] The research presented here demonstrates that this translates into a significantly reduced level of sexual satisfaction later in life and in marriage, higher risks of contracting an STD, getting pregnant, greater risk of divorce, and being less content overall.

CULTURAL CONSEQUENCES OF SEXUAL FREEDOM

While it's not difficult to see how the personal benefits of a sexual system of one man for one woman for life translate into comprehensive cultural benefits, it is important to focus on how such a sexual ethic affects the larger culture. Beyond the spread of STDs, more illegitimacy, more sexually frustrated individuals seeking to fulfill their unmet needs in increasingly deviant ways, and more marital breakdown, a liberal sexual ethic affects the very progress and cohesion of a culture. Sorokin, in his study of sex and culture, finds two generalities:

1. The regime that confines sexual life within socially sanctioned marriage and that morally disapproves and legally prohibits premarital and extramarital relations provides an environment more favorable for creative growth.
2. The regime that permits chronically excessive, illicit, and disorderly sex activities contributes to the decline of cultural creativity.[63]

Sorokin's conclusions are supported by the work of noted British anthropologist Joseph Daniel Unwin of the Universities of Cambridge and Oxford. Unwin's comprehensive, but largely ignored, *Sex and Culture*, written in 1934, is a study of how sexual mores impact the cultural process, drawing from the observation of eighty-six civilized and uncivilized cultures throughout several hundred years of history.[64]

Unwin introduces his presentation as follows:

Indeed the coincident facts are so impressive that in all probability we shall have to revise our old ideas in regard to the cultural process; for the cultural condition of any society at any time seems to depend on the amount of its mental and social energy, and this in its turn seems to depend upon the extent of the compulsory continence imposed by its past and present methods of regulating the relations between the sexes. So close, in fact, is the relation between sexual opportunity and cultural condition that if we know what sexual regulation a society adopted, we can prophesy accurately the pattern of its culture.[65]

To better understand Unwin's work, we should start by looking at his four main patterns of human culture and his definitions of each. The first is *zoistic*; the most primitive of cultures. It erects no temples, has no clear or well-thought-out beliefs about the powers at work in the universe, and employs no priests. It also doesn't pay any kind of postfuneral attention to its dead. The second is the *manistic* culture. Slightly more advanced than the former, a manistic culture's people do not erect temples, but do pay some sort of postfuneral attention to their dead. They also have a very rough belief in some external universal power. More advanced still is the *deistic* culture, which builds temples and employs priests in order to maintain a right relationship with the power or powers of the universe. The most advanced of all is the *rationalistic* culture. This group, the only one that can be called truly "cultured," has a well-developed and logical conception of the universe, which allows its people to control their environment to some degree. In addition, they possess a sophisticated set of rites and ceremonies concerning the passing of important life events for the individual and the society at large.[66]

Unwin contends that it is an "indubitable fact" that there is a close parallel between the social energy a culture expends and its manner of sexual regulation—a topic that will be examined later. Those cultures that confine sexuality to marriage are of a higher cultural order because they have more "expansive energy," which is dedicated to cultural enhancement. Such societies are interested in metaphysical questions regarding life and its meaning. They erect elaborate temples based on a sophisticated belief system. They think large thoughts about the physical world and even strive to control their environment and improve their standard of living.[67]

Those cultures that allow sexual freedom do not display this kind of social energy and are consistently of a lower order. They are slothful because their energy is consumed with meeting their physical appetites. Therefore, they do not have the interest or energy to invest in cultural improvements. They have not thought out a system of beliefs that requires even the simplest of temples or the most cursory funeral rites. In these cultures, life is for now. As Unwin summarizes, "If the compulsory continence be great, there will be great social energy; if it be small, there will be little social energy. If there be no compulsory continence, there can be no social energy."[68]

The heart of Unwin's thesis is nicely summed up in a number of what he calls universal primary and secondary laws regarding sexual opportunity and cultural change. Unwin's first primary law (1), which operates on all past societies, is:

The cultural condition of any society in any geographical environment is conditioned by its past and present method of regulating the relations between the sexes.[69]

49

This rule will remain constant, Unwin explains, as long as human organisms remain as they have over the past five thousand years. Unwin, in fact, was so convinced of the truth of this law that it plays a prominent part in his detailed plans to build the ideal culture (contained in his last book *Hopousia or The Sexual and Economic Foundations of a New Society*, published after his death).[70] This manifesto for the ideal secular humanist society maintains that the model society would consist of "alpha marriages," which demand premarital chastity for the sake of enhanced social energy. "Adultery," he said, "could not be condoned, not for any moral reason, but because it strikes at the root of social energy."[71]

His first secondary law (1a) is this:

Any society in which prenuptial sexual freedom has been permitted for at least three generations will be in a zoistic [primitive] cultural condition. It will also be at a dead level of conception if previously it had not been in a higher cultural condition.[72]

If Unwin's conclusion here is correct, it has serious implications for our nation, given our analysis of the history of the sexual revolution in American culture. Since the earliest days of the twentieth century, our society has become increasingly liberal in its sexual codes. The 1960s and 1970s especially witnessed a complete divorce between the exercise of sexuality and marriage. During these decades, sex became untethered. This ever growing ethic has limited the amount of "expansive energy" we can generate. And this limitation of creative energy will certainly grow greater the longer we operate under such an ethic.

Unwin's second secondary law (1b) is:

If in any human society such regulations are adopted as compel an irregular or occasional continence, the cultural condition of the society will become manistic. If the compulsory continence be slight, the post-funeral rites will partake of the nature of tendance [somewhat sophisticated]. If it be great, those rites will partake also of the nature of cult [highly sophisticated].[73]

The second primary law (2) offers hope and speaks to the regenerative powers of recovering sexual continence:

> No society can display productive social energy unless a new generation inherits a social system under which sexual opportunity is reduced to a minimum. If such a system be preserved, a richer and yet richer tradition will be created.[74]

When a society allows marriage ties to be severed at will, such as our divorce laws currently allow and our general family ethos tolerates, that system becomes one which Unwin describes as "modified monogamy." He warns that a "society which adopts a modified system of monogamy, or a modified polygamy, or an absolute polygamy cannot advance to the rationalistic [highest] cultural condition."[75] It is therefore logical to assume, based on the cultural processes Unwin has observed, that a rationalistic culture which has adopted a modified monogamy and sustained it for three generations as we have, *will experience cultural decline.*

By way of example, Unwin illustrates his conclusions with a number of once great civilizations. The Babylonians were a monogamous people and displayed great cultural energy. Great temples were built, commerce was strengthened, and the empire expanded. However, eventually marriages and sexual unions were entered and departed with great ease, and the decline of the great civilization followed close behind. Likewise with the great Sumerians, the Hellenes, and the Romans.

Clearly, our culture is also one in decline. Many of our cities are dying from the inside out. The number of places within our own borders where we cannot travel without fear for safety is increasing. We are becoming so self-indulgent and lacking any discipline that our national and personal debt is threatening to strangle our financial viability and freedom as a people. The loss of any objective moral compass is engulfing our once civil society. Local, state, and federal law enforcement organizations are expanding endlessly due to the heavy burden of an increased workload. We can't seem to build prisons fast enough or large enough. The dockets in our court systems grow longer and longer. Sexually transmitted diseases are ruining and/or ending more lives than ever imagined. In short, we are having to extend greater energy and resources toward the end of just holding our nation together, rather than using it to exert expansive, productive energy. Granted, it would be a hasty assumption to say that all of this is the direct result of the loosening of our sexual values. However, it would be equally shortsighted to dismiss any connection altogether.

The human personality is a personality of passions. We are a race of intense desirers. It is what we do the moment we enter the world and don't stop until we take our last breath. Our passion is a good thing. It is what we do with it that requires judgment. We spend our lives seeking to satisfy our passions and desires, be they good or bad, healthy or unhealthy. Our passions, because they are powerful things, must be bridled and brought under control if we want to channel them toward productive ends. The person who can be governed by two competing passions, display productivity in both, and still appear to keep his wits is an anomaly.

All of this holds true with one of the most powerful of all our passions: our sexuality. It is not a demon to be overcome and destroyed but a precious gift to be cared for, protected, and harnessed because, as we have seen, that is when it is most beneficial. Because our sexuality is so inherently a part of us, when we cease to cherish, confine, and protect it, we will cease to cherish and protect anything. Because our sexuality is so intimately attached to our deepest being and so very intrinsic to who we are as passionate beings, the widespread relaxation of sexual mores is the first sign of our personal and, therefore, societal disintegration. It reveals that we have "come apart" as a people in a fundamental way. This is the point Unwin's work revealed.

What is more, we each have only so much energy and passion. When that is consumed with something as intoxicating as sex, there is precious little left over for other things. This truth is captured unwittingly in a recent quote by comedian and "Tonight Show" host, Jay Leno. Explaining his passion for collecting highly prized cars, he says, "Most men in Hollywood have one car and lots of women; I have one woman and lots of cars."[76] Leno, the man, has only so much passion and energy, and it is going to be spent somewhere. He can spend it building a collection of women or a collection of cars. None of us have the energy or attention to build both.

CONCLUSION

Unwin's second primary law concludes that a society cannot display productive social energy unless a new generation adopts a system of sexual restraint. I believe that we are at a point in our society's lifespan where this is what we must do. If we don't, we are doomed to live in the kind of society Sorokin describes:

> The sex-obsessed society unhesitatingly breaks both divine and human law, blows to smithereens all values. Like a tornado, it leaves in its path a legion of corpses, a multitude of wrecked lives, an untold amount of suffering, and an ugly debris of broken standards. It destroys the real freedom of normal love; and in lieu of enriching and ennobling the sexual passion, it reduces it to mere copulation.[77]

The evidence documenting the comprehensive failure of this revolution and substantiating Sorokin's prophecy is overwhelming. People are acquiring sexually transmitted diseases in unprecedented numbers. More people are less satisfied with the physical and emotional natures of their sex lives and are less successful in nurturing meaningful relationships. With the great divorce between marriage and sexuality, the dream of a fulfilling sex life is more elusive to more people than it has been at any time in our nation's history. After years of observing this sexual revolution, we have found, ironically, that sex does not need to be liberated. Rather, it simply needs to be confined to its proper and most productive domain. Decades of research show that this place is lifelong, monogamous marriage. It is time to initiate a counterrevolution.

TWO

Troubled and Costly:

The Hidden Consequences of Cohabitation

"All you need is love."
—THE BEATLES, 1967

THE GREAT DIVORCE BETWEEN SEXUALITY AND MARRIAGE created new encouragement and opportunities for Americans to establish alternative forms of domestic life. "As the normative link between sex and marriage eroded, there was progressively less reason for unmarried couples not to share households," explains Professor Larry Bumpass.[1] This new form of domestic life was referred to, by the more Victorian among us, as "living in sin." Others called it "shacking up." But as more couples started entering this form of domestic life, it took on a more clinical name: cohabitation.

Webster defines cohabiting as "living together as lovers when not married." Cohabitation was the brainchild of two groups of cultural progressives who approached this idea with different rationales, one group taking a high view of marriage and the other a low view. The first group believes that because marriage is an important and special institution that requires a great deal of competency, people shouldn't enter it without significant thought toward compatibility or whether the couple has the emotional tools required to make their relationship work. Therefore, cohabitation was offered as a testing ground—a farm league for marriage—where people could determine whether they were ready to play ball in the big leagues. Or to use another analogy, cohabitation could give people a dress rehearsal, a dry run before the real show. If the trial run proved successful, people could move on to the real thing and enjoy the fruits of a well-tested relationship culminating in lifelong marriage. If not, the couple could part ways with the comfort and satisfaction of knowing the relationship wouldn't have worked.

The other group took a more cynical approach to marriage. It said that nothing about a marriage license was significant because it was only a piece of paper. All that really mattered was the love two people shared. Anything else forced upon the relationship was superfluous. To become legally married would weigh down a beautiful and unencumbered love with the ugly legalities of a business contract. Such baggage would only serve to choke out the lifeblood of the relationship. Does love require a legal document to legitimize itself? Without such entanglements, two people could remain together because they *desire* to be together, not because some legal entity says they must. Cohabitation would allow the warmth of love, not cold legalities, to regulate the temperature of domestic relationships.

Under either rationale, domestic relationships between men and women would clearly be the winners. Given enough time, homes across the country would be filled with equity, harmony, good will, and strong relationships. Because of these promises, cohabitation became the fastest growing family configuration over the past two decades, increasing at an astonishing rate of 700 percent since 1970.[2] This explosive growth has provided social scientists with a massive body of data to analyze, providing the opportunity to draw some strong and educated conclusions regarding the success of this experiment.

What have they learned? Does premarital cohabitation serve to ensure that couples are compatible before they tie the knot? Has it created stronger marriages and fewer divorces? Does cohabitation make for healthier, less-encumbered relationships?

To properly assess cohabitation, let's address three questions:

1. How do those who cohabit prior to marriage succeed once their marriage is established?
2. How healthy are nonmarital cohabiting relationships?
3. What is the cohabitor's level of contentment in that relationship?

EFFECT OF NONMARITAL COHABITATION ON MARRIAGES

Over 90 percent of all cohabiters report that they plan to marry someone, if not their current partner, at some point in their lives.[3] What is the likelihood that their cohabiting relationship will lead to a healthy marriage? The research data provides a decisive answer.

Sociologists at the Universities of Chicago and Michigan explain that the "expectation of a positive relationship between cohabitation and marital stability . . . has been shattered in recent years by studies conducted in several Western countries, including Canada, Sweden, New Zealand, and the United States." Their data indicates that those who cohabit before marriage have substantially higher divorce rates than those who do not. In fact, the recorded differences range from 50 to 100 percent higher.[4]

Sociologists at the University of Wisconsin-Madison agree: "Recent national studies in Canada, Sweden, and the United States found that cohabitation increased rather than decreased the risk of marital dissolution."[5] Zheng Wu of the University of Victoria, British Columbia, reports, "Contrary to the conventional wisdom that living together before marriage will screen out poor matches and therefore improve subsequent marital stability, there is considerable empirical evidence demonstrating that premarital cohabitation is associated with lowered marital stability."[6] Sociologists Elizabeth Thomson and Ugo Colella found that "cohabitation is associated with greater marital conflict and poorer communication."[7] This lack of communication and increased conflict contributes to the fact that "cohabitors perceived greater likelihood of divorce than couples who did not cohabit before marriage, and longer cohabitation was associated with higher likelihood of divorce."[8]

Research done at Macquarie University in Australia also found that couples who cohabited before marriage were more likely to divorce than those who did not. Couples who lived together before marriage also "separated more often, sought counseling more often, and regarded marriage as a less important part of their life" than those who did not live together before marriage.[9]

Alan Booth and David Johnson, working from the University of Nebraska, studied 2,033 married couples in a nationally representative sample and found that the data does "not support the model that cohabitation improves marital quality and reduces marital instability because it serves as a training period for marriage or improves mate selection."[10] They concluded this because "cohabitation is not related to marital happiness, but it is related to lower levels of marital interaction, higher levels of marital disagreement, and marital instability."[11] Further, they said, "On the basis of the analysis presented so far, we must reject the argument that cohabitation provides superior training for marriage or improves mate selection."[12]

Jan Stets of Washington State University, one of the most noted researchers on the issue of cohabitation, found that "after controlling for other factors (gender, race, education, alcohol abuse, social integration, the type of person with whom one has previously cohabited, the length of the relationships, and the presence of children), prior cohabiting relationships negatively influence current married *and* cohabiting relationships" (emphasis in original).[13]

The Measured Effects

How wide is the disparity of relational longevity between those who cohabit before marriage and those who do not?

Demographers Larry Bumpass and James Sweet from the University of Wisconsin-Madison, in cooperation with Andrew Cherlin, a sociologist from Johns Hopkins University, explain that "40 percent (of cohabitational relationships) will disrupt before marriage, and marriages that are preceded by living together have 50 percent higher disruption rates than marriages without premarital cohabitation."[14]

A joint study conducted by three Canadian universities found that of all couples married less than ten years, 31 percent of those who cohabited before marriage divorced, compared to a divorce rate of 14 percent for those who did not cohabit before marriage.[15] Researchers from Yale University, Columbia University, and the Institute for Resource Development at Westinghouse collaborated on a study examining the link between premarital cohabitation and subsequent marital relationships and published their work in the *American Sociological Review*. They found that divorce is significantly more prevalent for couples who cohabit with their future spouses:

> The overall association between premarital cohabitation and subsequent marital stability is striking. The dissolution rates of women who cohabit premaritally with their future spouse are, on average, nearly 80 percent higher than the rates of those who do not.[16]

The authors add that these findings are consistent with other studies conducted in Norway and Canada.

Of those who cohabit, marry, and then see their marriages dissolve, into what kinds of relationships are they most likely to transition? This is a question that Dr. Wu examined in a unique study. She found that those who cohabited before marriage are more likely to move back into a cohabitational situation after their marriage dissolves—nearly extinguishing their chances for a more successful subsequent relationship.[17]

Research done at the University of California, Los Angeles, and published in the *Journal of Personality Assessment*, looked at the difference in "problem areas" for married couples who did and did not cohabit prior to marriage. Of some twenty problem areas, drunkenness, adultery, and drug abuse (in that order) were the top three problems that distinguished married couples who lived together before marriage from couples who did not cohabit prior to marriage. The authors, Michael Newcomb and P. M. Bentler, explain:

> In regard to problem areas, it was found that cohabitors experienced significantly more difficulty in their marriages with adultery, alcohol, drugs, and independence than couples who had not cohabited. Apparently, this makes

marriage preceded by cohabitation more prone to problems often associated with other deviant lifestyles—for example, use of drugs and alcohol, more permissive sexual relationships, and an abhorrence of dependence—than marriages not preceded by cohabitation.[18]

A related factor, with the instability of cohabiting relationships, is what sociologists call "the nest-leaving process." Interestingly, although cohabitors desire to be more individualistic and independent, they end up returning to their parents' homes in much larger numbers than those who marry without first cohabiting.

Research done at Brown University and the University of Michigan on the nest-leaving process found that "only those leaving in conjunction with marriage were truly unlikely to return" to their parents' home. However, "Cohabitors were very likely to return home alone for an extended stay."[19] The difference in the rates is striking: 20 percent of cohabitors returned while only 2 percent of married individuals returned to their parents' home. Given this statistic, these sociologists conclude that "it is difficult to argue that cohabitors resemble married people."[20]

HEALTH OF NONMARITAL COHABITING RELATIONSHIPS

Not only do cohabitational relationships create hardships by fostering significantly higher divorce rates (50 to 100 percent), but research also shows that the relationships themselves are plagued by numerous problems even before the marriage ever takes place.

Dr. Stets' work indicates, in general, that "cohabiting couples compared to married couples have less healthy relationships. They have lower relationship quality, lower stability, and a higher level of disagreements."[21] Sociologists from the University of Kentucky, writing in the *International Journal of Sociology of the Family*, dispel the myth that marriage is an oppressive institution where the husband is an order-barking taskmaster while the wife plays the role of the dutiful servant. One of the goals of cohabitation was to put man and woman on equal footing and make the division of labor more harmonious. However, when married couples were compared to cohabiting couples, it was found that "married couples were significantly more equalitarian in their role expectations than cohabiting subjects."[22] Contrary to popular notions, married males were especially more likely to be equalitarian than their cohabiting counterparts. This gives credence to George Gilder's assertion in his book, *Men and Marriage*, that marriage is the one institution that effectively serves to domesticate men and turn them into useful contributors to civilized society.[23]

Domestic Violence

Not only are spouses more likely to receive help with household duties from their mates, they are also much less likely to become victims of domestic violence. The Family Violence Research Program at the University of New Hampshire, the nation's leading institution to study this subject, led by Murray Straus, conducted a major study of more than two thousand adults and the nature of their relationships. The findings regarding cohabitors are clear and distinct: "Cohabitors are much more violent than marrieds."[24] They specifically found that the overall rates of violence for cohabiting couples was twice as high and the overall rate for "severe" violence was nearly five times as high for cohabiting couples when compared with married couples.[25] A joint study conducted a few years later by Straus and Stets also found that cohabiting couples experience more frequent and severe assaults from one another than couples who were dating or married. These higher levels of aggression among cohabitors remained consistent even when controls for education, age, and occupational status were applied.[26]

People enter cohabiting relationships for many reasons, but the primary reason seems to be one of freedom—not wanting to be tied down. However, Stets and Straus explain this "freedom" might contribute to the increased levels of violence for two reasons.

The first reason is that cohabitors are less likely to be connected to a network of kin or peers who can serve to hold the couple accountable for their behavior toward each other.[27] Second, this increased level of aggression could also be tied to the issue of self-autonomy.[28] People who enter cohabiting relationships show greater tendencies toward individualism.[29] This is one reason why cohabiting seems more attractive than getting married, because cohabiting appears to offer more autonomy. However, there is less agreement among cohabiting couples as to how much freedom each will extend to his or her mate. Stets and Straus explain that "Married individuals may 'give in' to their partner's wishes, believing that they need to make sacrifices or compromises for the sake of keeping the relationship intact."[30] Cohabiting individuals may not be as likely to make these kinds of sacrifices and may therefore be more demanding. Besides, the cohabiting relationship, by its very nature, is less defined. So much so that University of Virginia sociologist Steven Nock describes cohabitation as "an incomplete institution suffused with ambiguity."[31] A cohabiting mate is faced with difficult questions regarding boundaries. "Does my mate really expect me home every night after work? Do I really need to call if I am going to be late? It's not like we're married!" the cohabitor may reason. Much of the increased violence can occur as attempts are made at defining these boundaries.

This leads to another interesting phenomenon that Straus discovered in his work. In a review of more than thirty studies on domestic violence, he consistently found that women initiated aggression (defined as an "unlawful physical attack by one person upon another") toward men at about the same rate as men toward women, even when controls were applied for the fact that men would tend to under-report attacks upon themselves by their partner. Some of the studies found a slightly higher number of assaults initiated by women while others report slightly higher numbers for men. Not surprisingly, men, because of their physical strength, inflicted more injury in their attacks.[32]

In addition, behavioral scientists at McMasters University in Canada found that, overall, domestic killings are perpetrated by females against males almost as often as the reverse. These killings (male to female and female to male) happen most frequently where the couples are not in registered marriages, but rather in common-law marriages (living together without being legally married). Margo Wilson and Martin Daly explain: "The rate of spousal homicide victimization is substantially higher in common-law marriages than in registered unions in Canada, in England and Wales, and in New South Wales."[33]

Regarding the specific measurements of the increase in domestic violence among cohabiting couples, Dr. Stets, in a recent study comparing cohabitational and marital aggression, discovered that "aggression is at least twice as common among cohabitors as it is among married partners." In a one-year period, 35 out of every 100 cohabiting couples have experienced some form of physical aggression, compared to 15 out of every 100 married couples. These numbers held constant, even after controlling for demographic factors such as education, age, occupation, and income.[34] Nearly 14 percent of those who cohabit admit to hitting, shoving, or throwing things at their partner during the past year, compared to 5 percent of married people.[35] Stets also found, along with UCLA researchers Newcomb and Bentler, in their study of relational problem areas, that "cohabitors are also more likely to exhibit depression and drunkenness than married couples."[36]

Other researchers have found much the same thing. Work done at Indiana University concerning domestic violence and the relationships between the batterer and victim yields what these authors call "some surprising results." Of course, these are really surprising only to those who have bought into the myth that marriage is a cauldron of battering and abuse. The study, published in the *Journal of Family Violence*, explains the following regarding the association between batterer and victim: "The most frequently cited relationship was cohabitation, with close to one-half (48 percent) of the couples living together."[37] The lowest rate was found among couples who were married (19 percent). The other major group consisted of those divorced or separated (27.3 percent).

When tracked over a longer period of time, the disparity of domestic violence among married and nonmarried couples is even more startling. The National Crime Victimization Survey, conducted by the U.S. Department of Justice, shows that of all violent crimes against women by their intimate partners between 1979 and 1987, about 65 percent were committed by either a boyfriend or ex-husband, while 9 percent were committed by husbands.[38] Given the increased level of safety within the marriage relationship, it's interesting to note that the U.S. Department of Justice reports that while men and women who are married are much less likely to be assaulted by their partners, they are also less likely to be assaulted by *anyone* else than those who are divorced or not married. Here are the rates per 1,000 for general aggravated assault in 1992 against:[39]

Males:	
Never Married	23.4
Married	5.5
Divorced or Separated	13.6

Females:	
Never Married	11.9
Married	3.1
Divorced or Separated	9.4

Additional data from the U.S. Department of Justice confirms that these rates are consistent over extended periods of time. From 1973 to 1992, the violent crime victimization rate for females (per 1,000 females age twelve or over) was 43 for unmarried women, 45 for divorced or separated women, and 11 for married women.[40]

In 1994, the Centers for Disease Control released a report revealing that 6 percent of all pregnant women are battered by their "husbands or partners."[41] What was not reported in the text, but is easily mined from the tables of the study, is that for every one pregnant married woman who was battered by her husband, four pregnant unmarried women were battered by their boyfriends. Marital status was the strongest predictor of abuse in this study—stronger than race, age, educational attainment, housing conditions, or access to prenatal health care.[42]

Clearly, men and women are physically safer when they are married. In the face of such facts, it is intriguing to note that whenever figures are given on the prevalence of domestic violence in public service announcements, boyfriends and husbands are lumped together in the same breath, with no distinction made between the two. The data reveals that this is a misleading presentation. As David Blankenhorn has noted, what is generically called "wife beating" could more precisely be termed "girlfriend beating."[43]

General Impact of Children Upon the Relationship

Children are present in 40 percent of all cohabiting relationships, and the number of cohabiting couples with children living in the home has increased nearly 550 percent since 1970.[44] This picture of cohabitation is certainly different from the stereotype of primarily college students or twentysomethings living together.[45] The high number of cohabiting families with children in the home has serious implications for the welfare and safety of children and the health of the environment in which they are raised, as we shall see in chapter four. Trouble in cohabiting relationships is increased with the presence of children. Just how much trouble typically is related to whose children they are.

Larry Bumpass, James Sweet, and Andrew Cherlin, after conducting a major study of nearly ten thousand individuals and their relationships, found that when children in the cohabiting relationship belong to only one of the partners,[46] the one who has the children claims that this situation "markedly increases the expectation of marriage and decreases the expectation of never marrying." Significant disagreement arises in the relationship from the fact that the partner to whom the children do not belong report increased "trouble and decreased marriage expectation."[47]

The partner who has children seeks marriage to legitimize the relationship, but the one who doesn't have children is not interested in making the commitment to children that are not his own.[48] Therefore, rather than being a force to bring the couple together, children in cohabiting relationships can serve as a wedge to drive the partners apart. This is likely to have serious negative consequences, even if subconsciously, for the children, who may see themselves as a source of tension and conflict in the family.

Specific Impact of Relationship Upon Children

A special issue of the *Journal of Comparative Family Studies*, addressing family violence, reports that "children living with caretakers other than two biological parents *are* at greater risk for child maltreatment"(emphasis theirs).[49] This idea is supported by other studies. Research done at the University of Iowa and published in the journal *Child Abuse and Neglect* reveals that even though boyfriends provide only about 2 percent of all nonparental child care, 64 percent of all cases of nonparental child abuse are committed by boyfriends, with 84 percent of all cases of nonparental child abuse occurring in single-parent homes. This data led Leslie Margolin to conclude, "A young child left with a mother's boyfriend experiences substantially elevated risk of abuse."[50]

Michael Gordon and Susan Creighton, presenting their research in the *Journal of Marriage and the Family*, explain that "a number of studies have shown that girls living with nonnatal fathers [boyfriends and stepfathers] are at higher risk for sexual abuse than girls living with natal fathers."[51]

The literature, presented here and in subsequent chapters, clearly shows that children are safer and better cared for by two biological parents who are married. These parents have a greater personal interest in committing to the emotional sacrifices necessary to raise children properly. While a biological father sees the continuation of his own genes in his children, the boyfriend or stepfather (as we shall see in chapter five) does not have this intense and natural motivation. They find that it is not as easy or rewarding to care for someone else's children.

SATISFACTION OF THOSE IN COHABITING RELATIONSHIPS

Beyond the significant increase of aggression in cohabiting relationships, there are other negative characteristics that greatly decrease the cohabitor's sense of satisfaction. While cohabitation was billed as the one institution that would liberate women, setting them free to pursue their passions and dreams, Drs. Bumpass, Sweet, and Cherlin report that a "fairly sizable proportion of cohabiting respondents, especially women, reported that their economic security and emotional security would be better if they were married."[52]

One of the most respected studies in the field of psychiatry, conducted by the National Institute of Mental Health (which will be discussed more thoroughly in chapter three), found that women in cohabiting relationships had much greater rates of depression than women in married relationships (second only to those twice divorced). The annual rate of incident of depression per 100 is as follows:[53]

Married (never divorced)	1.5
Never Married	2.4
Divorced Once	4.1
Divorced Twice	5.8
Cohabiting	5.1

The women in cohabiting relationships also show more anxiety about their relationships when compared with married women. Bumpass and his colleagues found that "compared with married respondents and adjusted for duration and age differences, cohabitors are almost twice as likely to report that they have thought their relationship was in trouble over the past year . . . and in three of every four cohabiting relationships, at least one partner reports having thought the relationship was in trouble."[54] And again, women are the most troubled by the cohabiting relationship: "Females are more likely than males to report trouble in the relationship."[55] Because the data shows that women are safer, enjoy better mental health, and feel more secure in marriage, it seems ironic that feminist leaders, from earliest days, declared the marriage union to be an institution where women cannot find peace, respect, or satisfaction.

Lowered Sexual Exclusivity

As we have seen in the previous chapter, sexual monogamy is an important contributor to higher levels of self-reported sexual satisfaction. Studies show that couples in cohabiting relationships maintain lower levels of sexual exclusivity; this is a significant hindrance to attaining sexual satisfaction both emotionally and physically. Doctors John Cunningham and John Antill showed that "generally speaking, [currently cohabiting and postmarital cohabitating] individuals have had wider sexual experience . . . and are less committed to their present partner as regards the possibility of sexual encounters with others" outside of the current relationship.[56] In addition, wives who cohabited before marriage showed "less commitment or exclusivity to their present or past partner(s)" than wives who had not cohabited.[57] This conclusion corresponds with what Newcomb and Bentler found in their study, with adultery being one of the top three "problem areas" separating cohabitors from noncohabitors. Perhaps this is due, in part, to the fact that sexually satisfied people, like we find among the first-time married, have no need to look to ancillary relationships.

Why Increased Troubles Among Cohabitors?

This counter-intuitive relationship between premarital cohabitation and the elevated risk of divorce is referred to by sociologists as the "cohabitation effect." While the existence of this effect has reached the level of a truism in the social science literature, the nature of this effect is not so clear. There are several hypotheses for why this effect exists, but the two main theories could be called the *selection* and *causal* hypotheses. The first theory states that since cohabitors display greater attitudes of individuality,[58] these attitudes tend to be pathological and are less likely to foster the kinds of behaviors necessary for a successful marriage: sacrifice, humility, flexibility, empathy, and the ability to delay gratification.[59] In addition, the cohabiting partners commonly have a lowered view of and commitment to the institution of marriage.[60] This disparity in attitudes toward marriage among cohabitors and noncohabitors is evidenced by the fact that "those who strongly agree with divorce enter cohabiting unions at a rate 144 percent higher than those who disagree strongly."[61] Therefore, as the theory goes, those most likely to divorce are selected into cohabiting relationships due to their individualistic and nontraditional values and attitudes. The second theory asserts that cohabitation, by its very nature, actually contributes to divorce.

There is an active discussion regarding the validity of these two hypotheses. While researchers have not come to strong agreement regarding selectivity or causality in the cohabitation effect, there seems to be some significant support for the causal theory. One study demonstrated that periods of cohabitation led to more individualistic attitudes and values, which could threaten the health of marital relationships.[62] Another major study found that cohabitation was selective of people more inclined to divorce, but it also found "that cohabiting experiences significantly increase young people's acceptance of divorce."[63] These researchers explain that, for people in their study sample, "nonmarital cohabitation between 1980 and 1985 produced significantly more acceptance of divorce in 1985. . . . The results support the conclusion that the effect of cohabitation on acceptance is not spurious."[64] Additionally, University of Wisconsin-Madison researchers, based on their work, report, "We can state that cohabitation for two years or more increases the perceived risk of divorce by approximately twice as much as cohabitation for less than six months."[65] Three additional studies, while unable to confirm the causal hypothesis, uncovered data that, as one stated, "seriously challenged if not refuted" the selection theory.[66]

HOW TO DISCOURAGE COHABITATION

It is clear from the research that cohabitation is a lifestyle that should be discouraged, not only because it falls short of the ideal of marriage and all the general benefits marriage offers (which we will explore in the next two chapters), but because it can also serve as a hindrance to the formation of successful marriages. Because of the negative picture of cohabitation the social science research reveals, it seems wise to discourage further formation of this domestic lifestyle choice. But how? By stigmatizing it—making it once again socially unacceptable.

This can have a significant impact on behavior. A report by Roy E. L. Watson and Peter W. DeMeo, published in *Family Relations*, noted that 96 percent of all people who are cohabiting expressed no regret about their relationship. In addition, 98 percent reported strong peer approval for their behavior, and 61 percent reported parental approval.[67] Additional data indicates that young people with positive attitudes toward cohabitation subsequently experience significantly higher rates of cohabitation than young people with negative attitudes.[68] Parental attitudes also affect the behavior of children. Young people whose mothers approve of cohabitation married at significantly lower rates than young people who had mothers who disapproved. They were also more likely to actually enter cohabiting relationships.[69]

Additionally, the role of religion is an important component of developing healthier intimate relationships. Research published in the *American Journal of Sociology* reveals that "strong support" exists for the proposition that "the cohabitational and marital behavior of young people is influenced by their religious commitment and participation."[70] Religious young people are much more likely to choose marriage over cohabitation than nonreligious young people. But there must be more than mere church attendance. The researchers explain, "the importance of religion and participation in it are more powerful and pervasive determinants of marriage . . . than religious affiliation."[71]

CONCLUSION

Cohabitation, like the sexual revolution, has not delivered on its promise to improve the way men and women interact in intimate relationships. To the contrary, a review of the published literature over the past few decades condemns it as a failure by every measure. Premarital cohabitation creates more broken and painful relationships, hinders the formation of successful subsequent relationships, is associated with more conflict and violence in the home, and leads to increased infidelity, less psychological well-being, and less equality in the domestic lives of men and women. Clearly, it is no alternative to marriage which, as we shall see in the next chapter, has no peer among alternative domestic configurations in providing for the health and well-being of adults. The data conclusively shows that marriage is more than a piece of paper.

THREE

Only a Piece of Paper?

The Benefits of Marriage for Adults

□

When we defend the family we do not mean it is always a
peaceful family; when we maintain the thesis of marriage we
do not mean that it is always a happy marriage. We mean that
it is the theatre of the spiritual drama, the place where things
happen, especially the things that matter.

—G. K. CHESTERTON, THE HOME OF THE UNITIES

A FEW YEARS AGO, A LEADING PSYCHOLOGICAL MAGAZINE
offered a contradictory companion cartoon to an article on the
health benefits of marriage. The cartoon presented two figures—
Sigmund Freud and Woody Allen—sitting in a bar, engaged in conversation. The filmmaker asks the psychoanalyst: "Is it indeed true
that married people live longer than the nonmarried?" The answer
from his sage companion: "No, it just seems longer."[1]

As modern Western culture has evolved, lifelong marriage has
become progressively suspect. It has even become quite popular to
poke fun at the institution. The promise and success of marriage is
doubted by many of the cultural elite. Judith Wallerstein, a leading
family researcher, highlights this by way of personal experience. In
the introduction to her book, *The Good Marriage: How and Why
Love Lasts* (a wonderfully refreshing book in its celebration of the
ideal of marriage), she tells of participating in a monthly meeting

with a hundred or so of her professional friends and colleagues. Sharing about their professional accomplishments and current projects, Wallerstein reported that she was interested in learning about what made a good marriage. She would do this by observing successful marriages and determining the characteristics and qualities that led to their richness and longevity. She then asked the group if any among them would find interest in participating in such a study. The room exploded in laughter. Wallerstein, of course, was troubled by the group's reaction. She explains, "Their laughter bore undertones of cynicism, nervousness, and disbelief, as if to say, 'Surely you can't mean that happy marriages exist in the 1990s. How could you possibly believe that?'"[2]

Others have tried to abolish the idea of traditional marriage to a warm reception. Nena and George O'Neill, in their very popular book, *Open Marriage: A New Lifestyle for Couples*,[3] open with a quote from Ambrose Bierce: "Marriage: a community consisting of a master, a mistress, and two slaves, making in all, two." The O'Neills explain that "those who doubt the necessity of marriage do have some powerful arguments on their side. Married bliss seems a mirage in the distance, ever more elusive, receding further and further beyond our grasp." This leads them to ask "Is marriage in fact worth saving?"[4] Not in the traditional, monogamous form, answer the O'Neills, and their book is a directive manual on how to create an "open marriage." All of these scorners seem to agree with Shelley:

I never was attached to that great sect
Whose doctrine is, that each one should select
Out of the crowd a mistress or a friend,
And all the rest, though fair and wise, commend
To cold oblivion, though it is in the code
Of modern morals, and the beaten road
Which those poor slaves with weary footsteps tread,
Who travel to their home among the dead
By the broad highway of the world, and so
With one chained friend, perhaps a jealous foe,
The dreariest and the longest journey go.[5]

But these and others who would condemn marriage to the trash heap of obsolescence do not have a sound foundation on which to stand. All of the social experimentation with marriage over the past few decades has produced a large research population for researchers to isolate, observe, measure, and report on. The social experimentation has proven to be an unqualified failure by every measure, and the evidence falls on the side of marriage.

As the researchers have gone to press with their work and produced an enormous literature, one of the most consistent findings is that men and women do markedly better in all measures of specific and general well-being when they are married compared to any of their unmarried counterparts. Married couples are healthier—physically and mentally—and they live longer, enjoy a more fulfilled life, and take better care of themselves (and each other). This has been shown consistently over decades, but it is rarely mentioned in the popular debate on the family. One of social science's best-kept secrets is that marriage is much more than a legal agreement between two people. *Marriage truly makes a difference in the lives of men and women.*

One of the most authoritative professional articles on the connection between marital status and well-being is a review of over 130 published empirical studies relating "marital status to various well-being indices." Published in the journal *Family Relations*,[6] this meta-analysis by Robert H. Coombs, Professor of Biobehavioral Sciences at the UCLA School of Medicine and Director of Education at the UCLA Neuropsychiatric Institute, reviewed studies spanning the history of sociology, beginning with the 1897 landmark study on suicide by Emile Durkheim to work done in the late twentieth century by social scientists.

This extensive review led Dr. Coombs to conclude that there is "an intimate link between marital status and personal well-being."[7] This finding was corroborated by research done at the University of Massachusetts, which concluded: "One of the most consistent observations in health research is that the married enjoy better health than those of other [relational] statuses."[8] This chapter will compare married couples with their unmarried counterparts and show the broad differences in the areas of alcoholism, suicide, morbidity and mortality, mental health, self-reported happiness, stress, and general well-being.

WHY IS MARRIAGE HEALTHIER?

Before we examine the research showing the connection between marriage and well-being, it's necessary to ask *why* married people experience better physical and mental health. Two major hypotheses are offered by social scientists in answer to this question. It is helpful to understand both theories before examining the data.

The two theories, the *protection/support hypothesis* and the *selection hypothesis*, each represent a different estimation of the efficacy of marriage. The selection hypothesis proposes that married couples enjoy increased health and well-being because people who are mentally and physically healthy are more likely to attract and keep a mate, and thus are selected into marriage. Therefore, marrieds are more likely to be healthy.

Here's an analogy that might help: Fresh produce that you find in a neighbor's home is the tastiest, most appetizing, best-looking fruit available. Why? Did it become desirable when your neighbors took it home? No, your neighbors took it home because it was desirable in the first place. The act of taking it home had no effect on the produce. Similarly, the selection hypothesis says that people select mates who are desirable. Therefore, the unhealthy and the mentally unstable are usually not found among this group. Just as the bad, bruised fruit is left back at the store to deteriorate further, the undesirable person is less likely to be "chosen" for a marriage. This could be thought of as the "natural selection" theory of human relationships.

Contrast this with the protection/support hypothesis which asserts that married people do better in all measures of health and well-being because a real and measurable benefit exists in permanent, married relationships. Plainly put, marriage provides genuine emotional and physical protection from the myriad pressures and afflictions of day-to-day life. As the wisdom of Ecclesiastes instructs us, "Two are better than one, because they have a good return for their work: If one falls down, his friend can help him up."[9] In marriage, a spouse provides support and encouragement in the midst of unexpected turmoils and tribulations. Facing life's furies alone is far more difficult than weathering the storm that can sometimes be the human experience while standing shoulder-to-shoulder, and sometimes leaning on, a faithful, loving spouse.

According to this theory, people are healthier, happier, and more likely to cope effectively with the problems of life because of the protection and support a spouse provides. Leonard Pearlin, of the National Institute of Mental Health, and Joyce Johnson, of the U.S. Department of Labor, writing in the *American Sociological Review*, say it well: "Marriage does not prevent economic and social problems from invading life, but it apparently can help people fend off the psychological assaults that such problems otherwise create."[10]

Each hypothesis takes a polar view on marriage—they seem to war with the notion that marriage is, in and of itself, a worthy institution. The contrast is stark: the protection/support hypothesis takes the higher appraisal, maintaining that marriage provides genuine benefits to both parties. The act of being—and remaining—married, actually does something good in the lives of individuals. Its impact is significantly positive and measurable.

The selection hypothesis takes a neutral view at best; at its worst, it paints a negative view of marriage. A proponent of this view might claim marriage doesn't really do anything to improve well-being. Any apparent beneficial results are not surprising and not a result of being married itself. In other words, those who are more healthy are more likely to be found among the married simply because of the selection process.

In fact, an even more negative view of marriage could be taken, claiming that marriage causes deleterious results and should be discouraged, at least in its present form. The reason? Marriage promotes "discrimination" against undesirable, potential mates, leaving them to lead even lonelier, sadder, and less healthy lives.[11] Ironically, this negative view is the mirror image of the protection/support hypothesis: When left alone, an individual's negative traits will be intensified.

Which hypothesis is most tenable? Does the data support the idea that marriage actually does something beneficial in the lives of people? Or does marriage merely select healthier, happier people into itself? While the question is not a distinct either/or, with all of the data falling to one theory, there are compelling reasons to favor one over the other. This will become clearer as we examine the interesting body of knowledge regarding the health and well-being that lifelong marriage provides. With that, let's examine how marital status affects the well-being of individuals.

Alcoholism

Periodic loneliness, perhaps, might be the most obvious negative aspect of not being married, but it is certainly not the only bane; the problems associated with not being married are much weightier than this. First we will examine alcoholism and problem drinking, which are much more common among the unmarried, divorced, and separated than among the married. One study found that 70 percent of chronic problem drinkers were either divorced or separated, while only 15 percent were presently married.[12] Other studies offer further support for this observation, consistently finding the highest rates of alcoholism among the separated and divorced and the lowest among the married.[13] Other reviews revealed that single people between the ages of twenty-five and thirty-four have more admissions for alcohol treatment than their married counterparts.[14] Single men are more than three times as likely than married men to die of cirrhosis of the liver,[15] which is most often caused by excessive alcohol intake.[16]

One of the most respected studies in mental health research is the Epidemiologic Catchment Area (ECA) study which was started by the National Institute of Mental Health (NIMH) in 1980. Completed in 1991, this study was instituted by the President's Commission on Mental Health (1978) to fill a gap in the nation's understanding of the prevalence of mental disorders in the United States. This type of survey was done previously in 1961 by the Joint Commission on Mental Health. However, since that time, many of the official definitions of psychiatric disorders had changed, making an updated study necessary.

Beyond being the first study to look at these newly defined disorders, the ECA study was groundbreaking because of its massive population sample and the extensive variety of disorders it examined. The study was a multisite analysis which conducted epidemiologic surveys in five different "catchment areas" around the country where the populations were at least two hundred thousand. The total sample size contained approximately twenty thousand people, producing "the most comprehensive report on psychiatric disorders in America ever assembled."[17]

This study, reported by Lee Robins and Darrell Regier, deals with a number of mental health factors, which will be examined later in this chapter. Presently, let's focus on their findings related to our current subject: alcoholism. To begin, Robins and Regier find that "marital history is distinctly related to lifetime prevalence of alcohol abuse and/or dependence."[18] Those who are not married are more likely to feel the strong need for alcohol and abuse this substance.

However, those in stable marriages showed the least need, and therefore had the lowest lifetime prevalence of alcoholism followed by those who never married and also never cohabited. The divorced and separated had higher rates, while the highest rate was found among those who cohabited without ever marrying. The specific percentages for lifetime prevalence of alcoholism by marital status are as follows:[19]

Marital Status Prevalence	Percentage of Lifetime
Stable Marriage	8.9
Never Married or Cohabited	15.0
One Divorce/Separation	16.2
More than one Divorce/Separation	24.2
Cohabited Only	29.2

Also striking is the fact that married individuals who do suffer from alcoholism suffer less in the midst of their illness than their unmarried peers. This was the finding of research done at Stanford University, showing that married alcoholics reported lower levels of depression and anxiety, had higher scores on tests of psychological well-being and self-confidence, and reported less physical discomfort in the midst of their alcoholism even prior to any form of treatment. When these married alcoholics were admitted for alcohol treatment, their experience was much more successful. These findings were found to be consistent among both males and females.[20]

Why do married individuals fare better when it comes to

alcoholism? A married couple can count on each other for mutual encouragement when it's needed most. A husband can give his wife the courage and comfort she needs to press on through the stresses of contemporary life. A wife can help her husband get over the conflicts he may have with fellow workers, financial crises, and the challenges of raising children. The support of a spouse can eliminate the perception that comfort can be received elsewhere—like from a bottle. And when a spouse does stumble, he or she doesn't suffer as severely as their unmarried counterparts.

The return to sobriety is aided by a supportive husband or wife—the protection/support hypothesis in action. More than support, though, spouses can insulate each other from the storms that rage around the home and family. In the midst of troubled times, a spouse can protect the other from engaging in dangerous behaviors, like alcohol consumption, that might be sought as a futile coping device.

Additionally, those who have the responsibility of caring and providing for a spouse and children are less likely to engage in dangerous behaviors that might threaten their health and well-being. They don't have the "freedom" to go out and drink at will because of the financial, emotional, and physical commitments to family.

Suicide

Just as a married person is not as likely to find the answers to life's problems in a bottle, the married person is also less likely to feel the need to choose suicide as an escape. Dr. Coombs found that "empirical support extending back to the nineteenth century shows that the highest suicide rates occur among the divorced, the widowed, and the never married, and lowest among the married."[21] This finding first surfaced in Durkheim's pioneering study of suicide and has been validated consistently in subsequent research.

Durkheim found evidence to reject the selection hypothesis in favor of the protection/support hypothesis,[22] citing a stronger social network of meaningful relationships among married individuals with friends and family that give them interpersonal connectedness, accountability, and a sense of belonging. This in turn, weakens the impulse toward suicidal tendencies. More recent studies have supported Durkheim's conclusion that unmarried individuals face more social isolation[23] which, tragically, can be a strong characteristic leading to suicide.

An article published in *Social Science Quarterly* showed that of all the variables analyzed, divorce has the strongest relationship to the suicide rate and marriage has the weakest.[24] Singles fell somewhere in between the divorced and the married. Research done by the Centers for Disease Control and published in the *American Journal of Public Health* supports these findings, with divorced individuals being three times more likely to commit suicide than those who are married. The relative risk for each marital status falls as follows:[25]

Marital Status	Relative Risk
Married	1.0
Never Married	1.9
Widowed	2.8
Divorced	2.9

Of the numerous works Dr. Coombs reviewed, only one study contradicted Durkheim's original finding with all the others supporting its basic conclusion. And this contradictory study was later discredited on the basis of statistical errors.[26]

Morbidity and Mortality

In an increasingly health-conscious culture, with people investing millions of dollars in exercise equipment, workout videos, health-club memberships, and expensive organic foods, it is interesting that there is no talk about the most important avenue to health. Marital status is a significant contributor to an individual's state of health and well-being—perhaps the most significant factor.

Married people suffer less from illness and disease and typically enjoy a longer life than those who are not married. This finding first appeared in the social science literature in 1858.[27] Research done recently at Erasmus University in Rotterdam still shows that "married people have the lowest morbidity rates, while the divorced show the highest."[28]

Naturally, the mortality rates are lower as well. This fact has led Linda J. Waite, an eminent social demographer at the University of

Chicago, to explain that the "relationship between marriage and death rates has now reached the status of a truism, having been observed across numerous societies and among various social and demographic groups." She adds that in her work, "we find a significant and sizable mortality disadvantage for both men and women who are not married compared to the married."[29] In her 1995 presidential address to the Population Association of America, Waite presented some surprising research showing that a married man with heart disease can be expected to live, on average, 1,400 days longer than an unmarried man with a healthy heart. This longer life expectancy is even longer for the married man who has cancer or is twenty pounds overweight as compared to his healthy unmarried counterpart. Being unmarried will shave more days off a woman's life than being married and having cancer, being twenty pounds overweight, or having a low socioeconomic status.[30] These findings regarding marital status appear to turn what we understand about health on its head. Yet it is marriage that makes the difference.

Dr. Coombs came to the same conclusion, adding that "virtually every study of mortality and marital status shows the unmarried of both sexes have higher death rates, whether by accident, disease, or self-inflicted wounds, and this is found in every country that maintains accurate health statistics."[31]

Recovery rates from illness are affected as well. Specifically, one study of nearly thirty thousand cancer cases, published in the *Journal of the American Medical Association* and conducted by James Goodwin and colleagues of the Medical College of Wisconsin, found that cures were 8 to 17 percent more likely for married cancer patients as compared to nonmarried cancer patients.[32] What is more, these researchers concluded that being married was "comparable with being in an age category 10 years younger" and that "the decreases in survival associated with being unmarried are not trivial and apply to a large population at risk."[33]

It is explained that married individuals have higher survival rates because they generally seek medical attention more quickly when symptoms have been detected. Those who are married have the benefit of a spouse to encourage them to seek medical attention and the internal motivation to remain healthy for the sake of their spouse and children. In addition, as seen earlier, married people have larger and more supportive social networks that contribute significantly to the process of healing. These findings led Dr. Goodwin and his team to favor the protection/support hypothesis.[34]

In a study that looked at patients fifty-five and older to see how well they recovered after hospitalization, Lois Verbrugge, of the University of Michigan, and Donald Balaban, of Jefferson Medical College in Philadelphia, found that "nonmarried people have worse health overall, with more days of feeling poorer and much poorer than their married peers."[35] Specifically they found that unmarried individuals spend twice as much time in the hospital as their married peers and also have lower activity levels. Additionally, the National Center of Health Statistics found that acute illness is less likely to keep married people confined to their beds, and that divorced women experience twice as many injuries as married women.[36]

Harold Morowitz, Professor of Biophysics at Yale University, uncovered some surprising data in the 1963 Hammond Report. This landmark study followed the smoking habits of nearly a half million men and led ultimately to warning labels being printed on tobacco products. Given the context of the times, the findings were stunning: Smoking was a serious health problem. However, Dr. Morowitz discovered something hiding in the Hammond Report. The relationship between smoking and individual health was not a simple one; marital status played a significant role. He found that "being divorced and a nonsmoker is slightly less dangerous than smoking a pack a day and staying married." With a bit of humor he concludes, "If a man's marriage is driving him to heavy smoking, he has a delicate statistical decision to make."[37] Dr. Morowitz presents the following age-standardized death rates per 100,000 men (ages 40–69), according to marital status:

Marital Status	Nonsmokers	20-plus cigarettes a day
Married	796	1,560
Single	1,074	2,567
Widowed	1,396	2,570
Divorced	1,420	2,675

James J. Lynch, Professor of Psychology at the University of Maryland, in his book, *The Broken Heart: The Medical Consequences of Loneliness*, asserts that the reason nonmarried persons may be more susceptible to poorer health is the lack of the tranquilizing influence continuous human companionship can provide.[38] Humans are social creatures. We intensely desire intimacy with others and we need the close, intimate companionship that only a spouse can bring.

Obviously, the decrease in levels of physical health among unmarried individuals contributes to a shortened lifespan. But for the skeptic who doubts the connection between marital status, physical health, and longevity, there is ample evidence. Consider research done at Brown University which shows "that the unmarried have higher mortality than the married."[39] Research done at the University of Colorado by Richard Rogers shows that unmarried individuals are twice as likely as married people to die a premature death.[40] Additional work done at the University of California–San Francisco established that those living with a spouse survive longer than those who live alone or live with someone who is not their spouse. The authors explain that "there was no additional survival advantage for persons who lived with someone other than a spouse compared with those living alone, and—particularly for men—the critical factor for survival was the presence of a spouse."[41]

Walter Gove, working from Vanderbilt University, found that those who are married are much less likely to die from diseases that require prolonged and attentive care. He specifically looked at two illnesses: tuberculosis and diabetes. Of those suffering from tuberculosis, "an infectious disease whose effective treatment requires the careful scheduling of one's life," single men, controlling for age, were 5.4 times more likely to die from it when compared to those sufferers who were married. The comparable figure for women was 3.3. Divorced men were 9.27 times more likely to die from the disease than their married counterparts, while divorced women were 3.1 times more likely than married women.[42]

Regarding diabetes, care for arranging one's life must also be taken, being mindful of diet on almost an hourly basis and tracking whether or not medication has been taken. This obviously is done much more effectively when a spouse is present who can help with the discipline and encouragement needed to stay on such a rigid schedule. Again, this gives further support for the protection/support hypothesis. Specifically, Gove found that single men were 2.7 times more likely to die of diabetes than married men. Single women were 2.0 times more likely than married women. Divorced men were 4.3 times more likely to die from diabetes, and divorced women were 1.7 times more likely, compared to their married counterparts.[43]

When measuring for all causes of mortality, the distinct disparity between married, single, and divorced individuals remained. Single males were 2.0 times more likely to die from any cause than married males, and single women were 1.7 times more likely than married females. The divorced male is 3.4 times more likely to die from any cause, while the divorced female is 2.0 times more likely.[44]

Dr. Waite also finds credence in the protection/support hypothesis of marriage regarding mortality and morbidity. In fact, Dr. Waite, one of the leading scholars in this field, encourages her fellow researchers not "to assign all responsibility to selectivity," and instead to "consider the possibility that marriage causes some of the better outcomes we see for the married."[45] She determines that marriage provides a benefit to individuals because it generally brings an increased state of economic well-being due to the combining of resources, thus making quality medical care more accessible. Marriage can also protect individuals by encouraging healthy behaviors such as regular balanced meals, periodic medical checkups, and the keeping of a regular schedule, which is conducive to getting a good night's sleep. Being married can also discourage negative behaviors such as smoking, excessive drinking, drug abuse, and other risky behaviors.[46]

Contrary to other studies, Waite found no significant difference between the marriage benefit for men and women. While men did benefit immediately from marriage, the plus side for women was not necessarily detectable during the early months of matrimony. It did, however, increase significantly over time. The husband's benefits continued to increase with time as well, balancing out and increasing the benefits for both as the years passed and the relationship matured.

Financial planners encourage us to invest our money wisely so that our "golden years" will be prosperous and financially worry-free. Society also encourages this. There is even a large and vibrant industry focusing on this goal. It's a good idea. Unfortunately, there seems to be much less encouragement to invest in a lifelong marriage, which will pay dividends in improved physical health, well-being, and longevity. The wise individual invests financially in diversified mutual funds, but emotionally in a consolidated marriage. Older married couples have wisely invested themselves in this lifelong relationship, and they are reaping the benefits in contentment, companionship, and good health. The love they share is still bringing forth a harvest of benefits with each new year. Sadly, growing old together is often a forgotten ideal, despite the proven benefits of such an arrangement.

Mental Health
I've always felt that Hollywood's portrayal of divorce is often glorified as an escape from a lifestyle that most assuredly would cause insanity. This is seen in the context of comments about the common struggles of life. The statement "I was so confined," or its myriad variables, is often heard. Translated to everyday reality, this comes out, "I had to help around the house, feed the children, fix the swing set, pick up groceries on the way home from work, and take the dirty laundry to the cleaners. My life was not my own! If I didn't get out, I would have gone crazy!" Fortunately, this portrayal is like everything else that comes out of Hollywood—mere fiction. The truth is that married people enjoy significantly better mental health than those who are single, divorced, or separated. To the contrary, marriage—and not the escape from it—is the key to tranquility and mental health.

Benjamin Malzberg, then senior statistician for the New York State Department of Mental Hygiene, reported as early as 1936 a connection between marital status and mental health. He found that first-time psychiatric admission rates for males suffering from schizophrenia were 5.4 times greater for nonmarried men as compared with the married individuals.[47] Malzberg concludes, "The evidence seems clear that the married population had, in general, much lower rates of mental disease than any of the other marital groups."[48] Dr. Coombs' exhaustive analysis discovered that

Malzberg's findings have been confirmed by more than a half-century of mental-health research: "All other schizophrenic studies report hospitalization rates lower among married patients than for the separated, divorced, widowed, or single."[49]

Drs. Robins and Regier, in their work with the ECA study, reveal that the lifetime prevalence for schizophrenic disorders is two to three times higher among the never married, and divorced, and separated than among the married. The actual prevalence percentages according to marital status are as follows:[50]

Marital Status	Lifetime Prevalence %
Married	1.0
Single	2.1
Separated/Divorced	2.9

Feminist pioneer Gloria Steinem once quipped that a "woman needs a man like a fish needs a bicycle." While I can't argue the utility of a bike to a fish, health researchers agree that a man, as a spouse, is very efficacious to a woman—and vice versa. They offer each other peace of mind and emotional comfort.

Research done in England and published in the *British Journal of Medical Psychology* points out that for women, greater psychological distress is associated with being unmarried.[51] How ironic then that feminist leaders, from earliest days, have declared the marriage union to be an institution where women cannot find peace, respect, or satisfaction. Feminist pioneer Elizabeth Cady Stanton declared in 1860: "In the best condition of marriage, as we now have it, to women come all the penalties and sacrifices. . . . In marriage, woman gives up all."[52] In 1972, feminist sociologist Jessie Bernard declared that "marriage may be hazardous to women's health."[53] More recently, best-selling feminist author Naomi Wolf said, "When I think of pledging my heart and body to a man—even the best and kindest man—within the existing institution of marriage, I feel faint."[54] Data, however, contrary to the sincere intentions of these feminist leaders, shows that married women are safer and do enjoy better mental health than their unmarried counterparts. What is more, women and men do know what is best for them, even if they don't always practice it. A fairly sizable proportion of presently cohabiting women in one study reported that their "economic security and emotional security would be better if they were married."[55] And they're right. It is mentally trying to live in a relationship that lacks commitment and security. The ties that bind also give peace of mind.

In addition, Robins and Regier also reveal that married individuals have the lowest rates of severe depression of people in any other marital category. The numbers are as follows (annual rate of major depression per 100):[56]

Marital Status	Rate of Major Depression
Married (never divorced)	1.5
Never Married	2.4
Divorced Once	4.1
Divorced Twice	5.8
Cohabiting	5.1

Depression is an effective measure of psychological well-being because it is something that everyone, to one degree or another, experiences as a result of involvement in normal daily life. So common is depression, it has been described as the "common cold of psychiatric practice."[57] The ECA data on depression indicates further support for the protection/support hypothesis, with Robins and Regier explaining "the strong protective effect of marriage against affective disorders is confirmed in much of the epidemiological literature on subclinical depression as was clinical research." They continue, "Solid marital relationships may reduce exposure to stressors and provide a source of support during times of difficulties."[58]

Marriage's protective effects held true not just for specific illnesses but for all psychiatric disorders. Robins and Regier found that the prevalence of suffering from *any* psychiatric disorder over a lifetime was significantly lower for those in a legal marriage. Cohabiting couples were more than twice as likely to suffer from *any* mental illness.[59] The variance was remarkable:

Marital Status	Lifetime Prevalence
Married, Never Divorced/Separated	24
Single, Never Cohabited	33
Divorced/Separated	44
Unmarried Cohabiting	52

Research conducted jointly at Yale University and UCLA reveals the superior psychiatric health of married individuals is consistent among both black and white populations. David Williams, David Takeuchi, and Russell Adair, from Yale University and UCLA, conclude:

One of the most consistent findings in psychiatric epidemiology is that married persons enjoy better health than the unmarried. Researchers have consistently found the highest rates of mental disorder among the divorced and separated, the lowest rates among the married, and intermediate rates for the single and widowed. Compared to the married, divorced persons are six to ten times more likely to use inpatient psychiatric facilities and four to five times more likely to be clients in outpatient clinics.[60]

Williams and his colleagues conclude that the "association between marital status and mental illness is robust and generalizable" among black and white populations. What's more, they also found that the tremendous benefits a spouse brings to one's mental health could not be replicated by a cohabiting mate. The legal status of marriage—that piece of paper known as the marriage license—made the difference.

Self-Reported Happiness

The last area Dr. Coombs looked at was the issue of self-reported happiness, an important indicator. This is a highly relevant measure of mental pathology because it allows the subject to give an evaluation of his or her *perceived* level of happiness, regardless of what might (or might not) appear to a trained observer. Dr. Coombs found evidence that "no part of the unmarried population—separated, divorced, widowed, or never married—describes itself as being so happy and contented with life as the married."[61] And while single women are generally happier than single men, these women are not happier than their married counterparts.

A Duke University researcher, Christopher G. Ellison, using data from the National Survey of Black Americans (NSBA), revealed that, for African-Americans, "marital status appears closely related to both dimensions of subjective well-being,[62] with divorced and separated respondents reporting lower levels of satisfaction and happiness than their married counterparts. However, widowhood is negatively associated with only life satisfaction."[63]

Does personal happiness carry over into other areas? Absolutely. An analysis at the State University of New York at Albany on the well-being of male and female factory workers found that "married persons are happier" in the workplace than those who are not married.[64] This means that married workers are less likely to miss work, are more productive on the job, are more likely to stay employed for longer periods of time, and are more likely to get along better with those they work with than their unmarried coworkers. Their improved health status will affect their productivity as well. It is certainly in the best interest of employers to actively encourage traditional marriages among their workforces.

Stress

We live in a high-stress society. For many in America, there is no such thing as the weekend. Our work continues on, unimpeded, in a constant flow, with few taking time to slow down and rest. It seems there is just too much to do. Even our vacations are so packed with activity that we must rest and recover when we return home. Contemporary life brings with it many struggles. We often look for ways to escape these struggles rather than work through them. In part, how we react to daily stressors is proportionate to the level of support we receive from those around us—particularly those close to us.

Studies show that individuals in stressful life stages cope better with those situations when they have the advantage of a spouse. Results from the University of Toronto and published in the *American Journal of Psychiatry* followed just over 1,800 interns, residents, and fellows in their medical training. The data showed that the married coped better with the tremendous stresses of training and showed less mild, moderate, or severe levels of depression.[65] The authors explain, "our data indicates that being married was associated with less distress for both men and women."[66] The specific percentages for mild, moderate, and severe depression among married and single residents, interns, and fellows, both male and female, are as follows:[67]

Level of Depression				
	Single Women	Single Men	Married Women	Married Men
Mild	12.8	10.0	10.1	9.6
Moderate	14.7	8.6	11.1	5.4
Severe	8.5	6.4	2.8	1.8

A similar examination of medical students found much the same thing, even when those with personal deficiencies were screened out, thus controlling for the selection hypothesis. This study, conducted by Robert Coombs and Fawzy I. Fawzy, was also published in the *American Journal of Psychiatry*.[68] This team found that early in the training period, no discernible stress difference was noted between married and unmarried students. However, as school pressures mounted, a gap appeared. The finding: Married students dealt with the pressure better than the unmarried students. Not only did unmarried individuals have problems dealing with the stress and anxiety, they were more likely to withdraw or consider dropping out of school. What's more, when formerly single students did marry, they reported a dramatic improvement in their overall sense of well-being.

Coombs and Fawzy explain that a "tenable explanation of the relationship between marital status and emotional stress is that marital partners provide emotional support for their mates and thereby reduce tension."[69] This was revealed in interviews with the medical students. As one male student related, "Sometimes I think it would be awfully nice to come home to a wife instead of an old empty room."

Further, Coombs and Fawzy point out, much of the stress of a medical student's training can come from not having a life separate from his or her grueling studies. A spouse can provide that other life. In medical school, the student is seen solely for what he can do, what he can produce, and not for what he is. A spouse balances this, seeing the mate as a total personality, giving the student a necessary and separate dimension to the daily academic grind. A husband or wife can serve as a healthy diversion. A spouse can also be an invaluable source of encouragement to a weary and often discouraged student. What's more, the married students have a significant sense of mission in their academic career: to please their spouses, to do well in their training, and to complete school so they can provide for their family.[70] One student explained, "Nobody wants to work just for oneself, at least not me. You have to have a feeling that you are working for someone besides yourself; it's an emotional concern, the feeling of having someone in your life that matters."[71]

General Well-Being
In addition to Dr. Coombs' meta-analysis, another notable inquiry examined every study published in English (ninety-three in all) touching on the issue of sex differences and predictors of general well-being.[72] This review, conducted by Wendy Wood, Professor of Psychology at Texas A & M, and her colleagues, agrees with the Coombs' findings. The authors explain that, "Perhaps the most consistent finding concerning the state of marriage is its association with enhanced positive well-being."[73] This finding was consistent with both males and females, but the outcomes proved slightly stronger for women than men. Psychologists from the University of California at Berkeley, Stanford, and the University of Washington, found stronger health outcomes for older women as compared to older men.[74] Research done at the University of Colorado-Boulder examined more than thirty-six thousand adults between the ages of twenty-five and sixty-four to determine the connection between marital status and well-being. Richard Rogers explains that his findings strongly support the protection/support hypothesis:

Marriage is believed to protect individuals by focusing on health, reducing risks, and increasing compliance with medical regimens. Those who are not married have higher rates of mortality due to drinking, smoking, risk-taking behaviors, accidents, and chronic diseases such as diabetes that require regulated behavior or treatment. Generally, compared with those who are not married, married individuals eat better, take better care of themselves, and live a more stable, secure, and scheduled lifestyle.[75]

Research conducted at the University of Idaho and published in *Psychological Reports* looked at a number of demographic variables to determine which was the strongest cause of feelings of loneliness.[76] These variables included gender, age, marital status, household income, educational attainment, ethnicity, employment status, and occupation. Loneliness was defined as "the absence or perceived absence of satisfying social relationships," and it is "not synonymous with aloneness, solitude, or isolation."[77]

Of these variables, "the strongest of all was marital status."[78] This random sample of more than 8,600 adults revealed the specific percentages of those who felt less lonely:

Marital Status	% Lonely
Married	4.6
Never Married	14.5
Divorced	20.4
Widowed	20.6
Separated	29.6

The finding that married people are less lonely is "consistent with other population-based studies of loneliness" report the authors.[79] This finding is even more striking given the author's definition of loneliness as being the "absence of satisfying social relationships" as opposed to merely the close presence of other people.

Catherine Ross, a sociologist at The Ohio State University, concurs, explaining that "the legal status of being married is associated with well-being because married people are more likely to have significant social attachments than are the single, divorced, and widowed."[80] Pearlin and Johnson also found that married people were significantly less socially isolated, but also concluded that when they were isolated, married individuals were considerably less likely to be depressed about their isolation compared to their unmarried counterparts.[81] This data flies in the face of the popular notion that marriage removes a person from the satisfying social circle of the larger world to a life of drudgery, boredom, and isolation. Just the opposite is true.

Marriage retains its positive relationship to well-being into a couple's later years. Research done at the State University of New York-Buffalo showed that for those fifty-five and older, being married was consistently associated with better overall health.[82] Work from the Department of Sociology at Texas A & M shows that those in the same age bracket who are married have a higher intake of vitamins and minerals, protein, and calories than those who are unmarried. While a network of friends or even a live-in companion can improve dietary habits, both of these groups still showed "less favorable food consumption patterns than those living with a spouse."[83] These authors report their findings have been replicated in other studies.

Married with Children
While we have seen that adults generally fare better when they are married, not surprisingly, adults also do better as parents when they are married. Ronald and Jacqueline Angel, both sociologists at the University of Texas-Austin, have done extensive research on the health of children in fatherless families (which will be examined in detail in the next chapter) as compared to intact families. They have also examined the impact of single-parenting upon adults. In their book, *Painful Inheritance: Health and the New Generation of Fatherless Families*, they explain that adults going it alone in the parenting role experience decreased general well-being due to "role overload" as the result of having to carry the entire economic, physical, and emotional load of caring for their children. "Role overload," the Angels explain, "refers to a situation in which being the sole breadwinner (or dependent on welfare), in combination with the demands of being both mother and father to [the] children, creates strains that undermine a [parent's] health."[84] Role overload is significant because

"there is convincing evidence that such role overload leads to higher rates of depression and diminished life satisfaction."[85] This was shown to be true in a number of studies that the Angels examined. One study looked at a large population of single mothers over a one-year period and controlled for the women's initial psychological state. This study, conducted by Sara McLanahan of Princeton (we will look at her highly important work in greater detail in chapter four), found that "single mothers suffered a significant decline in their subjective well-being over the course of a year."[86] In another study, single mothers reported "more chronic conditions, more functional disability, poorer health, and feeling more bothered by health problems than married mothers."[87]

Given the large body of data the Angels reviewed, they can "fairly confidently say that, in general, single mothers have poorer physical as well as mental health than do married mothers."[88] Given that many of the studies examined by the Angels controlled for the health status of women prior to becoming single mothers, they can also confidently conclude that the selection hypothesis is not strong here. They find that "'spouselessness' undermines many single mothers' overall sense of well-being."[89]

MARRIAGE FINDINGS ARE INTERNATIONALLY CONSISTENT

Work done at Princeton University on an international comparison of mortality differences by marital status found "the greater longevity of married people as compared with unmarried persons has been repeatedly demonstrated throughout the twentieth century in a large number of countries. . . . In fact, these differences persist even when the effects of socioeconomic status and other observable factors are controlled."[90] They also found that, unfortunately, the higher mortality rates for people who are divorced, single, or widowed have been increasing over the past two to three decades relative to those who are married.

An additional analysis of the connection between marital status and well-being in nineteen countries by Arne Mastekaasa, a sociologist at the University of Oslo, Norway, found the same international consistency.[91] This study measured well-being by observing several indicators, the most significant being attitudinal

measures of life satisfaction, mental-hospitalization rates, and suicide rates. Dr. Mastekaasa found:

> Clear evidence exists in most countries of a relationship
> between marital status and at least some psychological well-
> being measures. The previously married are clearly worse
> off, but differences are also found between the never mar-
> ried and the currently married. Not the least important,
> these differences among marital status categories are not
> limited to North American and Western European coun-
> tries. . . . There is no evidence that the relationship between
> marital status and well-being is particularly weak in the
> economically affluent and presumably most 'modern'
> countries.[92]

Mastekaasa also found "the relationship between marital status
and well-being appears to be slightly stronger for men than for
women, but the difference is very small." This implies that earlier
findings showing stronger marital benefits for women should be
tempered to some degree.[93] What we can conclude, given the differing findings, is that benefits are significant and largely equal for
both men and women.

To Marry or Not to Marry

Clearly, a nation obsessed with its personal health and well-being
should start to rediscover and develop a new appreciation for the
virtue of the institution called marriage. Why would a society
embrace—or even tolerate—the rapid growth of lifestyles that significantly decrease the lifespan of its people or discourage mental
health, well-being, and happiness? Why would we abolish the one
institution that markedly provides more positive outcomes in every
measure of health?

The simple and disturbing answer to these questions is that we
have lost the desire and ability to make definitive, well-reasoned
value judgments. As a culture, we must face up to the fact that marriage really does have a positive effect in the lives of those who commit themselves to it—as well as for the larger society. Further, the

numerous studies examined here overwhelmingly favor the pro-
tection/support theory as a reasonable explanation for the wide
health disparity between those who are married and their unmarried counterparts.[94]

As Dr. Catherine Ross concludes, "The positive effect of marriage on well-being is strong and consistent, and selection of the
psychologically healthy into marriage or the psychologically
unhealthy out of marriage cannot explain the effect."[95] This means
that marriage actually does something for its participants—and
what it does is very good.

Therefore, it is in our society's best interest to do what it can to
value and encourage marriage and have our community's mediating structures work to strengthen marriage on a family-by-family
basis. The benefit of marriage for children is even more pronounced.
While common sense would tell us this is so, the next chapter will
support this intuitive belief with solid empirical research. A culture
wise enough to favor marriage over the myriad "alternative" family structures will reap the benefits of citizens who enjoy healthy,
strong, happy, sound, productive, and long-lived lives.

FOUR

A Mom and a Dad:

What Every Child Needs

□

If our American way of life fails the child, it fails us all.
—PEARL BUCK, CHILDREN FOR ADOPTION

AMERICA'S GENERATION X, ALSO REFERRED TO AS GEN X or Xers (roughly those born between 1961 and 1976), is the first generation in any industrialized country to see widespread divorce among their parents. This seems to have affected them deeply and has marked their character.[1]

Kurt Cobain, a Gen X icon, killed himself after living a storied life as lead singer of grunge rock's pioneer band Nirvana. Some who have examined Cobain's life believe that the divorce of his parents was a turning point. Like many others of his generation, the death of his parents' marriage was a painful event that deeply affected every area of his life. He made a public commitment that his daughter would not suffer the same consequences of divorce that he had.

To ensure this, ironically, he reportedly told his wife while holding a gun to his own head, "I'd rather die than divorce."[2]

Did Cobain, because of his own experience, see divorce as more painful for his daughter than his own death? He explained, "I've been brooding and bellyaching about something I couldn't have, which is family, a solid family unit, for too long." In fact, as journalist Sarah Ferguson reports in the *Utne Reader*, "the dissolution of the American family has exerted a tremendous torque on the members of Cobain's generation." This generation "engages in a kind of mournful nostalgia for a childhood without violation," Ferguson concludes.[3] Given this, it is no wonder that someone as culturally progressive as Cobain would choose as his favorite television shows two programs as anachronistic as *Leave It to Beaver* and *The Andy Griffith Show*.

This nostalgia of suburbia and the nuclear family is a dream sought after by a generation of people who feel they were cheated by their parents, who were too busy pursuing their own dream of self-actualization and individual expression. Rachel Stevens, a senior at the University of Michigan, captures the heart of the problem: "Ronald Reagan was around longer than some of my friend's fathers."[4] Members of Generation X desire something different for themselves and their families.

David Popenoe, Associate Dean for Social and Behavioral Sciences at Rutgers University, and one of the nation's leading sociologists, has recognized this shift in thinking about the family in his research and among his students. He calls it a "new familism." Dr. Popenoe writes:

In 1990 more babies were born in America than in any year since 1964, the birth rate having returned almost to the replacement level, and there is nothing like having children to shift one's ideology in a pro-family direction. . . . A solid case can be made that the baby-boom generation, coming from the strong families of the 1950s, took the family for granted. To this generation, self-expression and self-fulfillment were the pressing values of the age—at least in their years of prolonged youth. To their children, however, often battle scarred from family turmoil, the world looks quite different. As many national studies—as well as the sentiments of my students—have indicated, the children of divorce, although their statistical chances of a successful marriage may not be so great, are outspokenly supportive of the importance of marital permanence and strong, divorce-free families. . . . It may be no coincidence that we are seeing the rise of a new familism just thirty years after the momentous cultural changes of the 1960s.[5]

As noted, Popenoe sees this shift reflected in the thoughts and sentiments of his students. A female student who comes from a divorced home proclaims, "I will be very careful when selecting a husband because I intend for my marriage to last forever. I really look forward to starting a 'traditional' nuclear family of my own because I think that will add an aspect of peace and stability to my life." A male, also from a divorced home, declares, "I would like to have two children and give them the family setting that I didn't have. The family means everything! I will do my best to obtain the precious family experiences."[6]

There are other indicators of this generational shift in appraising family life. *Working Woman* magazine has recognized that more female Xers are making a different evaluation regarding the balance between work and family than their mothers did. Author Pamela Kruger, talking to a number of recent female MBA grads, discovered a common theme. "Women in their twenties are looking at the failed superwomen. They're revolting against the mindless careerism they saw their sisters and mothers have."[7] They are seeking fulfillment elsewhere. As Liz Landau, 25, of Columbia University explains, "I want to have kids right away. I want a big family—four children. Maybe I'll find something to do part-time, but my children will come first."

Another student, Kim Erle, president of the student organization called Columbia Women in Business, turned down an exceptional position with a major bank because she is pregnant with her second child and wants to stay home and raise her children. She explains, "One high-level woman at the bank called me a traitor." In reaction, Erle says, "I think a lot of older women don't understand what we're doing because they think *they* have it all."[8] An MBA student from Georgetown University explains her thinking, "In my mind, I see the career track and the family track, and I just don't see any way to mesh them."[9] The reason for this shift in thinking among Xers is not complex. Management consultant Claire Raines, co-author of *Twentysomething: Managing & Motivating Today's New Work Force*, explains: "Generations are motivated by what they were deprived of when they were kids, and for this generation, that was time with their parents."[10]

This change in favor of the family has created what *Barron's* magazine labels "a change of place." Chief economist at Donaldson Lufkin & Jenrette, Richard Hokenson, calls this shift the beginning of a "demographic sea change" with "women of childbearing age flocking back home."[11] As Laurie M., a twentysomething "retired" school teacher, relates, "We want to be sure we have a strong family unit. My mother worked, my husband's mother worked; we want our child to have more parental guidance at home." Julie B. concurs, "I don't want to have to worry about my child. And I think if I stay home, we're less likely to divorce—more likely to keep the family whole."[12]

As David Blankenhorn has commented, Gen Xers are "not rebelling against the family values of the 1950s. They are rebelling against the family chaos of the 1970s."[13] They are rebelling against this chaos for good reason. Quite simply, they are products of the chaos, and as they might say, "It sucked!"

But they are not the only people reaching this conclusion. Social scientists are also realizing that marital breakdown is having real and detrimental consequences for children. The published evidence supporting the conclusions of this generation is absolutely overwhelming. As Karl Zinsmeister, the DeWitt Wallace Fellow at the American Enterprise Institute, relates:

> There is a mountain of scientific evidence showing that when families disintegrate, children often end up with intellectual, physical, and emotional scars that persist for life. . . . We talk about the drug crisis, the education crisis, and the problem of teen pregnancy and juvenile crime. But all these ills trace back predominantly to one source: broken families.[14]

What children need most is for their parents to be and remain married. Pitirim Sorokin, founder and first chair of the Sociology Department at Harvard, proclaimed the importance of marriage and family for children some fifty years ago: "The most essential sociocultural patterning of a newborn human organism is achieved by the family. It is the first and most efficient sculptor of human material, shaping the physical, behavioral, mental, moral, and sociocultural characteristics of practically every individual."[15] Sorokin qualifies the meaning of family by explaining that "from the remotest past, married parents have been the most effective teachers of their children."[16]

Anthropologist Bronislaw Malinowski explains the universality of the idea of marriage and the two-parent family unit:

> Yet through all the variations [of family] there runs the rule that the father is indispensable for the full sociological status of the child as well as of its mother, that the group consisting of a woman and her offspring is sociologically incomplete and illegitimate. The father, in other words, is necessary for the full legal status of the family.[17]

The data supporting this ideal is what we will concern ourselves with in this chapter. But first, let's examine how research on single-parent families has evolved over the past few decades.

EARLY RESEARCH ON SINGLE-PARENT FAMILIES

Throughout the 1950s and 1960s, the majority of social science research indicated that single parenting was harmful for children. However, these studies were based on small unrepresentative samples and were vulnerable to criticism. The most significant challenge to this early body of data came in 1973 when Elizabeth Herzog and Cecilia Sudia published their essay, "Children in Fatherless Families."[18] Herzog and Sudia contested these studies from earlier decades based on their methodological shortcomings and warned that conclusions regarding the harm of single-parent families should not be drawn from this data.

Although Herzog and Sudia conducted no empirical research themselves, and even concluded that—based on the previous critiqued research—some negative effects of single-parenting could be detected, their conclusion in "Fatherless Families" was widely interpreted that single parenting had no negative effect on children.

Herzog and Sudia's critique should have served notice that there was a significant need for wide-scale, reliable, empirical research determining the effects of single parenting on children. Instead, it helped to construct a myth, asserting that it didn't matter how children are raised. This irresponsible interpretation of Herzog and Sudia's work gave "scientific" justification for the family relativism that was building momentum in the 1970s.

In addition, research dealing with single parenting became unfashionable when in 1965, then Assistant Secretary of Labor Daniel Patrick Moynihan released his report on the shape and future of the black family.[19] He warned that even while the black community was gaining ground in the area of civil rights, it was being significantly repressed by the growing problem of single parenting. The Moynihan Report was roundly criticized by some black leaders and social liberals as a racist attack on the black community.[20] As a result, few researchers desired to gather additional data of this type. The reaction to the Moynihan Report still presents a problem today in the broader popular family debate. To bring attention to a serious problem among alternative families is seen to be an attack on the individuals who make up that particular kind of family, and therefore keeps us from drawing definitive qualitative conclusions.

In the late 1970s, however, research was being reported that dealt with single-parent families in a less controversial manner. This research dealt with the issue of divorce, analyzing the longitudinal impact of marital dissolution on children and adults. The best known of these studies was the work of Judith Wallerstein which was published in 1980.[21] Wallerstein's findings, which we will examine in great detail in chapter five, indicated that divorce is no casual matter; it has real and long-term effects in the lives of both children and adults. Her work, and the work of others, stimulated and reopened the debate on single parenthood.

THE COMING OF AGE OF RESEARCH ON THE SINGLE-PARENT FAMILY

One scholar who has done more than any other to deepen the study of single parenting and its impact upon children and adults is Sara McLanahan, a sociologist at Princeton University. Her work with single parenting began in 1981 when she read a three-part series by Ken Auletta in *The New Yorker*. These articles, later expanded and published as a book titled *The Underclass*,[22] claimed that of all the ills plaguing America's young people—such as drug addiction, poverty, and dropping out of school—there was one common thread linking each of these: single parenthood. As a single parent herself, McLanahan was outraged by this notion. "I was trained in graduate school in the days when the politically correct argument was that single-parent families were just another alternative family form, and it was fine."[23] She hypothesized that Auletta's negative findings for single-parent families could be explained away by economic disparities between single- and two-parent families. If studies could control for the economic inequity, the two family forms would look very similar.

McLanahan undertook the work that would control for the economic difference with the added benefit of basing her analysis on large representative data sets. This early study has led to a distinguished career marked by the publication of five highly acclaimed books and more than sixty professional articles on the sociology of the family. What McLanahan discovered was that the economic factor explained approximately half of the difference in well-being among children from two-parent families, but it could not account for *all* of the difference. The honest truth, McLanahan discovered, was that a father and husband is more than a breadwinner. His presence matters in the lives of his children, and his absence creates what Irwin Garfinkel and McLanahan have called "a new American dilemma."[24]

In *Growing Up with a Single Parent*, one of the most well-researched and authoritative books on single-parent families, McLanahan and Gary Sandefur, of the University of Wisconsin-Madison, explain that in a "market economy such as the United States, economic well-being is fundamental to all other forms of well-being. Thus, in our study we focus on economic success—being able to support oneself at a standard of living above the poverty line and being able to maintain a steady income throughout the year and from one year to the next."[25] They concentrate on three areas of achievement that can lead to or help ensure economic success.

Educational attainment is one of the strongest indicators for a solid earning potential, and the cost of not finishing high school today is much higher than it was twenty years ago. Worse, in today's highly technical workplace, an employee faces a severe disadvantage if he has spent little or no time in college. McLanahan and Sandefur report that in 1990, the average young man with a college education earns sixty-two percent more than a young man with only a high school education when both are working full-time.[26]

Another indicator of economic success is *idleness/labor-force attachment*. As they leave school, young adults must establish themselves in the job market and develop good work habits. McLanahan and Sandefur explain, "Sticking to the task and holding down a steady job are good indicators of people's motivation, ability, and skills, and ultimately of their long-term chances of earning a good income."[27] If this work habit is not gained early and made an integral part of one's life, it is significantly more difficult to acquire later in life. What is more, strong labor-force attachment diminishes idleness which, among many circumstances, can contribute to crime and other antisocial behaviors.

Early childbearing is a strong indicator of economic success for young women. If young women enter motherhood in their teens, they are less likely to finish high school and less likely to find good-paying jobs in the labor force. More than two-thirds of teen mothers bear their children out of wedlock, and those who do marry have a high rate of divorce. The majority of these teen mothers are forced to depend on welfare, and that dependence usually lasts until their children are grown.[28]

A Mountain of Scientific Data

In examining what the data says about growing up in a single-parent family, we need to look at the first three indicators McLanahan and Sandefur have isolated. We will use their work as the model and see how it agrees with the wider body of social science research. We will also address other measures of well-being that have been studied by various scholars. They include criminal and antisocial behavior, general health and well-being, child abuse, stress, and depression. For now, let us concern ourselves with three key areas: educational attainment, idleness/labor-force attachment, and premarital childbearing. McLanahan and Sandefur have based their work on four different nationally representative data sets[29] assuring their work is immune to the kinds of criticism that plagued the family research conducted in the 1950s and 1960s.

Educational Attainment

The data clearly shows that children who live with only one parent are at much higher risk of dropping out of high school. McLanahan and Sandefur report, "Regardless of which survey we look at, children from one-parent families are about twice as likely to drop out of school as children from two-parent families."[30]

According to each of the four surveys analyzed by McLanahan and Sandefur, with each data set adjusted for race, sex, parental education, number of siblings, and place of residence, the percentages of risk for dropping out of high school, according to family type, are as follows:[31]

Source	Two Parents	Single Parent
National Longitudinal Survey of Youth (NLSY)	13%	29%
Panel Study of Income Dynamics (PSID)	15%	25%
High School and Beyond (HSB)	9%	16%
National Survey of Families and Households (NSFH)	9%	17%

But family composition doesn't simply impact whether or not a child stays in school. It's also a significant indicator of how well he will do while he is there. Regarding the performance of students presently in school, children from two-parent families on average have test scores and grade-point averages that are higher, they miss fewer school days, and have greater expectations of attending college than children living with one parent. What is more, of those from either family type that do attend college, those from two-parent families are more likely to finish college with the differential ranging anywhere from 7 percent to 20 percent.[32]

Other research on educational attainment draws similar conclusions. Research conducted at the Center for Studies of the Family at Brigham Young University looked at a number of academic measures against three different family forms among a study population of 530 students, grades six through nine. The academic measures were: (1) school behavior ratings, (2) teacher ratings, (3) grade-point average, (4) absences, (5) tardies, and (6) social competence and citizenship ratings. Students from single-parent, step-parent, and intact families were examined. It was found that "students from intact families scored more positively on all the dependent variables than did those from both reconstituted and single-parent families."[33] This research team concludes that the academic success of children is enhanced when two parents who are married are able to influence the child's life, explaining, "The consistency of findings across seven different indicators provides persuasive support for this conclusion."[34]

Children also suffer serious academic consequences when they experience the death of their parents' marriage. Scientists at the Child Study Center at the University of Ottawa in Ontario, Canada, found that 30 percent of the children in their study sample whose parents divorced "experienced a marked decrease in their academic performance."[35] Deborah Dawson of the National Institute on Alcohol Abuse and Alcoholism, working with data from the National Health Interview Survey on Child Health (NHIS-CH), explains that 16 percent of children with formerly married mothers and 20 percent of those with never-married or remarried mothers had repeated a grade in school. Only 12 percent of those living with both biological parents ever repeated a grade.[36]

Of course, educational success can be undermined by behavior problems at school affecting the learning ability of the student, the rest of the class, as well as the effectiveness of the teacher. Research done jointly at the University of Michigan and Columbia University reveals that even after controlling for differences in family incomes, behavior problems were "persistent" in single-parent families and families experiencing divorce.[37] Dawson found that children from divorced homes were 70 percent more likely than those living with both biological parents to have been expelled or suspended from school. Children living with never-married mothers were twice as likely to be expelled or suspended. She also reveals that children who do not live with both biological parents were from 45 to 95 percent more likely to have required meetings between parents and teachers to deal with performance or behavioral problems than those who did live with both parents.[38]

Roger Wojtkiewicz, a sociologist from Louisiana State University, using data from the National Longitudinal Survey of Youth (NLSY),[39] found that while those from nonintact families had lower high school graduation rates, it didn't really matter how much time one spent in that family form. What was significant was that the child spent any time in the single-parent home. The author explains, "There is no additional effect for the number of years spent in mother-only families."[40]

In a study of New York City children to determine which were most likely to be at risk for special education placement, researchers at the New York City Department of Health write in the *American Journal of Public Health*, "Special education children were far more likely to be black males whose unmarried mothers lacked formal education beyond high school and who had Medicare coverage at the time they gave birth."[41] Notice the significant cyclical effect of family breakdown that McLanahan and Sandefur referred to. These boys are educationally disadvantaged because they were born to single mothers who are poor and have little education.

As the data shows in this chapter, these women are more likely to be poor and have little education because they are single mothers. The three consequences typically go together as a package and get passed on to a new generation who get a significantly disadvantaged start in life. This creates a bleak picture for future generations. In order for a new generation to be strong, the forces of composition have to be greater than the forces of decomposition. Marital breakdown makes this positive ratio difficult to achieve.

Additional research shows how family makeup can determine what kind of baton we pass to our children in the generational relay race of life. Work at the Western Psychiatric Institute and Clinic at the University of Pittsburgh explains that the number of students who are emotionally disturbed enrolled in public schools has increased steadily. In their population sample, these researchers found that "with regard to family background, 83 children (58 percent) lived in single-parent households, 44 (31 percent) lived in two-parent households."[42]

The type of family a child resides in is a strong factor in determining what academic standards will be set for that child. Nan Marie Astone, of Johns Hopkins University, and Sara McLanahan discovered that "children from nonintact families report lower educational expectations on the part of their parents, less monitoring of schoolwork by mothers and fathers, and less overall supervision of social activities than children from intact families." They explain, "Parental practices are related to *all* of the school-achievement indicators, including grades, attendance, attitudes, expectations, school retention, and degree completion."[43] Setting high standards and academic disciplines are important for children because seldom do they strive higher than the expectations that are set for them. How many children ask to have their homework time increased by thirty minutes every night? It is parents who must set high but reasonable standards that will challenge the child's intellect and ability. If children do not learn the habits of academic discipline in the early years, it's unlikely they'll develop good habits in later years.

When a young person drops out of school, it affects much more than his ability to find fulfilling work. This decline in educational attainment has serious societal implications. Ralph McNeal, an educational psychologist at the University of Connecticut, explains: "Macro-level examinations have found that higher dropout rates lead to lower tax revenues and increased expenditures for government-assistance programs. Rising dropout rates are also associated with foregone national income, increased crime rates, and reduced levels of political and social participation."[44] The personal and societal ramifications of lowered educational attainment are clarified by Sheila Fitzgerald Krein and Andrea H. Beller, both from the University of Illinois School of Human Resources and Family Studies. Specifically, they report:

> In general, the longer the time spent in a single-parent family, the greater the reduction in educational attainment. . . .

Controlling for income does not reduce the magnitude of the effect noticeably. . . . Thus, even after taking into account the lower income in single-parent families, the absence of a father has a significant negative effect on the educational attainment of boys.

Krein and Beller conclude:

Our findings have important implications for the growing number of female-headed families, for the perpetuation of poverty from generation to generation, and ultimately, for society as a whole. As indicated earlier, female-headed families make up a disproportionate and increasing share of the poverty population. Educational advancement is one route out of poverty, but the children in these families get significantly less of it.[45]

Idleness and Labor-Force Attachment

It is the social expectation that young people, as they leave school, join the work force and become productive economic contributors to their families and communities. This has always been essential for young men, and with the changing economic scenario and family mores, women are increasingly becoming attached to the workforce by necessity and desire. Certainly the completion of high school and college can make this attachment stronger and more rewarding, but the marital status of these young people's parents is a vital factor. McLanahan and Sandefur found in their analysis that "young men from one-parent families are about 1.5 times as likely to be idle (out of school and not working) as young men from two-parent families."[46]

One obvious consideration is that children from single-parent families are more likely to be idle because, as we have seen, they are most likely to drop out of school due to lowered ambitions. This diminishment of ambition is likely to carry over into reduced participation in the labor force. McLanahan and Sandefur recognized this and restricted their sample on this point to only those young adults who had completed high school. This control did not change the numbers. No matter how the data was examined, young men were 1.5 times more likely to be out of school and not working if their parents weren't married. Young women from broken homes were even more likely to be idle. The percentages for males and females at risk of being out of school and out of work fall as follows and all the differences were statistically significant:[47]

Study Population	Two-Parent Families	Single-Parent Families
Males		
NLSY	12%	17%
PSID	19%	29%
HSB	9%	12%
Females		
NLSY	16%	28%
PSID	26%	41%
HSB	18%	24%

What is more troubling is that McLanahan and Sandefur found this idleness persisted well into the mid-twenties, which indicates that this idleness is not a brief or passing predicament. They conclude that growing up with only one parent can have a "lingering effect on a young man's chance of finding and keeping a job."[48] This means that family breakdown can impact young men's chances for economic success *both* by decreasing their chances of finishing school and by reducing their ability to become adequately integrated into the labor force if they do finish high school.

Remember the saying, "Idle hands are the devil's workshop"? Based on this sociological finding, this aphorism becomes truth! When young men are not working productively, they are more likely to turn to crime for two reasons. First, it is a means of providing for one's material needs and desires. Second, it is a means of obtaining what pioneering child psychologist Erik Erikson described as the primary occupation of adolescence: establishing a sense of industry. Erikson explains this as learning "to win recognition by producing things" and becoming "an eager and absorbed unit of a productive situation."[49] Everyone needs community recognition (whether it be universally praiseworthy or not), and if a young man can't strive for or possess the values required to be the new manager at the tire store or the local pizza restaurant, at least he can try to establish an identity as the gang leader or a leading drug dealer.

A large body of data shows that married parents have a significant impact in decreasing crime in neighborhoods. The connection between family breakdown and crime is so tight that David Popenoe claims, "As the families go, so goes civil society."[50] This connection is what we will examine now.

Crime

One of the nation's leading scholars on crime, James Q. Wilson, of the University of California, Los Angeles, explains the relationship between crime and married parents in communities:

> Neighborhood standards may be set by mothers, but they are enforced by fathers, or at least adult males. Neighborhoods without fathers are neighborhoods without men able and willing to confront errant youth, chase threatening gangs, and reproach delinquent fathers. The absence of fathers . . . deprives the community of those little platoons that informally but effectively control boys on the street.[51]

Whatever the type of neighborhood or family children grow up in, one thing remains constant: Children will be socialized. The question is not whether they will be, but *how* will they be socialized? Data coming jointly from Columbia University and the University of Michigan takes Wilson's thoughts a step further. When single-parent families increase in a neighborhood, the supply of monitoring and positively socializing adults decreases. Given this vacuum, "adolescents from female-headed households seem to be more influenced by peers when it comes to expressing antisocial behavior."[52]

Michael R. Gottfredson and Travis Hirschi in their book, *A General Theory on Crime*, indicate how important marriage is in reducing neighborhood crime: "Such family measures as the percentages of the population divorced, the percentages of households headed by women, and the percentage of unattached individuals in the community are among the most powerful predictors of crime rates."[53]

A 1990 study conducted by Progressive Policy Institute, the research arm of the Democratic Leadership Council, explains that the "relationship between crime and one-parent families" is "so strong that controlling for family configuration erases the relationship between race and crime and between low income and crime. This conclusion shows up time and again in the literature."[54] This is because the family is the major control agency for the moral development of children. Hirschi explains: "The more strongly a child is bound to his parents, the more strongly he is bound to their expectations and, therefore, the more strongly he is bound to conformity with the legal norms of the larger system."[55]

Clearly, it is not merely social surrounding and economic stability that makes the difference as to whether young men get into trouble. Research conducted in 1993 by M. Anne Hill and June O'Neill at the City University of New York looked at young men whose families were on public assistance and lived in public housing. They found that "among men, the absence of the father has . . . statistically significant effects on reducing work attachment, going to jail, and using drugs heavily." The father's absence was associated with an increase of four percentage points in the probability of a jail sentence. And among black youths, this probability rises by ten percentage points.[56]

Research done at the Institute for Child Study at the University of Maryland compared adolescent males who were incarcerated with those who were not. In this study, males from mother-only families suffered a significant deficit of social skills, and a larger proportion of boys from these families were incarcerated. The authors conclude: "That a significantly large number of nonincarcerated adolescents came from real mother/real father homes illustrates that the intact family structure is more conducive to the development of appropriate social development."[57]

A meta-analysis examining fifty separate studies regarding "broken homes" appeared in the journal *Social Problems*. According to the authors, Edward L. Wells and Joseph H. Rankin, the intent of the analysis "was not to disprove what people already knew [about family makeup and delinquency] but rather to provide a systematic, cumulative, and empirically grounded evaluation of that knowledge, using available research." Wells and Rankin discovered specifically that "the prevalence of delinquency in broken homes is 10 to 15 percent higher than in intact homes."[58]

Researchers Douglas Smith and Roger Jarjoura, from the Institute of Criminal Justice and Criminology at the University of Maryland, note that the "percentage of single-parent households with children between the ages of 12 and 20 is significantly associated with rates of violent crime and burglary [in a neighborhood]. Additionally, this variable is important to the extent that it explains the association between other community characteristics and crime rates."[59]

As David Blankenhorn explains, "We have too many boys with guns primarily because we have too few fathers. If we want fewer of the former, we must have more of the latter. There is little evidence to suggest that any other strategy will work."[60] Boys need role models—an opportunity to observe their fathers controlling their anger and emotions and exhibiting their masculinity in productive and socially acceptable ways. Boys need dads to make them feel secure in their sprouting masculinity so they can exhibit their developing manliness in healthy ways. If adolescent boys are not affirmed in a positive masculine evolution, they will seek to "prove" their masculinity to the world through violence. That is what we see too much of today.

Girls also need fathers to help them learn the proper ways to interact with and receive affection from males. While boys without fathers turn to guns and crime, girls without fathers seem to turn to having babies. We will now examine how family breakdown similarly precipitates antisocial activity for adolescent girls.

Illegitimate Childbearing

What can be done to ensure that young women have the greatest chance of economic success in today's society? One is to make sure they finish school. We have already seen that having married parents can make a tremendous difference in whether or not this goal is realized. Obviously, premarital childbearing can influence whether a young woman finishes school on time, if at all. In McLanahan and Sandefur's study populations, they found that about 20 percent of adolescents from single-parent families became pregnant before reaching age twenty, and nearly 70 percent of these young mothers eventually earned their diplomas.[61] This number is compared to the fact that 90 percent of those who *did not* have children did finish school on time. This educational deficit only serves to further diminish the economic outlook of being a young, single parent.

The probability of a girl becoming a teen mother increases significantly when her father is not around. If he is not in the home, he cannot teach her what it means to be loved appropriately and to be respected by a man. If she is not getting the kind of proper masculine affirmative love she needs from her father, she will seek it elsewhere from a counterfeit source. As Wade Horn, a child psychologist and Commissioner for Children, Youth, and Families during the Bush administration, explains:

> If a girl experiences the love of a father who places her well-being above his own and who acts as a natural protector, then the girl is likely to delay sexual relations until she finds such a man herself. If she is denied such fatherly love, then the girl is likely to try to seek it elsewhere—often inappropriately and often at very young ages.[62]

Judith S. Musick agrees, explaining in her book, *Young, Poor, and Pregnant*:

> Girls for whom basic acceptance and love are primary motivating forces have little interest or emotional energy to invest in school or work-related activities unless they are exceptionally bright and talented. Even then, the pull of unmet affiliative or dependency needs may be more powerful than anything the worlds of school or work have to offer.[63]

What is more, if her mother and father are not married, the young woman does not have a consistent example of how a man should act toward a woman and vice versa. She will have no model upon which to operate when she does begin to establish relationships with boys. This parental deficit can have serious implications for an adolescent girl. Interestingly, E. Mavis Hetherington, a professor of psychology at the University of Virginia, found that girls who lost their fathers due to death became more sexually withdrawn and expressed anxiety sexually. They also reported fewer dates. However, girls whose fathers left due to divorce were more sexually aggressive and sought attention from males.[64]

The empirical data clearly shows that having two married parents who live in the same home reduces a girl's chances of being sexually active and bearing a child in her teens. Adjusting for such factors as race, mother's education, father's education, number of siblings, and place of residence, young women from single-parent homes are more likely to bear children in their teens than their counterparts in intact families. The risks for teen births for unmarried women are as follows:[65]

Study Population	Two Parents	One Parent
NLSY	11%	27%
PSID	14%	31%
HSB	14%	19%
NSFH	20%	30%

[Adolescent girls who became pregnant in school are less likely to finish high school. This accounts for the smaller disparity between the two-family forms in a school-based survey like The High School and Beyond Study (HSB).]

In earlier work with the 1982 National Survey of Family Growth, Sara McLanahan and Larry Bumpass determined that among whites, girls growing up in single-parent homes are 53 percent more likely to marry as teenagers, 111 percent more likely to bear children as teenagers, 164 percent more likely to have a child out of marriage, and—if they do marry—their marriages are 92 percent more likely to dissolve compared to their counterparts in two-parent families. For blacks, they explain, the trends are the same except early marriages are not as high.[66] Hill and O'Neill, in their previously mentioned study dealing with adolescent males and crime, found that girls from fatherless families living in public housing and on welfare were more than twice as likely to bear children out-of-wedlock than in nonwelfare intact families.[67]

Research done at Columbia University reveals that adolescent girls from intact families were more than twice as likely to be virgins compared to their counterparts from single-parent families. The authors of the study explain: "The risk of first sex prior to age 16 is

36 percent greater for women living in a nonintact family at age 14 than for those living with both biological parents."[68] Dennis P. Hogan and Evelyn M. Kitagawa of the University of Chicago found that black "girls from nonintact families have rates of initial intercourse that are one-third higher than those from intact families."[69]

McLanahan and Sandefur explain that living in a single-parent family can increase the likelihood of bearing a child as an adolescent in two significant ways. First, the young woman's future prospects for college or an interesting career are diminished due to lowered ambitions and poverty. This means she is less likely to put off childbearing than a woman who has plans for college or a career. In fact, having a child can seem to be a way to make things happen in the young woman's life, a mechanism to inaugurate the transition into adulthood.

Second is the effect of reduced parental guidance. Research has shown that one of the key factors contributing to teenage sexual abstinence is parental involvement.[70] As McLanahan and Sandefur explain, "It's easy to understand how parents who are experiencing high levels of stress or who are trying to raise their children alone might have more difficulty monitoring their children than parents who . . . are able to cooperate with one another and share the burden of vigilance."[71] As we have seen, without a father to help his daughter develop proper sexual expressions, the girl is likely to express her sexuality in ways that will increase the likelihood of becoming pregnant. Additionally, if the girl's unmarried mother is dating or cohabiting, the girl is likely to deduce that sexual relationships need not necessarily take place within the parameters of marriage. In addition, Arland Thornton of the University of Michigan found that young women from divorced homes had more liberal views toward premarital sexual engagement and this acceptance was even more pronounced if the mother was remarried. This finding indicates that the dating behavior of the mother influenced the daughter's sexual ethic more than the divorce itself.[72]

Lawrence Wu and Brian Martinson, both sociologists from the University of Wisconsin at Madison, have also looked at the question of why adolescent girls from broken homes are more likely to experience premarital births. They believe that it may be due to the upheaval and instability of the broken family milieu rather than any sort of deliberate socialization that may take place in single-parent family homes.[73]

Poverty in Single-Parent Homes
Each of these three factors we have examined—educational attainment, labor-force attachment, and out-of-wedlock births—are key factors in the ability of new generations to attain financial independence for themselves. But if children are going to grow and develop properly, their families must also be able to provide for them at a level above the poverty line. Such a modest goal is not possible for the vast majority of single-parent families. As David Ellwood, Professor of Public Policy at Harvard University, notes:

> The vast majority of children who are raised entirely in a two-parent home will never be poor during childhood. By contrast, the vast majority of children who spend time in a single-parent home will experience poverty.[74]

Garfinkel and McLanahan agree, explaining, "Families headed by single women with children are the poorest of all major demographic groups regardless of how poverty is measured."[75] In 1989, the last year for which there are figures, more than four times as many divorced women with children lived under the poverty line than married women with children.[76]

Historically, poverty has resulted primarily from unemployment and low wages. Today, however, it results increasingly from family structure. Considering that the radical shift in the American family began in the late 1960s, let's look at how childhood poverty has changed over the last few decades. In 1950, the poverty rate for children was 48 percent, and that number steadily decreased to 16 percent in 1970. As the family began to break down, the rate stopped decreasing. Then, in the 1980s, it started to increase. As Dennis P. Hogan and Daniel T. Lichter explain of this reversal, "The root of the problem is the increased percentage of children who have only one adult in their household."[77] In the 1980s, the United States experienced an important turning point. For the first time in recent history, a majority of all poor families were one-parent families.[78]

David Eggebeen and Daniel Lichter, both from the Population Issues Research Center at Pennsylvania State University, discovered many precise and startling factors concerning the relationship between family makeup and poverty. They found that:

Fifty-one percent of the 4.5 percentage-point increase in child poverty between 1980 and 1988 can be accounted for by changes in family structure during the 1980s. Changing family structure also accounted for 48 percent of the increase during the 1980s in deep poverty, and 59 percent of the rise in relative poverty among U.S. children. . . . In 1960, children in female-headed families were three times more likely to be poor (as measured by the official rate) than were children living with both parents. By 1988, these children were five times more likely to be officially poor.[79]

As we have seen, each of these consequences of single-parent families impacts each other. Just as education affects poverty, Eggebeen and Lichter explain the inverse is also true: "Poverty during childhood affects educational attainment and adult socioeconomic achievement. This means that family poverty is likely to be reproduced from generation to generation."[80] As a family disintegrates and is no longer able to care for its children, government finds the need to step in. Between 1960 and 1991, total spending per child (adjusted for inflation) on services such as schools and health care more than doubled.[81]

Societal observers have recognized, from various vantage points and perspectives, that family disintegration has a strong economic dimension. The noted financial paper *Investor's Business Daily* has observed:

A growing number of analysts of all political stripes believe problems with the economy—as well as a number of other social ills—could be best addressed by halting the disintegration of the traditional American family.[82]

The Progressive Policy Institute declares, "It is no exaggeration to say that a stable, two-parent family is an American child's best protection against poverty."[83] And sociologist Daniel Yankelovich, the recognized dean of public opinion researchers, has also commented on the connection between economics and family health:

There exists a deeply intuitive sense that the success of a market-based economy depends on a highly developed social morality—trustworthiness, honesty, concern for future generations, an ethic of service to others, a humane society that takes care of those in need, frugality instead of greed, high standards of quality, and concern for community. These economically desirable social values, in turn, are seen as rooted in family values. Thus the link in public thinking between a healthy family and a robust economy, though indirect, is clear and firm.[84]

Physical Health and Mental Well-Being
Finally, it needs to be noted that children living with only one parent experience lower physical and mental health scores. This is due in large part, as we have seen in the previous chapter, to the fact that their unmarried parents experience poorer health. Conversely, those children who live with married parents have better health, primarily because their parents are healthier and they are able to offer more care. The poverty of single-parent families can also have a significant effect on child health, and decreased parental supervision of single-parent families can increase the possibility of children being injured in an accident.

Ronald Angel and Jacqueline Worobey, in their analysis of single motherhood and children's health, found that single mothers report poorer overall physical health for their children than do mothers in intact marriages. They explain that "mothers in female-headed households reported the greatest number of chronic conditions for their children, regardless of racial or ethnic status."[85] The mother's "reported" health status of her children is an important indicator because it allows the researcher to detect the mother's own perception of how her child is doing, regardless of the child's actual clinical state. The mother is also the one who knows her child best and can detect and report on health abnormalities that others might not recognize.

Deborah A. Dawson, writing in the *Journal of Marriage and the Family*, reports that children living in one of three alternative family types (never-married mothers, formerly-married mothers, and mothers/stepfathers) had a greater probability of being "treated for emotional or behavioral problems . . . [and] have elevated scores for behavioral problems and health vulnerability" than children living in an intact family. In addition, "Children from divorced homes and single-parent families also have been found to be overrepresented among outpatient psychiatric patients and to be more likely than other children to have visited mental health professionals."[86]

Specifically, Dr. Dawson discovered the following about different family types:

- Health vulnerability scores were 20 to 35 percent higher than those for children living with both biological parents.
- The predicted risk of injury was about 20 to 30 percent greater for children from disrupted marriages than for other children.
- Children living with formerly married mothers had a 50 percent greater risk of having asthma in the preceding twelve months.
- There is increased risk of frequent headaches among both children living with formerly married mothers and those living with mother and stepfather.
- There is increased risk of speech defects among children living with never-married mothers.
- The observed proportion reported to have received professional help for emotional or behavior problems in the preceding year varied from 2.7 percent for children living with both biological parents to 8.8 percent for children living with formerly married mothers. For children living with never-married mothers or with mothers and stepfathers, the respective proportions were 4.4 percent and 6.6 percent.[87]

Babies born to single mothers are 2.4 times more likely to die of sudden infant death syndrome than babies born to married mothers.[88] As we have seen, babies born to single mothers are more likely to be born into poverty and therefore suffer its accompanying problems. These infants are more likely to have low birth weights, making them susceptible to respiratory distress syndrome, hypoglycemia, jaundice, and other metabolic and neurological maladies. They are also less likely to be fully immunized.[89]

Regarding mental health, a study conducted at the University of Vermont tracked psychological and social pathologies for children over a six-year period to determine whether there was any change over an extended time span. The authors explain:

> Parental marital status significantly predicted five syndromes for boys (Withdrawn, Somatic, Anxious/Depressed, Delinquent, Aggressive) and two for girls (Attention Problems, Aggressive). That is, children whose parents were separated, divorced, or never married as of 1986 scored significantly higher on these syndromes than did other children.[90]

Today, if children suffer from any type of health problem, it is increasingly of an emotional, cognitive, or behavioral nature as opposed to the traditional nature, which is infectious disease. The prevalence of this triad over infectious diseases has been called "the new morbidity" by researchers.[91] This calls for a closer look at the data on mental health and the children of unmarried parents.

Data published in the *Archives of General Psychiatry* reports that more than half of those adults who succeeded in taking their own lives and nearly two-thirds of those who attempted suicide came from broken homes.[92] James Peterson and Nicholas Zill, in a study of more than 1,400 children measuring childhood depression, found that children living in single-parent homes suffered greater levels of depression than their counterparts in two-parent families. This was true even when significant child and family characteristics were statistically controlled.[93] Other studies also indicate that children from fatherless and broken families are more subject to depression.[94]

Ronald Angel and Jacqueline Angel, in *Painful Inheritance: Health and the New Generation of Fatherless Families*, report on a classic two-year study at the University of Chicago Social Psychiatry Laboratory which found that children from fatherless families "experienced more psychological and emotional problems such as sadness, tension, and nervousness than children living with both parents."[95] These children manifested these problems over the two-year history of the study, indicating that the impact of family breakdown does have long-term health consequences. Children from single-parent families were more likely to use alcohol in early adolescence, and children from homes where their parents are married have better self-concepts, which can serve as a strong mechanism in preventing participation in unhealthy peer-driven behaviors like premarital sex, drug use, and chance taking.[96]

MARRIAGE DOES MATTER

Clearly it does matter how children are raised. Children need and desire a mother and a father who are married. Children raised in alternative family structures start out life with a distinct disadvantage. Given this overwhelming mountain of scientific data, McLanahan and Sandefur conclude:

> If we were asked to design a system for making sure that children's basic needs were met, we would probably come up with something quite similar to the two-parent family idea. Such a design, in theory, would not only ensure that children had access to the time and money of two adults, it also would provide a system of checks and balances that promoted quality parenting. The fact that both adults have a biological connection to the child would increase the likelihood that the parents would identify with the child and be willing to sacrifice for that child, and it would reduce the likelihood that either parent would abuse the child. . . . While we recognize that two-parent families frequently do not live up to this ideal in all respects, nevertheless we would expect children who grow up in two-parent families to be doing better, on average, than children who grow up with only one parent.[97]

FIVE

Shattering the Myth:

The Broken Promises of Divorce and Remarriage

□

This triangle of truisms, of father, mother, and child cannot be destroyed; it can only destroy those civilizations that disregard it.

G. K. CHESTERTON, THE SUPERSTITION OF DIVORCE

THE UNITED STATES OF AMERICA IS A DIVORCING CULTURE. Since our nation's inception we have been the unrivaled winners in the international divorce race.[1] In colonial days, our divorce laws were more liberal and our people more tolerant of divorce than those in the mother country, and the laws and tolerance have remained that way to date.[2] Until recently, however, lifelong marriage remained the overwhelming rule for family life in America. Divorce has always been the exception.

However, 1974 was a critical year. For the first time in our nation's history, more marriages were ended by divorce than by the death of a spouse.[3] The majority of family change became something we did to ourselves, rather than something beyond our control that happened to us. This marked a significant change in the way our society values marital permanence. Further evidence of this shift is seen in a survey taken in 1962, when 51 percent of young adult women thought that "divorce is usually the best solution when a couple can't seem to work out their marriage problems." In 1977, when this same group of women was interviewed again, the number agreeing with this statement had grown to 80 percent.[4]

One of the primary contributors to this slow but steady displacement of a marriage culture for a divorce culture is what Barbara Dafoe Whitehead calls the "Love Family Ideology." As she explains in her book, *The Divorce Culture*, this ideology "abandons the norm of permanence in marriage . . . in favor of a norm of unfettered choice, [where] individuals are free to pursue their love interests and choose their love partners outside the institutional confines of marriage."[5] This pervasive ideology values choice and its accompanying options as the highest good and relegates self-denying commitment to those who are either suckers or unrealistic dreamers. When this idea grows and takes hold in the minds of a people, you have the death of a marriage culture.

This loss of a marriage culture is not only negative because it discourages people from entering and enjoying the benefits of marriage, but some family scholars believe that the loss of the ideal of marriage may contribute to the increase of marital failure. Norval Glenn, a sociologist at the University of Texas, explains:

> Although many contemporary marriage ceremonies include traditional marriage vows, such as "till death do us part" and "as long we both shall live," it is doubtful that most brides and grooms mean what they say. More honest vows would often be "as long as we both shall love" or "as long as no one better comes along."[6]

Dr. Glenn explains that there are "strong theoretical reasons" for making a causal connection between a loss of the ideal of marriage and an increase in the probability of divorce. For instance:

1. People who see marriage as a temporary situation are not likely to make the kind of commitment necessary to work through the problems that the normal routine of life will inevitably throw their way.

2. One who has lost the ideal of marriage permanence will be comparing [his] present marital situation to a real or imagined situation that could be. Under this circumstance, the present relationship will seldom be as fulfilling as an imagined relationship, thus serving to undermine the real relationship.

3. Even people who hold personally to the ideal of marriage permanence might be afraid to commit strongly to their marriages if they perceive a general weakening of the ideal. This could serve as an unconscious protective mechanism against the possibility of being hurt by the rejection of a spouse. This could be one of the reasons that children of divorce are, themselves, more likely to divorce, even when they are ideologically committed to seeing their marriages work out better than their parents'.[7]

Given the overriding influence of the unfettered choice ethic that Whitehead spoke of, it was assumed by the majority of family therapists, researchers, and professionals that divorce, since it created more relational options and opportunities, must be a good thing—certainly much better than living in a lifeless relationship. In the late 1960s and early 1970s, the published research on the effects of divorce was quite similar to the current available research on same-sex marriage and parenting—limited in quantity and methodologically questionable.

Incredibly, in the absence of any available *bad news* on divorce, our nation ignored caution and entered headlong into this experiment with the American family, trusting that everything would work out wonderfully because choice was being expanded. Again, this is similar to the current debate on same-sex marriage and parenting (and perhaps it should be a caution to us as that debate continues). However, as more serious and accurate research was conducted, due primarily to access to larger study populations, researchers came to some striking and unsuspected conclusions. One of the early pioneers of the substantial study of the long-term effects of divorce on adults and children was Judith Wallerstein, a psychologist from the University of California-Berkeley. She explains the devastation divorce brings to a culture:

Divorce has ripple effects that touch not just the family involved, but our entire society. As writer Pat Conroy observed when his own marriage broke up, "Each divorce is the death of a small civilization." . . . Today, all relationships between men and women are profoundly influenced by the high incidence of divorce. Children from intact families are jittery about divorce. Teachers from all over the country tell me that their students come to school wide-eyed with fear, saying that their parents quarreled the night before and asking in terror, "Does that mean they are going to divorce?" Radical changes in family life affect all families, homes, parents, children, courtships, and marriages, silently altering the social fabric of the entire society.[8]

But Wallerstein is not alone in her concern. The Council on Families in America, a group of family scholars from various academic disciplines and institutions, released a report titled "Marriage in America: A Report to the Nation." Led by David Popenoe and Jean Elshtain of the University of Chicago, the report explains the failure of our divorce revolution:

The evidence of failure is overwhelming. The divorce revolution—by which we mean the steady displacement of a marriage culture by a culture of divorce—has created terrible hardships for children. It has generated poverty within families. It has burdened us with insupportable social costs. It has failed to deliver on its promise of greater adult happiness and better relationships between men and women.[9]

THE TOLL OF DIVORCE

What are the personal and societal consequences of divorce? To answer this question, we should start by looking at Wallerstein's work. She explains that when she started her study on the effects of divorce in 1971, little was known about how people coped with the death of a marriage. Common knowledge at the time was that divorce was a "brief crisis that would soon resolve itself," but very little serious work had been done in this area.[10]

Wallerstein recounts the evolution of her thoughts about divorce in the introduction of her book, *Second Chances: Men, Women, and Children a Decade After Divorce.* She was interested to discover whether divorce created long-term effects, and if so, what were they, how severe were they, and who suffered? She submitted a grant proposal for a study to observe sixty families who were presently experiencing divorce. Given the current thinking about divorce in the early 1970s, Wallerstein believed a year would be a sufficient observation period. She assumed the families would resolve their problems and move on with their lives, and during that year-long period, she would learn how families coped with and overcame divorce. However, when the follow-up interviews were conducted after a twelve- to eighteen-month period, Wallerstein found—surprisingly—that most of these families had not resolved their problems. She illustrates what she observed:

> Their wounds were wide open. Turmoil and distress had not noticeably subsided. Many adults still felt angry, humiliated, and rejected, and most had not gotten their lives back together. An unexpected number of children were on a downward course. Their symptoms were worse than before. Their behavior at school was worse. Their peer relationships were worse. Our findings were absolutely contradictory to our expectations.[11]

Wallerstein, realizing she needed a longer period of observation with her families, presented another grant proposal to extend the follow-up to five years. At the five-year mark, fifty-six of the original sixty families were contacted, and the results of follow-up interviews were reported in the book *Surviving the Breakup: How Children and Parents Cope with Divorce.*[12]

Wallerstein explains that while some of the individuals were doing better five years after the divorce, "we were deeply concerned about a large number of youngsters—well over a third of the group—who were significantly worse off than before." Many of these children were clinically depressed, were doing poorly in school, and had difficulty with peer relationships. They had degenerated to the point that some early disturbances, such as sleep, education, and behavior problems, were persistent. The majority of the adults believed their lives had improved at this five-year mark, "but a surprisingly large number did not." These folks "were either stalled or felt more troubled and unhappy than they had during the marriage."[13] One woman complained to Wallerstein that her health was failing and her children were becoming uncompassionate. Rather than seeing her divorce as a positive event, despair is evident in her words: "I have no one to take care of me, no one to check on me. I am totally alone."[14]

Wallerstein also found that the divorce was *not* welcome news to the children. Though they knew their parents were unhappy in their marriage, the children in her study overwhelmingly preferred that their parents remain together rather than divorce.

> Many of the children, despite the unhappiness of their parents, were relatively happy and considered their situation neither better nor worse than that of other families around them. They would, in fact, have been content to hobble along. The lightning that struck them was the divorce, and they had not been aware of the existence of the storm.[15]

The death of their parents' marriage was a significantly negative event in these children's lives. Wallerstein reports that a large number of these children spoke regrettably of their emotional and economic poverty but wistfully about the years when their family was intact. Many of these children continued to cling to the hopeless idea of parental reconciliation, even ten years after the divorce. An alarming number of children were hounded by graphic recollections and flashbacks of the traumatic breakup of their parents' marriage. Almost half of these children at the ten-year mark were "worried, underachieving, self-deprecating, and sometimes angry young men and women." Wallerstein continues that they "spoke of divorce as having cut their life short."[16]

When it came time for Wallerstein to present her data, this negative appraisal of divorce was unwelcome news in some quarters. She got angry letters from therapists, parents, and lawyers telling her the data simply had to be wrong. They sought to assure her that children were better off seeing a bad marriage die than to remain in it, and that divorce was really an emancipating experience. Undeterred, Wallerstein realized that she needed to extend the follow-up to ten years and acquired an additional grant. This ten-year follow-up resulted in her highly acclaimed book, *Second Chances*. The conclusion of Wallerstein's work is summed up as follows:

> The earlier view of divorce as a short-lived crisis understood within the familiar paradigm of crisis theory has given way to a more sober appraisal, accompanied by the rising concern that a significant number of children suffer long-term, perhaps detrimental effects from divorce, and that others experience submerged effects that may appear years later.[17]

Given the data Wallerstein discovered, it was her cultural observation that "there is an extraordinary reluctance to acknowledge [divorce's] seriousness and enormous impact on all our lives. We have been afraid to look at what is happening in our midsts."[18] Wallerstein saw the logical progression of her work as the establishment of the Center for Family in Transition, which provides support and counseling for families experiencing divorce. In the first ten years of the Center, Wallerstein worked with more than two thousand families. Given this vast experience, she explains that on the divorce front, things are not getting better. Instead, they are getting worse.

Although Wallerstein's work is among the earliest and longest study examining the effects of divorce, it is by no means the only work done in this field. Other studies were also conducted that were based on more representative samples than Wallerstein's work.[19] The following is a look at a significant portion of this larger body of knowledge.

CHILDREN AND ADULTS OF DIVORCE: THE LARGER BODY OF DATA

E. Mavis Hetherington, a psychologist from the University of Virginia, is another early pioneer in study of divorce and its impact on adults and children. She conducted a six-year follow-up on a sample of 180 families which compared divorced and intact families.[20] Her observations support the findings presented in chapter three, concluding that the stress of separation and divorce can place both men and women at increased risk for a host of psychological and physical problems. Hetherington observed increased levels of alcoholism, substance abuse, depression, psychosomatic problems, and accidents among divorced adults compared with non-divorced adults. She explains that marital breakdown can even hamper the immunologic system of an individual, making the divorced individual more susceptible to disease, infection, chronic and acute medical problems, and even death.[21] Catherine Riessman and Naomi Gerstel, from the University of Massachusetts, agree with Hetherington, reporting that the health disparity between people who are married and those who are divorced is "one of the most consistent observations in health research." And they found that marital dissolution does not have a greater effect upon one sex in comparison to the other.[22]

Hetherington found that loneliness was a significant problem for divorced women, using the word *pervasive* to describe its prevalence and impact.[23] This loneliness persisted for the entire six years of her study, in spite of the fact that many of these women had built up new social networks and maintained more contact with their families. What is more, this loneliness is much greater for divorced women than for women who have never married. As James Lynch reminds us in his work, *The Broken Heart: The Medical Consequences of Loneliness*, this pervasive loneliness can have significant health consequences, serving to widen the health and wellness disparity between the married and divorced.[24]

Additional research reveals that divorced women do less well in other areas when compared to single and married women. This study, published in the *American Journal of Orthopsychiatry*, explains:

It was found that the divorced single woman reported a significantly greater need for support in the areas of finances, childcare, and career; these women were significantly less satisfied with the support they actually received in the areas of finances, social life, sex and physical intimacy, and household. . . . It is also surprising that the divorced single woman also reported poorer social adjustment with respect to current partner, family unit, extended family, and social and leisure activities. These divorced single women seem remarkably aware of their own distress and their areas of greatest vulnerability and need.[25]

But men also suffer uniquely from the consequences of divorce, especially as fathers. Research done at the University of Texas supports the idea that men are generally better off when they are married and worse off when they are divorced. Researchers Debra Umberson and Christine Williams explain:

Numerous studies indicate that divorced men exhibit more [general well-being] problems than do other gender/marital-status groups. Official statistics and epidemiologic data indicate that divorced men exhibit higher rates of mental illness and mortality than their married male counterparts. The mortality rate differential between divorced and married men is greatest for cause of death involving a behavioral component; for example, suicide and accidents. . . . Fathers who live separately from their children are more likely to engage in risky health behaviors than are fathers who live with their children.[26]

They also report that men who live with their children are less likely to abuse alcohol because they have an increased sense of responsibility.

Parental Role Strain
Not only do divorced adults do less well when it comes to their health, they do less well in their ability to parent their children. Divorce creates an increase in parental role strain leading to a period of "diminished parenting."[27] Hetherington found it is not uncommon for mothers (with whom 90 percent of children reside after divorce) to "become self-involved, erratic, uncommunicative, nonsupportive, and inconsistently punitive in dealing with their children."[28] These mothers are also less likely to be successful in nurturing, controlling, and monitoring their children.[29] She also

found sex differences in how mothers relate with their children. Divorced mothers experience twice as many combative and angry interactions with their sons compared to mothers of intact families, and this relational unrest remained consistent for the six years following the divorce. In addition, a single incident of a flair-up between mother and son lasted longer in divorced homes compared to intact homes. Sons of divorced women recognized their own aggressive, rebellious behaviors toward their mothers and admit that their mothers have little control over them.

However, these boys also report high levels of warm affection toward their mothers. Given this irony, Hetherington explains that "it might be best to view this relation between divorced mothers and sons as intense and ambivalent rather than purely hostile and rejecting."[30] Hetherington's description of this relationship conveys more of a feeling of confusion and an inability to adjust to a difficult family situation rather than one of pure rebellion. It appears as if both want the situation to work, although neither knows quite how.

Divorced mothers showed more expressive attention to their daughters than to sons. Girls also exhibit noncompliance, anger, and selfishness, but these problems diminish in girls after two years following the divorce. While boys have more difficulty with their divorced mothers, girls have more problems with their remarried mothers.[31] We will examine the dynamics of these steprelations later in this chapter.

These sex-differentiated problems exist not just for custodial mothers. Hetherington reports the same types of problems for fathers who receive custody of their children; however these men have less strained relationships with their sons. The isolation both parents experience after divorce can serve to intensify these problems with their children.[32]

Obviously, the needs of adults and children are not always the same following divorce, and finding a balance between meeting each individual's needs can be difficult. In Hetherington's examination of divorced mothers and fathers and their preschool children at the two-year mark following divorce, she found that there was a group of women in her population that reported recovering a meaningful sense of well-being one year after the divorce. These women reported that their lives now were vastly preferable to their married lives before. They described their new situation as satisfying, happy, and stimulating, and they exhibited a greater degree of self-esteem and internal control over their lives.[33] However, Hetherington reports, "They gained their satisfaction at the expense of their children's well-being."[34] Their children had the most frequent, intense, and persistent signs of emotional disturbances and behavior problems at home and at school. Hetherington explains:

> This was in part because, in their relentless pursuit of self-gratification and search for a resolution of their own emotional problems, the mother[s] spent little time with their children and often did not recognize or were unresponsive to their children's needs and distresses. The quality of the mothers' relations with their children was hurried, preoccupied, erratic, uncommunicative, and frequently emotionally disengaged. In addition, substitute child care and supervision were often inadequate.[35]

Impact Upon Children
Generally, it is common for children of divorce to display a wide variety of unhealthy emotional behaviors. At the onset of the parental separation, children of all ages can experience and exhibit feelings of anger, anxiety, pervasive sadness, loneliness, grieving for the lost parent, and feelings of rejection. But the intensity and duration of these feelings varies relative to the age of the child. Further along in emotional development, older children can cope a little better with their feelings as time passes. Younger children, with their egocentrism and undeveloped cognitive and social skills, tend to be more self-blaming in assessing the cause of their parents' separation. The younger children are also more likely to be overly and unrealistically optimistic in entertaining thoughts of parental reconciliation, or these children may grossly distort their fears of total abandonment by either parent.[36] Hetherington also found that young boys exhibit great ambivalence in their interpersonal relationships with other adults. This is marked by a clinginess and indiscriminate displays of affection toward males. Young boys from mother-headed families made overtures toward male teachers nearly

twice as often as did boys from nondivorced families.

This is in part because boys have an intense desire and need to associate closely and regularly with other men in order to affirm their "boyness" and to productively guide it into "manness." Therapist Michael Gurian explains this need in great detail in his book, *The Wonder of Boys*. He warns, "Without male role models, boy culture feels lost, and human culture in general is put in danger."[37] Divorce dampens this vital interaction between a boy and his father.

According to Hetherington, children can adjust to the broken home better if they are provided with a stable, orderly, and predictable household, as well as when the custodial parent is nurturing, displays consistent authoritative control, and sets reasonable expectations for his children. However, these criteria are very difficult to achieve in a broken home. A single-parent home following divorce is seldom orderly and stable, but rather chaotic and in a period of re-definition. As Ann Goetting summarizes from her observations:

> Members of divorced households were likely to eat erratically, and divorced mothers and their children . . . were less likely to eat together. Bedtime activity was more irregular; the children were read to less before bedtime. Also they were more likely to arrive at school late.[38]

Custodial parents will often make more demands on a child beyond the ability of his years. For example, these parents may make age-inappropriate, emotional demands on their children, treating them as confidants. This can cause the child to develop feelings of incompetence and resentment.[39] Divorced mothers proved to be less successful in controlling their children than mothers from intact families. They showed comparatively less affection to their children, communicated less with them—except for nagging and complaining—and punished them more often and less consistently.[40] Children from divorced homes also are monitored less often than children from intact homes. As Hetherington explains, divorced mothers "know less about where their children are, who they are with, and what they are doing than do mothers in two-parent households."[41]

Boys from divorced homes reported being involved in more antisocial behavior that their mother was unaware of than did children in any other family group.[42] In fact, an Illinois State University meta-analysis of fifty studies on the connection between family makeup and juvenile delinquency admits that "the topic of broken homes has been a central part of delinquency theory since the emergence of criminology in the nineteenth century." The authors explain the intent of the literature review "was not to disprove what people already knew [that family makeup is closely connected to delinquency], but rather to provide a systematic, cumulative, and empirically grounded evaluation of that knowledge, using available research."[43] These researchers found that delinquency in broken homes was from 10 to 15 percent higher than in intact homes, and they learned that the race of the adolescent did not change the outcome appreciably.

This higher rate of delinquency can be attributed to the fact that these boys reported spending significantly less time at home and more time alone with peers than any other groups of children. Children in these broken homes were less likely to have any adult supervision when the parent was away from home. They were also more likely to have smaller social networks consisting of unrelated role-modeling adults, such as scout leaders, coaches, adult neighbors, and parents' friends.[44]

Striking Fear in the Hearts of Children

Nicholas Zill, another leader in the field of the long-term consequences of divorce, has focused his work on divorce's effect on children. Zill agrees with Wallerstein that the pandemic of divorce is causing unrest among our nation's youth, even while their parents are married. Children, seeing that divorce is so universal, fear that their parents may not remain married. Relying on data from the National Survey of Children,[45] Zill observes more than half of all elementary school-age children become afraid for the future of their families when their parents have arguments.

The same survey also revealed that children of divorced or separated parents have poorer relationships with either parent than children who live with both biological or adoptive parents. Whereas 55 percent of children from intact families had positive relationships with both parents, only 26 percent of children from broken homes reported the same positive relationship with both parents.[46] This may not seem significant since children from broken homes are likely to have strained relationships with either parent due to the death of the marriage. The children might, for real or imagined reasons, blame one of the parents for the breakup of the home and are more likely to have a strained relationship with that parent. Given this, it is significant to consider that for intact families, only 18 percent of children reported having *negative* relationships with *both* parents, while 30 percent of children from broken homes reported the same.[47]

Zill also notes that children from divorced homes are much more likely to become depressed and withdrawn, display antisocial, impulsive, and hyperactive behaviors, and exhibit behavioral problems at school (ranging from having a note sent home to being expelled).[48] But while children face limitations from parental divorce when they are young, they also suffer some impact as they enter adulthood.

Children of Divorce as Adults

Zill found that adult children (ages eighteen to twenty-two) from divorced families were twice as likely to exhibit problems than those who came from intact families, even after controlling for demographic and socioeconomic differences.[49] Zill explains that "the common belief that parental divorce poses long-term hazards for the children involved is supported by this analysis of longitudinal data from . . . a nationally representative sample of American youth." He continues, "Effects of marital discord and family disruption were visible twelve to twenty-two years later in poor relationships with parents, and [there is] an increased likelihood of dropping out of high school and receiving psychological help."[50]

Teresa Cooney, of the University of Delaware, finds that adult children of divorce have poorer relationships with their parents than do their peers from intact families.[51] Looking at eighteen- to twenty-three-year-olds, Cooney reports from her study that "approximately 15 percent of nonresident adult children of divorce had less than monthly contact with their fathers—something that was virtually unheard of in intact families."[52] Less than 60 percent of these children had weekly contact with their fathers in contrast to 80 percent from intact families.

Divorced Parents and Diminished Well-Being over a Lifespan
Another leader in the field of divorce research, Paul Amato, a sociologist from the University of Nebraska, also finds that divorce affects children when they are young, into adulthood and beyond. The *Journal of Marriage and the Family* reports on two meta-analyses conducted by Amato, one looking at how divorce impacts children while they are young and the other examining how divorce influences children as they enter adulthood.[53] As we have seen in previous chapters, the meta-analysis is an effective conclusion-drawing tool because it allows researchers to look at a large number of studies that come to various conclusions due to methodological variations and then arrive at a median finding. In effect, it analyzes the work of a large number of researchers through their published studies, considers all of their inconsistencies, discrepancies, and disagreements with each other, then comes to an educated conclusion as to what the academic community is collectively saying on a particular issue.

Effect of Divorce on Adolescents
Amato's first analysis pooled the results of ninety-two separate studies involving a collective research population of more than thirteen thousand children, ranging from preschool to late teens.[54] In order for a study to be included in this analysis, Amato required that each of the studies contains a sample of children living in both a single-parent family created by divorce and a sample of children living in continuously intact families. Looking at a total of eight different measurements of well-being, Amato found that children of divorce, on average, experience greater problems than children from intact families in each area.[55] He explains that "these problems include lower academic achievement, more behavioral problems, poorer psychological adjustments, more negative self-concepts, more social difficulties, and more problematic relationships with both mothers and fathers."[56] This led Amato to conclude that "the view that children of divorce adapt readily and reveal no lasting negative consequences is simply not supported by the cumulative data in this area."[57]

In addition to all the data examined in the previous chapter, and beyond the ninety-two studies analyzed by Amato, there are various studies that support the conclusion that divorce does have a real impact upon children's lives. Regarding the academic accomplishments and behavior of children, Sylvie Drapeau of the University of Laval, Quebec, and Camil Bouchard from the University of Quebec at Montreal, in their study of six- to twelve-year-old Canadian students from divorced and intact families, found that children from disrupted families were seen as "less competent" and their behavior was more likely to be judged "in the average" by their teachers. The behaviors of students from intact families were considered above average by the same teachers. The parents of children from disrupted families rated their own children's school performance and behavior less satisfactorily than parents of children from intact families.[58]

Work done jointly at Georgetown University and Johns Hopkins University also found that behavior problems were more consistent among children from disrupted families than those from intact families. This study looked at a sample of 1,123 children whose parents were married in 1986 and how they fared at that time in the areas of behavior and school performance. They were re-examined in 1988 to see if their families were still intact and how family cohesion or disruption affected either measure. At re-examination, 129 children of the original sample had experienced the divorce of their parents. These researchers found that children from divorced families, on average, ranked worse in their behavior and academic accomplishments than children with married parents.[59] Other work showed that high school students who experience the breakup of their parents' marriages exhibited more aggression and more depression than children with alcoholic parents.[60]

Amato mentioned that children of divorce experience more negative psychological outcomes, but the breakup of a marriage can also influence physical well-being. Research done jointly at Kent State and the University of Akron, polling parents and teachers of children from intact and divorced families, found that reported "health ratings for intact-family children, as well as their parents and siblings, were higher than ratings assigned to divorced-family children and their parents and siblings."[61]

A study in Australia, at the University of Queensland, examined some two thousand Australian adolescents from both divorced and intact families. This work found that "adolescents from disrupted families reported higher levels of general health problems, were more neurotic, less extroverted, had poorer perceptions of their bodies, were more impulsive, and had more negative views of their school performance."[62] They were also more likely to have requested the help of health professionals for emotional problems and were more likely to be sexually active. Additional work has confirmed that children of divorce are more likely to have lower self-concepts compared to children from intact families, leading to an increased likelihood of participation by these youths in harmful and antisocial behaviors.[63]

Similar findings come from research conducted in New Zealand, which followed a sample of nearly one thousand children during a fifteen-year period. This data shows that children of divorce were between 1.11 and 4 times more likely to be sexually active than children living with both parents and 2.75 times more likely to abuse substances. These negative outcomes remained consistent even when controls were made for other outside social factors.[64]

ADULT CHILDREN OF DIVORCE

The second meta-analysis conducted by Paul Amato was comprised of thirty-seven separate studies which examined, as Zill's did, how children of divorce did as adults with a collective study population of more than eighty thousand adults.[65] As in his first meta-analysis, Amato required that the studies he examined involve children from both intact and divorced families and include at least one qualitative measure of well-being. In addition, the respondents had to be at least eighteen years old or over, and studies based entirely on college students were discarded. Amato looked at fifteen categories of well-being and found that "adult children of divorce generally exhibited a *lower* level of well-being when compared with other adults (emphasis in original)."[66]

Compared with their peers from intact families, adults from divorced homes "had lower psychological well-being, more behavioral problems, less education, lower job status, a lower standard of living, lower marital satisfaction, a heightened risk of divorce, a heightened risk of being a single parent, and poorer physical health."[67] Amato concludes that "the long-term consequences of parental divorce for adult attainment and quality of life may prove to be more serious than the short-term emotional and social problems in children that are more frequently studied."[68]

Additional studies, conducted since the time of Amato's meta-analysis, support his findings. Compared with their peers from continuously intact families, adult children of divorce were found in these additional studies to be less likely to finish high school or attend college. They are more likely to be idle when out of school. They are more likely to engage in sex at an earlier age, cohabit, form families earlier without the benefit of marriage, and face a greater likelihood of divorce when they do marry. Adult children of divorce exhibit more depression and report less satisfaction with their lives. They are more likely to report needing psychological help.[69] These grown children are also more likely to be hospitalized for some physical ailment and face an increased risk of mortality.[70]

Although his work is not based on empirical scientific research, Professor Allan Bloom, in his book, *The Closing of the American Mind*, makes some interesting observations about the college students from divorced homes he encountered in his many years at the University of Chicago. As a liberal arts teacher, he explained that he was keenly aware of his students' limitations to entertain self-probing questions which are essential to a significant humanities education. Of these students, Bloom lamented:

> I find they are not as open to the serious study of philosophy and literature as some other students are. I would guess this is because they are less eager to look into the meaning of their lives, or risk shaking their received opinions. In order to live with the chaos of their experience, they tend to have rigid frameworks about what is right and wrong and how they ought to live. They are full of desperate platitudes about self-determination, respect for others' rights and decisions, the need to work out one's individual values and commitments, etc. All this is a thin veneer over boundless seas of rage, doubt, and fear.[71]

Why the Disparity?

Why do children of divorce do less well—both as children and adults—than their peers in two-parent families? Amato explains that the mechanisms responsible for this disparity are just beginning to be understood. He cites five contributing factors to the difficult road facing children of divorce.[72]

The first factor is *parental absence*. Just as we saw in the previous chapter, children need two parents in order to succeed in the measures that mark personal well-being. Divorce affects this because the breakup of a marriage usually decreases the amount of time a child spends with both parents due to separated living arrangements. The quality of time with the custodial parent usually decreases, as well, because of the increased stress and household duties that fall on this single parent. "Quality time" with the noncustodial parent decreases simply because the quantity of time is less.[73]

This increased strain and responsibility leads us to the second factor: *parental adjustment*. Following a divorce, parents often exhibit signs of anxiety and depression which affect their ability to parent. As we have seen from Hetherington's work, subsequent to a divorce, parents were less affectionate to their children, tended to make more age-inappropriate demands of their children, were less aware of their whereabouts and activities, and were inconsistent and arbitrary in their discipline.[74] Children need to draw stability from their parents, and if the parents are not able to provide this, the child matures with a deficit.

The third factor is what Amato calls *interparental conflict*. Children who experience the heated conflict of their parents on a regular basis tend to become children who settle conflicts with others via fighting and aggression. Effective conflict resolution skills are not being modeled for these children. They are not learning to talk through and resolve problems with reason and compromise. This can significantly interfere with a child's ability to start and maintain meaningful relationships in childhood and as adults. It can also determine how these children deal with their own spouses.

The fourth factor coming to bear on why children of divorce fare worse than children of intact families is *economic hardship*. Divorce usually brings a radically decreased standard of living for custodial mothers and their children. As we saw from Sara McLana-han's work in the previous chapter, the economic impact of family breakdown is indeed serious for the well-being of children. Lenore J. Weitzman originally reported in *The Divorce Revolution* that men average a gain of 42 percent in their standard of living, while women experience a decline of 73 percent in theirs.[75] However, in 1996 she admitted that there were some errors in her computations due to a computer data file mix-up. Another researcher, Richard R. Peter-son, of the Social Science Research Council, recalculated Weitz-man's figures and found a 27 percent decline in women's post-divorce standard of living and a 10 percent increase in men's.[76]

But this conclusion, that women suffer and men benefit finan-cially from divorce has been contradicted by the work of other researchers. Writing in the *Journal of Divorce and Remarriage*, Atlee Stroup and Gene Pollock found that men and women both suffer financially from divorce. They explain that for "both genders, incomes of divorced persons are lower than incomes of married persons."[77] Using national probability samples, they found that divorced women will experience an income decline of about 30 per-cent, while the divorced male will experience about a 10 percent drop in income. However, neither of these findings contradict the observation of William J. Goode, who notes that international stud-ies consistently find that divorced women are universally disad-vantaged compared to divorced men.[78] It appears that both men and women lose financially in divorce, but to differing degrees.

Children are both directly and indirectly affected by the eco-nomic impact of divorce, often to such a degree that "they share many of the emotional problems experienced by the children who went through the Great Depression."[79] Economic problems within families can mean elevated levels of psychological and behavioral problems for children, decreased nutritional intake, and lack of available medical care. A decrease in family income can determine that a family will live in a neighborhood with a higher prevalence of crime, making the children more susceptible to negative peer influences and increased physical harm. Economic status can also make a good education more difficult to attain.[80]

The fifth factor is *life stress*. Each of the previous four factors create stress in the lives of those seeing their families break down.

However, divorce brings additional stresses. These include the mere act of moving and changing schools. In addition, remarriage and coping with stepparents and siblings can, as we will see later in this chapter, be a source of strain.

Adults also suffer from their own divorces. Their distress has consequences for their relationship with their children. Frank Furstenberg, of the University of Pennsylvania, and Andrew Cherlin, of Johns Hopkins University, in their book, *Divided Families: What Happens to Children When Parents Part*, explain that children at different ages react to their parents' breakup in different ways. For instance, preschoolers interpret their world in a very egocentric way, therefore deducing that the breaking of their family must be their fault because they did something very bad to "make Mommy (or Daddy) leave."

Older children are able to understand that the divorce is not their fault, but still cannot understand why Mom and Dad are not living together. They exhibit great concern as to what this divorce will mean for their lives. Adolescents commonly show a great deal of anger at one or both of their parents for breaking up the family.[81]

Given these troubles in children's lives, the broken family is at a great disadvantage in providing what a child needs most. First, children of divorce need extra attention and emotional support in order to soften this significant blow to their entire world. Second, they need the predictable structure of a regular schedule. They need to be able to depend on things.[82] But divorce, by its very nature, lessens a parent's ability to provide these things. Depressed and troubled parents do not have the extra emotional capital to provide adequately for a hurting child. Concerning a regular routine, divorce shatters this, at least for a time. In the first year following a divorce, women are seven times more likely to move than married women.[83] Furstenberg and Cherlin conclude that "researchers agree that almost all children are moderately or severely distressed when their parents separate, and that most continue to experience confusion, sadness, or anger for a period of months or even years."[84]

Remarriage

If married people enjoy enhanced general well-being, and divorce decreases this well-being, wouldn't it seem reasonable that divorced

143

individuals could recover this sense of well-being by remarrying? Unfortunately, research shows that this does not occur, indicating instead that remarriages are less stable than first marriages and more likely to end in another divorce. Given the increased problems created by divorce that we just observed, rather than ameliorate the problems of divorce, remarriage can serve to reinforce and amplify them. Remarriage is a genuine cause for concern. Let's examine it in greater detail.

Those remarrying would seem to have a number of seemingly advantageous characteristics (older, more mature, more time to search for a spouse who can satisfy their needs and preferences, and greater work skills). Yet in his study of remarriages, Andrew Cherlin found that "the divorce rate is higher in remarriages after divorce."[85] He explains that this finding has appeared consistently over twenty years of research and that several recent studies have shown that levels of satisfaction and happiness are lower among the remarried. The *Journal of Divorce and Remarriage* reports that "remarried respondents generally do report elevated levels of tension and disagreement, in comparison with first-married respondents."[86] Cherlin found that the differences among those who are married the first time and those who remarried are more distinct for women.[87]

David Popenoe explains that the most recent census data reveals that more than 62 percent of remarriages among women under age forty will end in divorce, and the likelihood of this end is increased if children are involved.[88] Popenoe contrasts this with the fact that from 40 to 50 percent of first marriages among this age group can be expected to die.

James H. Bray, of the Texas Woman's University, draws conclusions that align with Popenoe's. Bray explains that the fragility of remarriage is because "stepfamilies had less cohesive, more problematic, and more stressful family relationships than nondivorced families."[89] Hetherington and Kathleen M. Jodl report that "stepfamilies have more conflict about childrearing and the financial support of children, less cohesion, ambiguous or disparate role expectations, more stress, and more problems in childrearing and child adjustment than families in first marriages."[90] Frank Furstenberg explains that "second marriages have a higher risk of divorce than do first marriages," and he offers two reasons: First, that step-parents have a difficult time defining new parenting roles and this can create significant tension in a home. Second, the population of those remarrying consists of individuals who have already demonstrated a willingness to leave an unhappy relationship.[91]

Stepfamilies: Remarried with Children
In fairy-tale literature, as in the stories of Snow White, Hansel and Gretel, or the legendary Cinderella, stepparents are the perennial antagonists. But this negative characterization of stepparents is not confined culturally. A consultation of the interesting and massive *Motif-Index of Folk Literature* will reveal that in Irish myth, "Evil stepmother orders stepdaughter to be killed," or in India, "Evil stepmother works stepdaughter to death in absence of merchant husband," and similar classifications continue, whether looking at Eskimos or Indonesians.[92] What is the real-world appraisal of steprelationships?

While many stepfamilies lead peaceful, productive home lives and are successful in raising well-adjusted children who become significant contributors to society, a large number of these families are facing considerable problems. Remarriages and stepfamilies involving children can provide more problems for adults by producing more divorce. But we shall also see that the role of stepparenting can be less satisfying for adults. And while we have seen that children need two parents, remarriage does not provide a cushioning effect from the negative impact of divorce for the children. Ironically, a growing body of research indicates that children might be better off in a single-parent family than living in a stepfamily. As Popenoe explains:

> Social scientists used to believe that for positive child outcomes, stepfamilies were preferable to single-parent families. Today, we are not so sure. Stepfamilies typically have an economic advantage, but some recent studies indicate that the children of stepfamilies have as many behavioral and emotional problems as the children of single-parent families, and possibly more.[93]

145

Stepfamilies and Parenting

In his survey research, Andrew Greeley found that two-thirds of the respondents in their first marriage say they agreed with their spouse on the particulars of raising children, while only half of spouses in their second (or third) marriage agreed on how to perform this vital task. Additionally, he reports, 85 percent of those in first marriages rate their spouse as a good parent compared to 68 percent of couples in their second marriage.[94] Research done at the University of Western Ontario found that couples raising stepchildren faced a risk of divorce more than four times greater than couples without stepchildren.[95] A nationwide sample of more than fifteen hundred married individuals revealed that "respondents with stepchildren report significantly less satisfaction with their family life than respondents with biological children."[96] Based on these findings, Lynn White and Alan Booth conclude:

A comparison of parents with stepchildren and those without shows a strong and consistent pattern: Parents with stepchildren more often would enjoy living away from their [step]children, perceive their [step]children as causing them problems, are dissatisfied with their spouse's relationship to their [biological] children, think their marriage has a negative effect on their relationship with their own children, and wish they had never remarried.[97]

Researchers, working jointly from the University of Wisconsin-Madison and Princeton University, found that "stepmothers, stepfathers, and cohabiting male partners reported significantly less frequent activities with and positive responses to children than did original parents."[98] They add that "stepparents engaged in child-related activities and/or expressed positive feelings toward children less frequently than did original parents," explaining that their findings are consistent with previous research.[99] Furstenberg and Cherlin report that stepparents who are raising both biological children and stepchildren reported that stepparenting was less rewarding and more difficult, while stepchildren consistently described negative relationships with stepparents more often than did children from intact families.[100]

A nationally representative sample of some two thousand children from more than fifteen hundred households revealed that a majority of stepparents reported having more difficulty in that role and indicated some reservations about their ability to give love and discipline to their stepchildren. A large number said their stepchildren did not accept them as parents.[101] Hetherington and Jodl's findings confirmed this, explaining that close stepfather/stepchild relationships were difficult to develop at best, and if the remarriage occurred while the child was in adolescence, the relationship might not form at all.[102] This is compounded by the fact that biological parents in stepfamilies felt, to a larger degree than in intact families, that their spouse did not take enough responsibility in rearing their collective children and did not have adequate control over their stepchildren.[103]

When asked who they included in their family, only 1 percent of parents failed to mention their biological children, while 15 percent of those parents with stepchildren residing in the house did not list them as family members. When children were asked the same question, 7 percent excluded a biological mother while 9 percent excluded a biological father. Regarding residential stepparents, 31 percent of children failed to mention these. When asked about siblings, 19 percent of children did not mention biological siblings compared to 41 percent who did not mention stepsiblings living in their home.[104] Controlling for length of time spent in stepfamilies did not affect any of these numbers.

Psychology Today gave a sobering appraisal regarding the health of stepfamilies:

> Stepfamilies are such a minefield of divided loyalties, emotional traps, and management conflicts that they are the most fragile form of family in America, breaking up at an even greater rate than first marriages.[105]

Children also report more conflict and more distant and less supportive relationships with their stepparents, and stepparents usually agreed with the child's assessment.[106] Regarding parental conflict in stepfamilies, girls show a higher percentage of problem behaviors in stepfamilies, especially in a biological mother/stepfather scenario, while boys exhibited more problem behavior during the divorce phase.[107]

Stepfamilies and Children

While we saw in the previous chapter that children need two parents for proper development and socialization, it is not merely the presence of two adults that matters, but the adult's relationship to the child. Biology matters. Zill found that children living in stepfamilies experienced more developmental problems, were three times as likely to have sought or required psychological help in the last year,[108] ranked a little lower in their classes at school, were nearly twice as likely to have repeated a grade, and were less likely to be described as being in excellent health when compared with children from intact families.[109]

Specifically, working with a sample from the *National Household Education Survey* (NHES) of more than ten thousand students in grades six through twelve, Zill reports the following on the percentage of children experiencing specific difficulties in their academic achievement:[110]

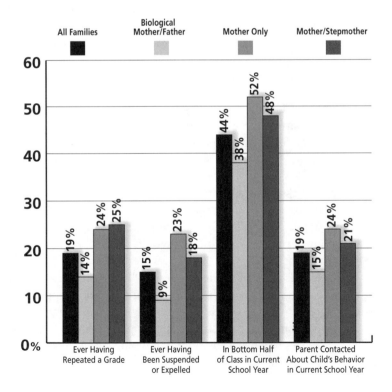

148

Zill summarizes that "students from mother-stepfather families were 80 percent more likely to have repeated a grade, and twice as likely to have been suspended or expelled, than were those from mother-father families. They were 25 percent more likely to be in the bottom half of their class, and 50 percent more likely to have had their parents contacted about school behavior problems in the last year."[111] These differences remained significant even after controlling for differences in child and family characteristics such as age of child, educational attainment of parents, and racial and ethnic backgrounds of families. These findings are consistent, reports Zill, with other studies taking both longitudinal and cross-sectional approaches.

Some argue that it is not the type of family that children come from that determines whether they will succeed in school, but how involved the parent or parents are in the educational life of the child. Data from the *National Household Educational Survey* indicates that this is true—or at least to some degree. Children do, in fact, perform better when their parents are involved in their education, regardless of what type of family they come from. *However*, family type can significantly determine how involved a parent might be. Parents participating in the *National Household Education Survey* were asked three questions about the extent of their involvement in their child's education. The questioning began:

"Since the beginning of the school year, have you or [child's other parent]:

1. Attended a general school meeting, for example, back-to-school night or a meeting of a parent-teacher organization?
2. Attended a school or class event, such as a play, sports event, or science fair?
3. Acted as a volunteer at the school or served on a school committee?"[112]

Parents who participated in none or only one of these areas were scored as having "low involvement," and those participating in two were classified as having "moderate involvement." Those answering affirmatively to all three were categorized as parents with "high involvement." These three categories were broken down among the different family types as follows:[113]

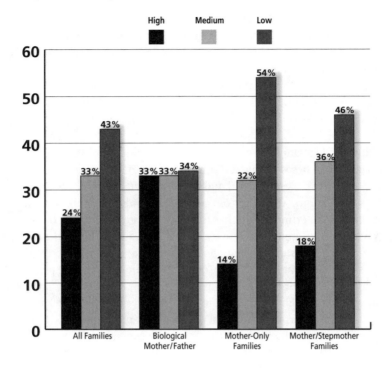

Zill's extensive research in this area leads him to conclude that "there is no clear evidence that remarriage has a protective or ameliorative effect against the negative consequences of family discord and disruption," and that "remarriage, which usually brings a reliable second income to the family, did not appear to have an overall protective effect."[114]

As we saw in the previous chapter, antisocial behavior is exhibited differently for boys and girls. Boys without fathers to teach them proper masculine behavior will tend toward crime and violence in an effort to display their power and independence, while girls without fathers tend toward premature sexual activity in search of masculine love. But the question is not, "Is there a father in the home?" but "Whose father is in the home?" The data shows that the presence of a stepfather in the home is a significant indicator of delinquent activity on the part of young males and "a strong predictor" of earlier sexual experiences for adolescent girls.[115]

Barbara Mitchell, of Simon Fraser University in Vancouver, British Columbia, reports that when examining the process of leaving the nest, young people exposed to stepfamilies are five to six times more likely to leave home at earlier ages than those in single-parent and intact families. Young adults in single-parent families and stepfamilies were more likely to report leaving home due to conflicts. In addition, these young adults were also less likely to leave home to attend school or enter marriage.[116]

Relying on data from the 1988 National Health Interview Survey on Child Health, Deborah Dawson found that the percentage of children receiving professional help for emotional or behavioral problems in the year preceding the health interview were as follows:[117]

Children Living With:	Percentage Receiving Help:
Both Biological Parents	2.7%
Formerly Married Mothers	8.8%
Never Married Mothers	4.4%
Mothers and Stepfathers	6.6%

David Popenoe reports that the National Child Development Study in Great Britain, a longitudinal analysis of seventeen thousand children born in 1958, found that the chances for stepchildren to suffer social deprivation before becoming adults are even greater than for children living with one divorced parent.[118] It is the parent's particular type of relationship to the child that matters.

Sara McLanahan's research agrees, explaining that for children, "living in a stepfamily appears to be just as risky as living with a single mother, and in some cases, the risk is even greater."[119] She also reports that children in stepfamilies show lower grade-point averages, diminished school attendance, and receive less help at home with their homework.[120]

Furstenberg explains that "most studies show that children in stepfamilies do not do better than children in single-parent families; indeed, many indicate that, on average, children in remarriages do worse."[121]

WHY INCREASED TROUBLES IN STEPFAMILIES?

One of the reasons indicated for elevated problems in stepfamilies is that couples in first marriages usually benefit from having some time between their wedding and the arrival of their first child. This period in marriage gives couples a chance to adjust to one another and their new life together.[122] Often this time can be a significant adjustment even without children. But at least during the adjustment period, the couple is able to anticipate and prepare for the arrival of their first child, having time to discuss and agree upon childrearing techniques and philosophies. Stepparents, on the other hand, have at the most a honeymoon by themselves. When they return home, a ready-made family is waiting, and significant adjustments must be made in the midst of working out the inevitable problems their new life together will bring. Without the time period first-marrieds enjoy, stepfamilies are forced to work out their childrearing tactics as they go along. They must also determine how much authority the stepparent will employ with their stepchildren and what they will do if the children do not respond to it. As we have seen, this can be a point of significant tension.

But the biological relationship of child and parent is important in intact families simply because the children are *theirs*. Both mother and father have an equal emotional stake in their children's lives, allowing them to extend a tremendous amount of grace to their children. Popenoe explains, based on the biosocial theory of family, that along with most species, the human being is "genetically selfish" and is more inclined to invest in its own biological offspring than in the offspring of others.[123] Popenoe continues:

> The reason why unrelated stepparents find their parenting roles more stressful and less satisfying than biological parents is probably due much less to social stigma and the uncertainty of their obligations, as to the fact that they gain fewer intrinsic emotional rewards from carrying out these obligations.[124]

Parenthood is a complex relationship, not merely a role that one just steps into and plays, even with proper training. In agreement with Popenoe's biosocial argument, Margo Wilson and Martin Daly of McMasters University in Ontario explain that stepparents parent less effectively, not because they do not know what to do; rather just the opposite. They know *what* to do, but they don't have the internal motivation because they don't receive the same emotional rewards from their stepchildren as biological parents do.[125] They explain that parent-child bonds are individualized, complex, and cannot be established at will. It is the biological process that properly develops these ties, and they are very difficult to develop otherwise. The biological tie also helps the parents become more consistent in their discipline because they are more likely to be committed to the long-term well-being of the child.

Norval Glenn offers another explanation for the instability of the stepparent/stepchild relationship. It relates to the simple matter of relationship selection. The adults in the relationship are attracted to one another and choose to enter into the relationship of their own free will. The children and stepparents do not usually enter their relationships under the same terms. It is a forced deal. The screening and testing process for compatibility has not taken place as it did on the adult/adult level. The two parties, stepparent and stepchild, have to make the best of the situation and the stepchild usually does not have the maturity or internal motivation for making such a commitment.[126] These three issues—lack of adjustment period, biological attachment, and selection process—are the reasons why stepfamilies face more problems and contribute to an increased breakup rate compared to first marriages.[127]

Stepfamilies and Abuse

Research on the issue of stepfamilies and abuse is relatively new, with most of the work coming to publication in the mid-1980s. Two researchers who have done the most significant work in this area are Martin Daly and Margo Wilson. Their work ascertained that preschool children who live with one biological parent and one stepparent were forty times more likely to become an abuse case than children living in an intact home. They tested for the theory that child abuse in stepfamilies is simply more likely to be reported than abuse that happens in biological families, explaining that such a reporting bias would be least influential in extreme abuse cases. But it is there that stepparent overrepresentation is at its maximum.[128]

Another theory of explanation is that the stepparents could be more abusive due to resentment toward the child for not accepting the new marital union. Wilson and Daly considered this and found it untenable since most of the abuse cases in stepfamilies involved infants.[129] These findings bring this team to strong conclusions, stating that, "stepchildren are not merely 'disadvantaged,' but imperiled."[130]

Again the issue of biology comes to bear on this discussion. Daly and Wilson report that abusive stepparents are highly discriminate as the stepchildren suffer the brunt of abuse and the biological children are often spared.[131] They also found that adoptive parents were not likely to abuse their children because they actively sought their present role as parents and found it rewarding.[132]

Regarding sexual abuse, Michael Gordon, from the University of Connecticut, reports that a girl is seven times more likely to be molested by a stepfather than a biological father. When biological fathers did molest their daughters, this happened most often when a mother was not residing in the home. The molestation by stepfathers was more severe than that of biological fathers. These findings were based on data from the 1983 National Study on Child Neglect and Reporting.[133]

DIVORCE VERSUS DEATH

Single parenting is not really a new phenomenon. In fact, some scholars tell us that the family is not undergoing any significant change because single-parent and stepparent families have been with us for quite some time.[134] And they are right . . . but they are also wrong. Families have been changing and evolving throughout the history of our nation, and the rate of remarriages in America has remained about the same since the seventeenth and eighteenth centuries.[135]

What is new, however, is the way these families change. While they used to change by chance, they now change by choice. Historically, fate delivered children and adults into single-parent and stepfamily situations. Steven Mintz and Susan Kellogg, in *Domestic Revolutions*, report that in the Chesapeake colonies of the seventeenth century, two-thirds of all children lost one parent due to death by the time they reached the age of 18.[136] Today we enter single-parent families mostly by our own doing. Andrew Cherlin explains in his monograph, *Remarriage as an Incomplete Institution*, that while "remarriages have been common in the United States since its beginnings, until this century almost all remarriages followed widowhood."[137] In colonial Massachusetts, for example, only forty divorces were granted between 1639 and 1692. But around the time of the Civil War, the divorce rate started to climb, so much so that the *Report of the Commissioner of Labor* (1889) lamented a 157 percent increase in the number of divorces granted between 1867 and 1886. This rise was already noted by some and was the impetus for the founding of the New England Divorce Reform League in 1881.[138] The rate continued to rise into the twentieth century, which prompted another national survey in order to grasp the magnitude of the problem. The *Marriage and Divorce Report* of 1909 estimated that from one in twelve to one in sixteen marriages would end in divorce at that time. Cherlin reports that in 1900, only 3 percent of all marrying brides were divorced; in 1930 this number rose to 9 percent, and in 1978, 28 percent of all marrying brides were divorced.[139]

Interestingly, however, remarriages and stepfamilies preceded by death are much different from those preceded by divorce. This, of course, means that the consequences and repercussions of family dissolution and re-formation have changed as well. Remarriages preceded by death don't show the kinds of problems revealed above. While children and adults suffer at the death of a parent or spouse, that suffering isn't as pathological as when a marriage dies by divorce. Cherlin explains that "remarriages after widowhood appear, in contrast to remarriages after divorce, to have a lower divorce rate than first marriages."[140] Additionally, children who lose a parent by death don't experience the type and severity of problems that children of divorce suffer.[141]

Marilyn Ihinger-Tallman and Kay Pasley, in their historical analysis of divorce and remarriage in American history, cite a number of studies showing that these two forms of family dissolution are quite different. Stepparent and stepchild relationships were reported as more positive by adults from death-created stepfamilies, and the marital quality of these remarriages was higher also. A survey of college students from stepfather families reported their family relationships more positively when their original family had been broken by their father's death rather than by divorce. Controls for the sex differential of the respondents did not change this.[142] Young adults whose parents separated due to divorce have nearly a 40 percent greater chance of divorce themselves, in any year of marriage, than those young adults who grew up in a family with a deceased parent.[143] Additional work revealed that adults in Great Britain found their task as stepparents easier if the previous marriage ended in death rather than divorce. British children also reported the same thing regarding their relationship with their stepparent.[144]

Research conducted at the Department of Public Health at Erasmus University in Rotterdam, the Netherlands, and published in the *International Journal of Epidemiology*, reveals that the "widowed do not differ significantly from the married in their perceived general health and subjective health complaints."[145] These researchers explain that this finding is consistent with other studies. Bryan Rodgers, a social psychiatrist at the Australian National University, writes that even early investigations of adult psychiatric patients dating back to the early 1950s found that the divorce of a parent was more closely related to emotional disorders and psychopathic personalities than was the death of a parent.[146]

Kathleen Kiernan, of the Family Policy Studies Centre in London, England, in her long-term study of the impact of divorce on the lives of adult children whose parents divorced when they were young, concludes that:

It is clear that losing a parent through death has a less adverse effect on children's subsequent life courses than experiencing the breakdown of their parents' marriage. Children who lose a parent through death are not significantly more likely to leave school, nor to begin work at an early age, than their contemporaries who live with both natural parents. They are also (in the main) no more likely to enter a union, nor to become parents at a young age, than children from intact families.[147]

In the conclusion of their meta-analysis on the connection between family breakdown and delinquency, Edward Wells and

Joseph Rankin recount that there is "higher delinquency in families broken by divorce compared to those by parental death."[148] Regarding Barbara Mitchell's work on the nest-leaving process, she found that children of a widowed mother were as likely to remain home until ready as children whose mother was still married, but more likely than children from divorced, separated, or never-married mothers.[149]

James Egan, a child psychiatrist at the Children's Hospital National Medical Center in Washington, D.C., explains the reason for the disparity between families affected by death and divorce. The difference has to do with choice versus fate. Children who lose a parent due to divorce, by choice, cannot understand why their parent left and might blame themselves or feel the departure was because Mom or Dad no longer loves them. Children who lose a parent due to death certainly don't understand it and they struggle with it for years, but they rarely see it as their fault. They know it is part of the larger life process that is beyond them and not easy to understand.

The other distinction between death and divorce is that even though the dead parent or spouse is gone, he still maintains a positive moral influence on, as well as a place in the life of, the family. These individuals are talked about in a positive light and their pictures remain on the walls. Friends like to hear stories and memories about the deceased, and the spouse or children like to tell them. This is not as true for the divorced. Deceased parents maintain a great deal of moral authority over the children—in some cases, more than when they were alive, due to inflated positive recollections. Behavioral problems on the part of children can be corrected with a simple, "Would your father/mother approve of that type of behavior?" This is not as true for a parent who has left due to divorce. Even though a parent or spouse has died, they are still present in a very important psychological and emotional sense.[150]

THE BEST MARRIAGE IS FIRST-TIME MARRIAGE

It's tragic when a marriage breaks down. Adding to this tragedy is the truth that the benefits of marriage for adults and children are not likely to be recovered in remarriage. When a first marriage breaks down, so do the benefits of marriage. Remarriage is not a replacement. Subsequent marriages break up at a higher rate than first marriages, and children and adults face more difficulties when they enter stepfamilies. The roles of stepparent and stepchild are hard to define, and the emotional attachment of these two parties is quite different from the emotional attachment between a biological or adoptive parent and child. This added trouble and conflict is why children, in general, do better in single-parent homes, since they don't experience relationship confusion. While a stepparent provides another pair of hands to help around the house and often a second paycheck to help out financially, a parent is much more than a second pair of hands and a paycheck. Therefore, it is in the best interest of individuals and society to work diligently to preserve first marriages and to secure the incomparable benefits that institution brings.

The Future of Marriage

*If we wish to preserve the family we must
revolutionize the nation.*

—G. K. CHESTERTON, WHAT'S WRONG WITH THE WORLD

BROKEN HOMES. THOSE TWO WORDS STARTED THIS DISCUSSION.
Broken homes. Broken promises. Broken hearts. Broken marriages. Broken ideals. Broken lives. Broken minds. Broken laws. Broken bodies. Broken societies. Broken people. Broken . . . everything is broken.

What is so grievous about the current state of family in America is not that our nation is missing out on all the inestimable benefits of marriage. Certainly, this is tragic. Worse than we can imagine. As we have seen, because marriage is in steep decline, more adults are living shorter, less healthy lives. They are less happy, suffering from greater amounts and degrees of mental illness, and finding less fulfillment in their sexual lives. By these measures, *life is good for fewer adults.*

Similarly, more children are growing up with serious emotional, physical, and intellectual handicaps. They are less secure, do more poorly in school, have more trouble with the law, engage in riskier sexual behaviors, conceive more babies. And their relationships with their parents are worse than they have ever been. By these measures, *the prospects for a good life are dimmer for more children than at any other time in America.*

The collection of research in this book has served to demonstrate how all of these personal and societal pathologies can be placed at the feet of the slow, systematic death of marriage in our culture.

Slow death. This is what is so grievous about the current state of marriage in America. The death of marriage is not some natural disaster beyond our control that has come upon us suddenly. It has been happening for more than forty years. It has happened right before our eyes and we have done nothing to stop it. In fact, there is very little indication that it even bothers us. At best, we have been passive observers. At worst, we have served as active facilitators.

Culpa Nostra—the fault is our own.

An Early Alarm Ignored

In the early 1960s, an unknown social scientist serving as Assistant Secretary of Labor in the administration of President Lyndon B. Johnson wrote a confidential report on the seriously troubled state of the black family in America. This report was released by the government in 1965. In less than fifty pages of text and tables, this young analyst—who went on to become the distinguished senator from New York, Daniel Patrick Moynihan—declared, "The evidence, not final, but powerfully persuasive, is that the Negro family in the urban ghettos is crumbling."[1] Moynihan's research showed that 23.6 percent of all births in the black community were illegitimate in 1963, up from 16.8 percent in 1940. He compared this to the percentage of illegitimate births among whites in 1963, which was 3.07.[2] Ringing our cultural "emergency bell" with great fervor and alarm, Moynihan concluded his report by declaring it was time for "national action"—a concerted effort—to slow the rate of decay of the black family. On the cultural side, no one really paid much attention to Moynihan's call. As mentioned earlier, the greatest attention paid to Moynihan's diagnosis was to denounce it as a racist attack on the black community.

On the policy side, however, when President Johnson announced his War on Poverty in 1964, his program was significantly influenced by Moynihan's report. This initiation of the "Great Society" led to one of the sharpest governmental growth spurts our nation has ever seen. When President Eisenhower left office in 1961, there were only 45 domestic social programs, and federal spending (excluding Social Security) in 1960 was $9.9 billion. These numbers had grown to 435 domestic social programs and $25.6 billion in spending in 1969 when Johnson left the White House.[3]

If nobody else took Moynihan's call seriously, Johnson did. And while we can argue cause and effect, no one can deny that while the government has increasingly become that much-touted "village" supposedly required to raise a child effectively, the problem of family decline has gotten much worse, far beyond what concerned Moynihan. As Steven Mintz and Susan Kellogg write in their social history of the American family, "Indeed, these problems have so worsened since Moynihan wrote his report that they now affect the entire society and can no longer be addressed solely in terms of race."[4]

Defining Family Deviancy Down

The perspicacious Moynihan now says that we have done with family what we have done with crime. In his equally important essay, "Defining Deviancy Down," published in 1993, Moynihan explores a sociological rule laid down by Emile Durkheim in his 1895 work *The Rules of Sociological Method*. Durkheim states that while crime is constant (a normal factor in every society), deviancy marks the level of crime a society will tolerate. Moynihan explains, "Despite occasional crime waves (in the early years of our nation), as when itinerant Quakers refused to take off their hats in the presence of magistrates, the amount of deviance in this corner of seventeenth-century New England fitted nicely with the supply of stocks and whipping posts."[5] In other words, while we have always had criminal activity, we didn't tolerate much deviance and we knew how to deal with it when it reared its ugly head. This level of acceptance has changed over time.

The amount of deviant behavior in American society has increased dramatically. Moynihan claims—and it is difficult to counter his statement—that "we have been redefining deviancy so as to exempt much conduct previously stigmatized, and also quietly raised the 'normal' level in categories where behavior [would have been] abnormal by any earlier standard."[6]

To illustrate this phenomenon, Moynihan asks us to consider the St. Valentine's Day Massacre of 1929. Seven gangsters were killed by four rival gangsters, and the nation was horrified. So horrified that the event was deserving of the descriptor "massacre." Today, however, such a crime is "normal" and earns minimal attention. James Q. Wilson, the noted UCLA criminologist, explains that we see the equivalent of the St. Valentine's Day Massacre most weekends in Los Angeles, and we are no longer outraged.[7] We have simply learned to live with it. In the dire warning of Judge Edwin Torres of the New York State Supreme Court:

> This numbness, this near narcoleptic state, can diminish the human condition to the level of combat infantrymen, who, in protracted campaigns, can eat their battlefield rations seated on the bodies of the fallen, friend and foe alike. A society that loses its sense of outrage is doomed to extinction."[8]

This is precisely what we have done with family. Marital and family dissolution have been "normalized" down to the level where we are not really shocked by much of anything and we will tolerate everything. We have lost our sense of outrage about the breakdown of the family. We have become a nation of family relativists, unable or unwilling to make any kind of definitive judgment concerning family. And we just continue to define family deviancy down.

This must change. We must revolutionize the nation.

REVOLUTIONIZE THE NATION

Of course, it is paramount that we show great gentleness to individuals who find themselves in broken homes. Many of them are there through no choice of their own, and they need the care and compassion of their communities. Yet, we must also rediscover a sense of moral outrage at the devaluation of marriage as an institution. We must rouse ourselves and find the courage and ability to make moral judgments. When a culture does not permit itself to make value statements about one thing being qualitatively better than another, that culture has removed the primary organ allowing it to make progress and better itself. Regarding compassion for those in broken homes, precisely because we understand the comprehensive negative consequences of marital breakdown and what it does to those involved is why we must rage against this cultural trend away from marriage. *It is bad, not because it fails to live up to some nostalgic ideal, but because it hurts people.*

We must recognize that marriage is too precious and its social and personal utility too valuable to allow it to suffer under this slow death. We must resolve that we are not going to ignore this problem any longer. Then, we must roll up our collective sleeves and get down to the critical task of recovering a marriage culture.

The First Order of Reform

First, our nation must gain a realistic picture of what marriage is and is not. One of the primary causes for marital breakdown is that marriage does not meet the expectations of its participants. Of course, fault lies with our expectations of the institution rather than the institution itself. As Norval Glenn suggests, "The very importance that people place on marriage as a source of gratification has contributed to the decline of marriage as an institution."[9] We seem to view marriage as we view other consumer products—something that exists for the sole purpose of meeting our needs. This is evident in Robert Bellah and colleagues' discussion of the pervasiveness of individualism in American culture in *Habits of the Heart*.[10] Americans act as if we have purchased marriage and carried it home from the Sears store with the guarantee that if we are not completely satisfied, we can return it for a full refund, no questions asked. We come to marriage the way we approach a date. If it doesn't work out, we can exercise our option to call it quits. But marriage is more than an extended date.

The Four Loves

To understand the nature of marriage, it is vital to understand that it is a complex mixture of four loves. These loves are not all equal, and some are more necessary than others. But none of them individually makes a true marriage. Instead, marriage is the only relationship where all four come together and have the opportunity to display themselves. Let us briefly look at each.

The first type of love that might immediately come to mind is *Eros*, which is sexual desire, but it is also more than that. As C. S. Lewis explains in *The Four Loves*, "Sexual desire wants *it, the thing in itself*; Eros wants the Beloved. . . . Now Eros makes a man really want, not a woman, but one particular woman. In some mysterious but quite indisputable fashion, the lover desires the Beloved herself, not the pleasure she can give."[11] Eros is a distinctive spice which enhances the marital relationship, setting it apart from all other love relationships.

Marriage also includes, but is more than, what the Greeks called *Storge*. Our English word is *affection*. This love doesn't immediately happen; rather, it is gradually cultivated. It is the kind of love that develops between family members: husband and wife, parent and child, brother and sister, and even good friends. It is a comfortable love and makes us feel at one with another, even when we might be in serious conflict. It is a love that allows us to say, "I love you even though I don't like you right now." It nearly always finds its source in what the other people mean to us because of the time they have invested in us and us in them.

Marriage love is also more than *Philia*. While it is ideal that marriage partners be each other's best friends, the marriage relationship is far more mature than friendship. Philia is another spice that enhances the marital relationship. It makes a relationship deeper when our spouse is the one we would choose, above all others, to sit and share a good movie with, to see a beautiful sunset, or to discuss the latest struggles in our lives. When those whom we love in this way are absent, it makes these events of life a bit less fulfilling.

Marriage consists of these three kinds of love: Eros, Storge, and Philia—all situated on the foundation of the fourth—*Agape*. This love serves as the cauldron that holds all the others (passion, affection, and friendship) together into a unique and magical stew that cannot be replicated in any other relationship. Agape serves this larger purpose because it is the highest order of love. In the historic Judeo-Christian ideal, it is the love of God for his people. This is love that is unmerited—love that we extend to another regardless of how it will (or will not) benefit us. It is a love that needs and seeks primarily to give, not receive. It is selfless and desires the highest good for the one loved. It is unconditional. Most importantly, it is something we *choose* to do. It is an act of our will, not just a feeling or emotion that simply appears.

This love is described in a text from the Bible that is read at many weddings, 1 Corinthians 13. Yet this love is exhibited in precious few marriages. Agape love "is kind and is not jealous . . . it is not arrogant, does not act unbecomingly, it does not seek its own . . . does not take into account wrong suffered . . . bears all things, believes all things, hope all things, endures all things."

This depth and quality of love can only be sustained by a conscious act of will; it never simply happens. It is an action, something we decide on and exhibit effort to do. It is a love that cannot be sustained by emotion. In fact, *Agape* love acts in opposition to feelings, which are transitory! It acts contrary to human nature. Eric Fromm, in his book *The Art of Loving*, discusses this form of love in the modern context so succinctly that I ask your forbearance in quoting him at length:

> Love should be essentially an act of will, of decision to commit my life completely to that of one other person. This is, indeed, the rationale behind the idea of the insolubility of marriage, as it is behind the many forms of traditional marriage in which the two partners never choose each other, but are chosen for one another—yet are expected to love one another. In contemporary Western culture this idea appears altogether false. Love is supposed to be the outcome of a spontaneous, emotional reaction, of suddenly being gripped by an irresistible feeling. In this view, one sees only the peculiarities of the two individuals involved— and not the fact that all men are part of Adam, and all women part of Eve. One neglects to see an important factor in erotic love, that of will. To love somebody is not just a strong feeling—it is a decision, it is a judgment, it is a promise. If love were only a feeling, there would be no basis for the promise to love each other forever.[12]

A true promise means something only in the context of the possibility that we would not naturally produce the thing promised. We promise our love and commitment to our spouse because we recognize that it is not likely to sustain itself upon our original emotions. Our love is sure to be imperfect because we, as lovers living in the fallen shadow of humanity's original parents, are imperfect. In this context, we make a commitment to our beloved to continue the hard work of refining and cultivating our love.

The recognition of this aspect of marriage is imperative because it goes right to the heart of why so many marriages don't last. Marriage is hard work and takes a commitment to our spouse and to the *idea* of marriage. As Chesterton observes,

> If Americans can be divorced for "incompatibility of temper," I cannot conceive why they are not all divorced. I have known many happy marriages, but never a compatible one. The whole aim of marriage is to fight through and survive the instant when incompatibility becomes unquestionable. For a man and a woman, as such, are incompatible.[13]

This "real world" view of marriage needs to be recovered so people know what they are committing to. Otherwise, disappointment will be inevitable and people will continue to exit marriage when their false dream has gone bad. It should be the widespread understanding of our culture that marriage is the "toughest job you'll ever love" and that it is this very process that, paradoxically, makes it so rich.

RECOMMENDATIONS FOR REVOLUTION

There are two primary grids for understanding how we have lost a marriage culture and it is imperative we understand them as we discuss steps toward its recovery. One is theoretical in nature and the other is more practical.

On the theoretical side, a strong marriage culture requires two things: personal commitment and societal expectation. As we have just seen, people need to have a proper view of the nature of love and a realistic appraisal of the commitment it requires. But equally important is societal expectation. We must have a societal norm that esteems marriage and *expects* it as the foundation for the practice of sexuality and establishment of domestic life. A healthy marriage culture demands both the societal and the personal ethic, and we have lost both.

Practically, we lose a marriage culture because (a) domestic life is established without the benefit of marriage, either through cohabitation and/or illegitimacy, or (b) domestic life is established on marriage, but the marriage is later dissolved through divorce. Both of these are currently happening at equal ratios in American culture. As we saw at the beginning of this book, a child living today in a single-parent family is just as likely to be living with a never married parent as with a divorced parent.

Clearly, the two grids intersect and impact one another. Together, they give us a clear way of understanding the nature of the problem. People live together and have babies out of wedlock because they lack commitment, and society doesn't appreciate and demand the priority of marriage. Also, marriages are often ended because people lack commitment and society doesn't expect lifelong, monogamous unions as a norm. In isolating recommendations for the recovery of a marriage culture, we will look at solutions through these two grids. The two main categories in our discussion will be (1) stemming cohabitation and illegitimacy, and (2) strengthening marriage, while the recommendations for doing both will fall along the lines of strengthening the personal and societal commitment to both.

Amelioration's first demand is a sober recognition of the problem, which is something I have sought to create over these pages. Its second demand is open and rigorous debate about solutions, subjecting all serious and sincere recommendations to the open-air and scrutiny of the public give-and-take. The recommendations I offer below are not all necessarily esteemed equally by me. Some I disagree with. Others I would enact tomorrow if someone made me king—admittedly a scary thought! Many fall somewhere in between. But what they all have in common is that they have been recommended here and there by serious and thoughtful people and deserve a testing in the crucible of the public square. I offer them here with that end in mind. Given that, let us examine some means toward recovery of a marriage culture.

Stemming Cohabitation and Illegitimacy

We live in a contemporary society that has proven we can change our behavior if it proves harmful. As research continues to come to light about the harmful effects of tobacco use, more and more people choose not to smoke. We have also learned that we must care for the environment. As a result, we are radically changing the way we interact with our natural world. While we once laughed at the drunken antics of Otis on the *Andy Griffith Show,* drunkenness and the many ways it can cause death (including disease and drunk driving) are no laughing matter. In addition, we have changed our dietary habits, cutting out or cutting down on fat, cholesterol, and consumption of red meat because the research tells us we will live longer, healthier lives without them.

In the ways that we are willing to change to better our health and that of our society, we must be willing to change regarding marriage. We must shrink the growing trends of illegitimacy, cohabitation, and divorce. As a nation of problem-solvers facing the problem of illegitimacy, we must:

- Encourage a serious study of the psychology behind out-of-wedlock childbearing. What motivates unmarried women to conceive children without getting husbands first? What part does the welfare check play? How significant is the need to have a child that needs you? Does the problem go deeper than these? Serious answers to these questions must come before we start discussing serious solutions.
- Encourage institutions of faith and community organizations to develop and strengthen peer-run programs through local hospitals that reach out to unwed fathers when the mother makes contact with the hospital. Help these new fathers connect in meaningful ways with the formation of this new family. Already-established, married fathers can model for the new father what it means to be a dad, and support the mother and child. As the research documented in this book shows, marriage is the best context in which to do this.
- Show swift and decisive action in removing high school

168

and college athletes from sports teams when they impregnate girls to whom they are not married. Sports figures are cultural heroes, and this would have a significant teaching effect on the rest of culture as the young seek to emulate their sports heroes. It would also send a strong message to the athletes themselves that this behavior is not consistent with the ideals of athletic discipline.

- Refuse to allow child-support payments to become dad-replacement. The idea that all a good dad needs to do is pay up is wrong-headed. An effective father is so much more than an on-time paycheck. In fact, the idea of not allowing a woman to get support from the government for a child she conceived with a man she is not married to would compel the woman to obtain the security of marriage to ensure the father will be there to care for the child. This would go further in ensuring that the father will care for his own children, which as we have seen, is more beneficial for the child, mother, and father. This has the appearance of a double standard upon the woman, and that must be conceded. But we must also realize that *it is women who are the gatekeepers of marriage.* If they don't insist on it, it is very unlikely that men will. They must exercise that power.

- Isolate both high school girls who are expecting children and the boys who are the fathers, taking them out of the regular school atmosphere and placing them in a special educational setting. Develop parenting programs by faith institutions and community groups for both mothers and fathers in these special schools. As parents, these children are in an exceptional phase of adolescence and should be treated exceptionally. They should not be treated as outcasts necessarily, nor should they be kept in the mainstream of adolescent life. They have special needs and require specific attention to cope with their changing life responsibilities.

- Encourage all-male schools, especially in inner cities, which are staffed primarily by men (with as many of them married as possible). This will assist young adolescent men in concentrating on school rather than girls and everything that interest entails. Having a primarily male, married staff will ensure that these young men have access to the proper male role models they are currently lacking.

■ Change our educational focus for our young people from seeking to curtail out-of-wedlock *births* to stopping out-of-wedlock *sexual activity*. In fact, as Barbara Whitehead carefully illustrated in a celebrated *Atlantic Monthly* article on the subject, our current sex-education efforts are failing miserably.[14] We should take the ennobling high road for humankind and replace our comprehensive sex-education efforts with comprehensive marriage education. Let us be unequivocal in stating with moral authority that sex belongs in marriage. Among other benefits, it is the only way to ensure the physical and emotional sexual fulfillment of our younger generations. Other mores produce more frustration, disappointment, and pain.

■ Convene a council of religious leaders, each representing specific ethnic groups, who can take the message of sexual abstinence and marital responsibility to the young males of their particular neighborhoods. If our churches, synagogues, and other places of worship don't champion this message and speak with a moral voice, how can we expect others to do the same?

■ Continue to favor the adoption rights of married adopting parents over the rights of the single, nonmarried adopting parent because children need two parents. Further, we should favor the rights of married adopting parents over the unmarried birth mothers or fathers once the child has been placed in the adoptive home. It is tragic when a child, once placed with two married adoptive parents, can be removed from the home, after the adoption was agreed to, because of the whims of an unmarried mother or father. The child needs a mother and father, and our adoption laws should ensure they get both.

- Regulate sperm banks so they service *only* married women with fertility problems. Unmarried women should not be facilitated in having children without the benefit of husbands. We should not be aiding scenarios which we know create children who start out life with significant deficits. Admittedly, such regulation would only affect a small number of people, yet it would also strike at the root of the problems plaguing marriage today: The current primacy of individual choice versus societal responsibility.
- Initiate and conduct a serious discussion about re-instituting the orphanage program for out-of-wedlock children. Orphanages are not the ideal situation, but then, we are finding that neither is single-motherhood. We must come up with alternatives for raising these children. Orphanages have worked well in the past. They shouldn't be ruled out in the present.

Regarding cohabitation, we must:

- Widely disseminate the information in popular media that cohabitation is a comprehensive failure as a testing ground for marriage. It should become a truism, as the research gathered in chapter two clearly shows, that cohabiting relationships are the most unhealthy of domestic relationships and they do not lead to successful marriages. Cohabitation should therefore become restigmatized.
- Structure our tax, social welfare, and Social Security policies so that they do not provide financial encouragements for couples to live together. Currently, in most income scenarios, it is cheaper for two people to live together than to marry. A government ought to encourage, through its policies, what is best for its citizens and the nation. It ought to encourage, not hinder, marital formation.
- Support the rights of landlords to limit offering leases to cohabiting couples if they so choose. Apart from an issue of conscience, these "discriminating" landlords are

strengthening the community fabric by not facilitating the formation of harmful domestic lifestyles, and they ought to be encouraged, not penalized.

Strengthening Marriage

Before the work to strengthen marriage can really begin in any substantive sense, we must repair the legal foundation of marriage. No-fault divorce laws, which exist in nearly all of the fifty states, effectively abolish marriage in any legal or social sense. When a spouse can leave any marriage, at any time, for any reason—or no reason at all—the only thing holding marriage together is the simultaneous commitment of two individuals to the marriage. While this personal commitment is important, we also need not just societal, but legal, expectation. We no longer have that. If one partner wavers at all in this commitment, current laws say the marriage contract can be abolished more easily and quickly than a business contract with the people who care for your lawn! The law is a teacher. Currently, it is teaching us that marriage only matters if two people simultaneously want it to matter. If one party loses faith temporarily, the marriage can end. The law must teach that marriage matters, *period*. As we have seen, we shouldn't only seek to keep marriages together for "the sake of the children," but also for the sake of the adults.

To accomplish this, we must reform (though not necessarily repeal) our nation's no-fault divorce laws so that they are considerate of the spouse who wants to hold the marriage together. We must adopt laws that are considerate of the marriage first, then the family as a unit, and then the individuals involved. We can do this and not necessarily go back to the old divorce laws that required proof of fault. We could extend the waiting period for divorce during periods of legal separation, which are both linked to mandatory joint counseling (with counselors of the parties' own choosing), informed consent education on the impact of divorce, and required parenting plans as to how the children will be cared for after the breakup. This would go far in protecting children and adults in danger while requiring people to assess the option of divorce more soberly. This is a major area of reform, but there are many other significant ideas.

Since the great majority of people get married in churches and synagogues, it is reasonable to look to the religious community for our thinking in strengthening marriage. This community of faith is uniquely positioned and individually commissioned to care for the cultural and domestic well-being of marriage. In light of this, we should:

- Have Christian and Jewish theologians work out a fuller theology of marriage. Without a theoretical framework for thinking about marriage, the storehouse of actions on marriage will be greatly impoverished. Catholics possess a sturdy theology of marriage. They should pull it out, dust it off, and get it out into the pews. Protestants, especially evangelicals, have a psychology of marriage, but no theology. A literature search and the questioning of colleagues and professors has yielded no significant Protestant work on the issue. The faith communities must have a theological foundation to build their work on. Only then will they be the peculiar, distinctive community they are meant to be. Currently, they are not much different from the non-believing, nonprogressive world on marriage.
- Convene an interfaith National Council of Religious Leaders on Marriage, which serves to direct the religious communities' attention to marriage. Due to denominational and doctrinal differences, this group could not direct policy but could speak with a clear and authoritative voice on the virtue, importance, and health of marriage. Our nation needs more custodians of a marital tradition. Such a Council would provide encouragement and leadership to the most important custodian of all: the faith community.
- Encourage individual denominations and religious communities to address seriously the question of what they can do to make sure the people getting married under their authority are equipped with the competencies necessary to successfully handle the troubles and trials normal life brings to marriages. They must ensure that couples have a realistic idea of what marriage is, including the highs and the lows. They must teach the concept of *Agape* love as the basis for marriage. In addition, a well-thought-

out and effectively run program can be a wonderful way to reach out to the unbelieving community while providing for their critical needs.

- Encourage all seminaries to train leaders to initiate well-thought-out pre- and post-wedding counseling programs that are both clergy and laity run. This will ensure that these workers have the competency and encouragement to serve as custodians of marriage once they are placed in their field of work.
- Encourage a policy which dictates that marriages initiated by faith communities can only be dissolved by that community of faith. If a couple chooses to marry at city hall, city hall can grant the divorce. If they choose to marry in a church, synagogue, or mosque, only that community can dissolve the marriage. Such a policy would allow these distinctive communities to act as more serious custodians of the marriage tradition due to the fact that they exercise full power over the blessing or sacrament they are charged with. It could cause the couple coming to the particular institution for its blessing to appraise seriously their own commitment: "Wow, these people really take marriage seriously. Are we ready for that?" It would also help our society see marriage as more than a legal institution which currently offers the minimalist ethic of no-fault divorce, and that the religious aspect is much more than sentimental adornment.
- Encourage—through churches and community organizations—the formation of mentoring couple groups that take younger couples by the hand and walk them through the marriage process. Nothing is as empowering and instructive as a successful example. Couples need to be tied into a community of other couples who can encourage and instruct them through marital growth. We should also encourage vocation-specific mentoring groups. Husbands and wives in the legal, pastoral, medical, business, and other professions can help other couples cope with the specific problems those professions bring to bear on a marriage. Perhaps employers themselves could encourage this as well.

174

- Have churches and synagogues survey their local divorce filings (which are public record) and contact these couples with great compassion and concern, offering the services they have developed to help marriages on their last thread. Chances are high that no one has encouraged these couples to give their marriage a fighting chance or offered the skills to do so. A few might respond to such an offer of help and accept assistance to avoid much unseen pain.
- Produce materials that teach the faith community leadership and laity about the comprehensive benefits of marriage so this information can inform their work and allow them to share it with others. While many leaders possess a conviction about the importance of marriage, knowledge of the wealth of research findings can serve to strengthen and animate this conviction, helping them to speak and act more authoritatively, compassionately, persuasively, and effectively.
- Give serious thought to how our nation's various racial and ethnic faith institutions can work to promote marriage among their communities. Often, these communities possess so many distinct cultural qualities that only those within the community can speak to, recognize, and appreciate. Many of these cultural distinctives impact the way marriage is viewed.

In regard to general marriage initiatives, we should:

- Stimulate a morally serious discussion on the essential character, virtue, and significance of marriage. This process is vital, given the pandemic confusion at all levels of our society as to what marriage really is and does. It should be widely known and understood that the most happy, healthy, safe, sexually fulfilled, and productive people are found among the married.
- Encourage municipalities to write and adopt "community resolutions" that affirm and encourage lifelong marriage and strong intact families as a community goal and norm.

Such a goal will reduce crime, domestic violence, teen pregnancy, prevalence of gangs, alcoholism, suicide, mental and physical illness, and improve educational enrollment and attainment as well as economic productivity. Local churches and synagogues could provide their resources and expertise to help meet this goal.

- Encourage state and federal governments to conduct and take seriously "marriage and family impact studies" to determine whether legislation under consideration would negatively impact the health of marriage or family. Government examines how its work will impact the physical environment. It ought to examine how its work will impact the equally vital marriage environment.

- Produce public service announcements for television and radio that highlight influential people from a number of different backgrounds: business leaders, sports heroes, actors, musicians, and opinion-shapers who talk about the joys of being faithful spouses and parents. These stories capture the imagination of what could be, rather than telling people what ought to be. It is often easier to pull someone to where you are, rather than push them from where they are. These stories, shared tenderly, would be very inviting and offer an irresistibly strong pull.

- Encourage employers to make materials and programs available to employees to help strengthen their marriages. Incentives should be given for attending marriage-improvement weekends and programs. Extending other policies to employees that allow more time with family and spouse would be helpful. Some ideas are flex-time, compressed work weeks, telecommuting when appropriate, and job-sharing. In addition, the trend toward policies that extend benefits to single employees with "significant others," which have traditionally been afforded exclusively to married workers, is wrong-headed and ill-informed. As we have seen, the research consistently reveals that these domestic relationships are completely different. Marriage affords more benefits to the employer in healthier, happier, more productive employees who miss less work and are able to concentrate more on work while they are there. "Diversified lifestyles" bring pathologies to the employer by diminishing the overall well-being of workers. Therefore, it is in the employers' best interests to encourage the formation of traditional, lifelong, monogamous marriage.

■ Encourage responsibility from "Hollywood" (the film and television industries) in promoting marriage as virtuous and necessary. Encourage them to increase the number of TV families portraying a realistic view of what it means to be "Married with Children." Television, for good or bad, is a teacher. The health and well-being of our nation needs it to be a teacher of the virtues of marriage rather than denigrating the institution. However, there are the hopeful signs of new television and movie writers, producers, and executives who want to create positive marriage/family shows. These people need to be greatly applauded and encouraged.

■ Encourage the textbook publishers from grade school to grad school to educate students about the comprehensive benefits of marriage for individuals and society. While most books do not offer explicitly anti-marriage statements, they do offer an overall negative view of marriage and offer none of the social science data on the beneficial consequences of marriage.[15] Genuine education demands that students receive a more realistic picture of marriage.

■ Encourage the development of high-school courses that take marriage seriously and give students a realistic picture of what purpose marriage serves. This will guide their expectations for establishing their domestic lives toward more beneficial ends.

■ Encourage professional organizations like the American Association for Marriage and Family Therapy to talk about how to strengthen first-time marriages at their conferences and in their literature (which they *actually* seldom do), and when they do, discuss ways they can encourage lifelong commitment among those they work with.[16] If the large professional affiliations, which are supposed to be the authorities on marriage, never talk about

177

it, what can we expect from other less interested sectors of society? As with social workers, these professionals need to stop focusing solely on ameliorating the effects of family breakdown and start working proactively to build good marriages. The payoff is matchless.

■ Encourage a wider celebration of World Marriage Day, which falls on the second Sunday of February, or even declare June as National Marriage Month. During this time, we could hold up married couples who have durable, long-lasting marriages of fifty-plus years. It would offer them a forum to tell the rest of us their secrets for successful marriage and what their many years together have taught them. It would also offer opportunities for our nation to recognize, discuss, and celebrate the virtues of marriage. For goodness' sake, there's a national frozen food month (really!), so marriage should at least receive equal billing.

■ Hold "No-Divorce" days in courts around the country like a town in Texas did. Fed up with the high divorce rate, one city said on this one day, "Today, we will not have any divorces in our town." Certainly it's a gimmick, but it's a start, and it has a teaching effect which says, in a small way, "We're not going to define family deviancy down any longer. We're fed up and are taking steps to reverse the trend!"

■ Work for more publicity for programs and people who are working to strengthen marriage in unique and creative ways. These programs may not be replicable, but their examples are instructive, encouraging, and ennobling. People who yearn for strong marriages need exposure to these uplifting examples. We need to know there is hope, and real-life examples of success offer hope as nothing else can.

■ Have a serious discussion on the benefits and possibilities of recovering a family wage so that a family man can have a greater chance of providing for a family, thus making him a more attractive marital prospect. Too often, a welfare check is a much better provider than a semi-skilled full-time laborer. Why would a woman with children trade the former for the latter? We must create opportunities and incentives for men to become better providers.

■ Begin efforts by foundations to fund the strengthening of marriage rather than continuing to offer money to ease the impact of family breakdown through "family services" funding. Let's address the problem on the front end. Upon looking at the entries in the 1995 edition of *The Foundation Directory*, under "family services" funding foundations, each of the categories deal with addressing family issues only after problems have occurred. Looking for foundations that fund marriage work? You'll not find a single entry between "Marine Science" and "Mathematics." The wise foundation that cares about the future of our civilization should seek to change this.

Finally, we must seek to challenge the notion of radical individualism that discourages long-term commitment and instead drives cohabitation, illegitimacy, and much divorce—all of which contribute to the death of marriage. Alexis de Tocqueville observed the individualism of early nineteenth-century American culture and saw many good things about it, but he also saw some harmful aspects. He saw the family as one of the primary spheres that could moderate the negative side of individualism. He observed and remarked:

Certainly, of all countries in the world, America is the one in which the marriage tie is most respected and where the highest and truest conjugal happiness has been conceived.[17]

This is no longer true of marriage in America because individualism is "moderating" marriage more than marriage is moderating it. Ann Swidler explains in *Habits of the Heart*, if "love and marriage are seen primarily in terms of psychological gratification, they may fail to fulfill their older social function of providing people with stable, committed relationships that tie them to a larger society."[18]

They will fail to fulfill their social function. This is why the death of marriage is so comprehensively harmful to adults, children, and society. We are social creatures who need one another. We need to interact on extended intimate levels with others. We need others to make demands of us that call us to change. However, just like a child who "needs" candy, we seek to maintain control over our own lives because of the immediate satisfaction it brings us. But we miss the more valuable long-term benefits it provides. And we are left impoverished. When we are watching out only for ourselves, we can afford precious little toleration for others. In a nutshell, this is why marriage dies.

We must become like adults who now realize that a well-balanced diet takes some discipline and repression of whim to maintain, but also know that the benefits are matchless. We must realize two things: Even though it is difficult to commit ourselves to someone else, humanities' dilemma really is, as the ancient wisdom of Genesis 2:18 tells us, "it is not good for man to be alone." And first-time, lifelong, monogamous marriage—not any of its alternatives—is the ideal solution to this dilemma.

Recommended Reading List

GENERAL READING ON MARRIAGE AS A SOCIAL INSTITUTION

Bumpass, Larry. *The Declining Significance of Marriage: Changing Family Life in the United States.* 1995 National Survey of Families and Households Working Paper No. 66, University of Wisconsin-Madison: Center for Demography and Ecology.

Gallagher, Maggie. *The Abolition of Marriage: How We Destroy Lasting Love.* Washington, D.C.: Regnery Gateway, 1996.

Goldscheider, Frances K. and Linda J. Waite. *New Families, No Families? The Transformation of the American Home.* Berkeley: University of California Press, 1991.

Davis, Kingsley, ed. *Contemporary Marriage: Comparative Perspectives on a Changing Institution.* New York: Russell Sage Foundation, 1985.

Lasch, Christopher. *Haven in a Heartless World: The Family Besieged.* New York: Basic Books, 1977.

Mintz, Steven and Susan Kellogg. *Domestic Revolutions: A Social History of American Family Life.* New York: The Free Press, 1988.

Murdock, George Peter. "The Universality of the Nuclear Family," in Norman W. Bell and Ezra F. Vogel, eds. *A Modern Introduction to the Family.* New York: The Free Press, 1968.

Popenoe, David, Jean Bethke Elshtain, and David Blankenhorn, eds. *Promises to Keep: The Decline and Renewal of Marriage in America.* Lanham, Md.: Rowman and Littlefield, Publishers, 1996.

Scott, Kieran and Michael Warren. *Perspectives on Marriage: A Reader.* New York: Oxford University Press, 1993.

MARRIAGE AS THE PROPER CONTEXT
FOR SEXUAL EXPRESSION

Cutler, Winnifred. *Love Cycles: The Science of Intimacy.* New York: Villard Books, 1991.

Greeley, Andrew. *Faithful Attraction: Discovering Intimacy, Love, and Fidelity in American Marriage.* New York: Tom Doherty Associates, 1991.

Kass, Leon. "The End of Courtship." *The Public Interest.* 126 (1997): 39–63.

Laumann, Edward O. and others. *The Social Organization of Sexuality.* Chicago: University of Chicago Press, 1994.

Michael, Robert T. and others. *Sex in America: A Definitive Survey.* Boston: Little, Brown, and Company, 1994.

Sorokin, Pitirim. *The American Sex Revolution.* Boston: Porter Sargent Publisher, 1956.

Unwin, Joseph Daniel. *Sexual Regulation and Human Behavior.* London: William & Norgate, Ltd., 1933.

THE NATURE OF COHABITING RELATIONSHIPS

Axinn, William G. and Arland Thornton. "The Relationship Between Cohabitation and Divorce: Selectivity or Causal Influence." *Demography.* 29 (1992): 357–374.

Bennett, Neil, Ann Klimas Blanc, and David E. Bloom. "Commitment and the Modern Union: Assessing the Link Between Premarital Cohabitation and Subsequent Marital Stability." *American Sociological Review.* 53 (1988): 127–138.

Bumpass, Larry, James A. Sweet, and Andrew Cherlin. "The Role of Cohabitation in Declining Rates of Marriage." *Journal of Marriage and the Family.* 53 (1991): 913–927.

Cunningham, John D. and John K. Antill. "Cohabitation and Marriage: Retrospectives and Predictive Comparisons." *Journal of Social and Personality Relationships.* 11 (1994): 77–93.

Newcomb, Michael D. and P. M. Bentler. "Assessment of Personality and Demographic Aspects of Cohabitation and Marital Success." *Journal of Personality Assessment.* 44 (1980): 11–24.

Nock, Steven L. "A Comparison of Marriages and Cohabiting Relationships." *Journal of Family Issues.* 16 (1995): 53–76.

Segrest, Margaret A. and M. O'Neal Weeks. "Comparison of the Role Expectations of Marriage and Cohabiting Subjects." *International Journal of Sociology of the Family.* 6 (1976): 275–281.

Stets, Jan E. "The Link Between Past and Present Intimate Relationships." *Journal of Family Issues* 14 (1993): 236–260.

Thomson, Elizabeth and Ugo Colella. "Cohabitation and Marital Stability: Quality or Commitment?" *Journal of Marriage and the Family.* 54 (1992): 259–267.

IMPORTANCE OF MARRIAGE FOR THE GENERAL WELL-BEING OF ADULTS

Coombs, Robert H. "Marital Status and Personal Well-Being: A Literature Review." *Family Relations.* 40 (1991): 97–102.

Coombs, Robert and Fawzy I. Fawzy. "The Effect of Marital Status on Stress in Medical School." *American Journal of Psychiatry.* 139 (1982): 1490–1493.

Gove, Walter. "Sex, Marital Status, and Mortality." *American Journal of Sociology.* 79 (1973): 45–67.

Goodwin, James S., William C. Hunt, Charles R. Key, and Jonathan M. Samet. "The Effect of Marital Status on Stage, Treatment, and Survival of Cancer Patients." *Journal of the American Medical Association.* 258 (1987): 3152–3130.

Lillard, Lee A. and Linda J. Waite. "'Til Death Do Us Part: Marital Disruption and Mortality." *American Journal of Sociology.* 100 (1995): 1131–1156.

Lynch, James J. *The Broken Heart: The Medical Consequences of Loneliness.* New York: Basic Books, 1977.

Malzberg, Benjamin. "Marital Status in Relation to the Prevalence of Mental Disease." *Psychiatric Quarterly.* 10 (1936): 245–261.

Robins, Lee N. and Darrel A. Regier. *Psychiatric Disorders in America: The Epidemiologic Catchment Area Study.* New York: The Free Press, 1991.

Waite, Linda J. "Does Marriage Matter?" *Demography.* 32 (1995): 483–507.

Wood, Wendy and others. "Sex Difference in Positive Well-Being: A Consideration of Emotional Style and Marital Status." *Psychological Bulletin.* 2 (1989): 249–264.

IMPORTANCE OF MARRIAGE FOR
PROPER SOCIALIZATION OF CHILDREN

Angel, Ronald J. and Jacqueline L. Angel. *Painful Inheritance: Health and the New Generation of Fatherless Families.* Madison: The University of Wisconsin Press, 1993.

Blankenhorn, David. *Fatherless America.* New York: Basic Books, 1995.

Dawson, Deborah. "Family Structure and Children's Health and Well-Being: Data from the 1988 National Health Interview Survey on Child Health." *Journal of Marriage and the Family.* 53 (1991): 573–584.

McLanahan, Sara and Gary Sandefur. *Growing Up With A Single Parent: What Hurts, What Helps.* Cambridge: Harvard University Press, 1994.

Popenoe, David. *Life Without Father: Compelling New Evidence That Fatherhood and Marriage are Indispensable for the Good of Children and Society.* New York: Free Press, 1996.

Whitehead, Barbara Dafoe. "Dan Quayle Was Right." *The Atlantic Monthly.* (April 1993), 47–84.

THE NEGATIVE CONSEQUENCES OF
DIVORCE AND REMARRIAGE

Legal and General Sociological Aspect

Glendon, Mary Ann. *Abortion and Divorce in Western Law.* Cambridge: Harvard University Press, 1987.

Nakonezny, Paul A. and others. "The Effect of No-Fault Divorce Law on the Divorce Rate Across the 50 States and Its Relation to Income, Education, and Religiosity." *Journal of Marriage and the Family.* 57 (1995): 477–488.

Parkman, Allen M. *No-Fault Divorce: What Went Wrong?* Boulder, Colo.: Westview Press, 1992.

Peterson, Richard. "A Re-evaluation of the Economic Consequences of Divorce." *American Sociological Review.* 61 (1996): 528–536.

Weitzman, Lenore. *The Divorce Revolution.* New York: The Free Press, 1987.

The Impact of Divorce on Adults and Children
Amato, Paul R. "Children's Adjustment to Divorce: Theories, Hypotheses and Empirical Support." *Journal of Marriage and the Family.* 55 (1993): 23–38.
Amato, Paul R. and Bruce Keith. "Parental Divorce and Well-Being of Children: A Meta-Analysis." *Psychological Bulletin.* 110 (1991): 26–46.
Amato, Paul R. and Bruce Keith. "Parental Divorce and Adult Well-being: A Meta-Analysis," *Journal of Marriage and the Family.* 53 (1991): 43–48.
Cherlin, Andrew. *Marriage, Divorce, Remarriage.* Cambridge, Mass.: Harvard University Press, 1992.
Furstenberg, Frank Jr. "Divorce and the American Family." *Annual Review of Sociology.* 16 (1990): 379–403.
Hetherington, E. Mavis and others. "Marital Transition: A Child's Perspective." *American Psychologist.* 44 (1989): 303–312.
Hetherington, E. Mavis. "Family Relations Six Years after Divorce," in Kay Pasley and Marilyn Ihinger-Tallman eds. *Remarriage and Stepparenting: Current Research and Theory.* New York: Guilford Press, 1987, pp. 185–207.
Hetherington, E. Mavis and others. "Effects of Divorce on Parents and Children," in Michael Lamb ed., *Nontraditional Families.* Hillsdale, N.J.: Earlbaum and Associates, Publishers, 1982, pp. 233–288.
Riessman, Catherine and Naomi Gerstel. "Marital Dissolution and Health: Do Males or Females Have Greater Risk?" *Social Science and Medicine.* 20 (1985): 627–635.
Wallerstein, Judith and Sandra Blakeslee. *Second Chances: Men and Women A Decade After Divorce.* New York: Ticknor & Fields, 1990.
Wallerstein, Judith. "The Long-Term Effects of Divorce on Children: A Review." *Journal of the American Academy of Child and Adolescent Psychiatry.* 30 (1991): 349–360.
Whitehead, Barbara Dafoe. *The Divorce Culture.* New York: Alfred A. Knopf, 1997.
Zill, Nicholas and others. "Long-Term Effects of Parental Divorce on Parent-Child Relationships, Adjustments and Achievement in Young Adulthood." *Journal of Family Psychology.* 7 (1993): 91–103.

REMARRIAGE AND STEPFAMILIES

Booth, Alan and Judy Dunn eds. *Stepfamilies: Who Benefits? Who Does Not?* Hillsdale, N.J.: Lawrence Erlbaum Associates, Publishers, 1994.

Bray, James H. "Children's Development in Early Remarriage," in E. Mavis Hetherington and J. D. Arasteh eds. *Impact of Divorce, Single-Parenting, and Stepparenting on Children.* Hillsdale, N.J.: Earlbaum Associates, Publishers, 1994, pp. 55–79.

Cherlin, Andrew. "Remarriage as an Incomplete Institution." *The American Journal of Sociology.* 84 (1978): 634–650.

Furstenberg, Frank F. "The New Extended Family: The Experience of Parents and Children After Remarriage," in Kay Pasley and Marilyn Ihinger-Tallman eds. *Remarriage and Stepparenting: Current Research and Theory.* New York: Guilford Press, 1987, pp. 42–61.

White, Lynn K. and Alan Booth. "The Quality and Stability of Relationships: The Role of Stepchildren." *American Sociological Review.* 50 (1985): 689–698.

DOMESTIC VIOLENCE AND CHILD ABUSE IN COHABITING AND STEPFAMILY SITUATIONS

Daly, Martin and Margo Wilson. "Child Abuse and Other Risks of Not Living with Both Parents." *Ethology and Sociobiology.* 6 (1985): 197–210.

Gordon, Michael. "The Family Environment of Sexual Abuse: A Comparison of Natal and Stepfather Abuse." *Child Abuse and Neglect.* 13 (1989): 121–130.

Malkin, Catherine and Michael Lamb. "Child Maltreatment: A Test of Sociobiological Theory." *Journal of Comparative Family Studies.* 25 (1994): 121–133.

Margolin, Leslie. "Child Abuse and Mother's Boyfriends: Why the Overrepresentation?" *Child Abuse and Neglect.* 16 (1992): 541–551.

Stets, Jan E. and Murray A. Straus. "The Marriage License as a Hitting License: A Comparison of Assaults in Dating, Cohabiting and Married Couples." *Journal of Family Violence.* 4 (1989): 161–180.

Stets, Jan E. "Cohabiting and Marital Aggression: The Role of Social Isolation." *Journal of Marriage and the Family.* 53 (1991): 669–680.

Straus, Murray A. "Physical Assault by Wives: A Major Social Problem," in Richard J. Gelles and Donileen R. Loseke eds. *Current Controversies on Family Violence.* Newbury Park, Calif.: Sage Publications, 1993, pp. 67–87.

Wilson, Margo and Martin Daly. "Risk of Maltreatment of Children Living with Stepparents," in Richard Gelles and Jane B. Lancaster, eds. *Child Abuse and Neglect: Biosocial Dimensions.* Hawthorne, N.Y.: Aldine De Gruyter, 1987, pp. 215–232.

Yllo, Kersti and Murray Straus. "Interpersonal Violence Among Married and Cohabiting Couples." *Family Relations.* 30 (1981): 339–347.

Notes

Preface and Acknowledgments
1. "Data" is a grammatically confusing word, one which various sources use differently. Even style guides and dictionaries disagree on what part of speech it is: a singular, plural, or collective noun. Of course, it is all of these, depending on how it is used. With rare exceptions, however, I use data in this book as a collective noun (much like team, committee, or group), and therefore have assigned it singular verbs and pronouns.
2. G. K. Chesterton, *What's Wrong With the World* (San Francisco: Ignatius Press, 1910, 1994), p. 47.
3. Charles Péguy, as quoted in Alvaro de Silva, ed., *Brave New Family: G. K. Chesterton on Men & Women, Children, Sex, Divorce, Marriage, & the Family* (San Francisco: Ignatius Press, 1990), p. 12.

   Fr. Silva has done the student of the family a great service in providing a very respectable survey of writings on various marriage and family topics from one of the world's most insightful thinkers on these subjects. Chesterton has done more than any other thinker to shape my thinking on the virtue and value of family. That influence is manifest in this book.

Prologue
1. Arlene F. Saluter, *Marital Status and Living Arrangements: March 1994*, U.S. Bureau of the Census, March 1996; Series P20–484, p. ix.
2. Gary S. Becker, *A Treatise on the Family* (Cambridge: Harvard University Press, 1991), p. 1.
3. Saluter, 1996.
4. Saluter, 1996, p. vi.
5. Lawrence Stone, "The Road to Polygamy," *New York Review*, (1989) March 2, p. 14. Cited in David Popenoe, "Where's Papa? Disappearing Dads are Destroying our Future," *Utne Reader*, (1996) September/October, p. 68.
6. Saluter, 1996, table A-1.
7. Saluter, 1996, table A-2.
8. Saluter, 1996, p. vi.
9. Saluter, 1996, table A, p. vi.
10. Saluter, 1996, p. vii.
11. Saluter, 1996, table A-9.
12. Saluter, 1996, table A-9.
13. Larry L. Bumpass, James A. Sweet, and Andrew Cherlin, "The Role of Cohabitation in Declining Rates of Marriage," *Journal of Marriage and the Family* 53 (1991): 913–927; L.S. Loomis and Nancy S. Landale, "Nonmarital Cohabitation

and Childbearing Among Black and White American Women," *Journal of Marriage and the Family* 56 (1994): 949–962.

14. Larry L. Bumpass and James A. Sweet, "Children's Experience in Single-Parent Families: Implications of Cohabitation and Marital Transitions," *Family Planning Perspectives* 21 (1989): 256–260.

15. Saluter, 1996, table A-5.

16. Saluter, 1996, p. ix, xi.

17. David Popenoe, Jean Bethke Elshtain, and David Blankenhorn, eds., *Promises to Keep: Decline and Renewal of Marriage in America* (Lanham, Md.: Rowman & Littlefield Publishers, 1996), p. ix.

18. Larry L. Bumpass, *The Declining Significance of Marriage: Changing Family Life in the United States,* National Survey of Families and Households Working Paper No. 66 (University of Wisconsin-Madison: Center for Demography and Ecology, 1995), p. 6.

19. Saluter, 1996, table A-5.

20. Saluter, 1996, table A-1.

21. Kingsley Davis, "The Meaning and Significance of Marriage in Contemporary Society" in *Contemporary Marriage: Comparative Perspectives on a Changing Institution,* Kingsley Davis, ed., (New York: Russell Sage Foundation, 1985), p. 21.

Kingsley's book is valuable and unique in that it was one of the first volumes to draw attention to what was happening in our midst regarding the decline of marriage. See especially Chapter One, "The Future of Marriage," pp. 25–51.

22. Frances K. Goldscheider and Linda J. Waite, *New Families, No Families? The Transformation of the American Home* (Berkeley: University of California Press, 1991).

This book offers a very interesting discussion of the social factors driving our culture away from marriage, with most of it being the changing relationships of how men and women relate to one another domestically along with women's growing participation in the marketplace.

23. Steven Mintz and Susan Kellogg, *Domestic Revolutions: A Social History of American Family Life* (New York: The Free Press, 1988), p. xvii.

This book, from a husband and wife writing team, is highly recommended as the best concise history of the various "domestic revolutions" that have evolved in the American family since our nation's founding. It offers a great education for all students of the family.

24. Christopher Lasch, *Haven in a Heartless World: The Family Besieged* (New York: Basic Books, 1977), p. xx.

25. This incredible shift is due in large part to a number of gifted thinkers and communicators: David Blankenhorn, Barbara Dafoe Whitehead, David Popenoe, and the band of scholars making up the Council on Families in America. Each of these are responsible for initiating and fueling this significant revolution in our nation's thinking.

26. Jonathan Alter, "Get Married, Madonna," *Newsweek* 29 April 1996, p. 51.

For an interesting treatment on the need to recover the lost art of making value judgments, see Jean Bethke Elshtain's "Judge Not?" in *First Things* October 1994, pp. 36–40.

27 Aristotle, *Politics* trans. Benjamin Jowett, Book I, Chapter II (New York: Walter J. Black, 1943).

28. David Popenoe, "Modern Marriage: Revisiting the Cultural Script," *Promises to Keep,* 1996, p. 248.

Chapter One: A Time for Every Purpose: Rediscovering the Need for a Sexual Ethic

1. Steve Mintz and Susan Kellog, *Domestic Revolutions: A Social History of American Family Life* (New York: The Free Press, 1988), pp. 208–209.

2. Neil Howe and William Strauss, *13th Gen* (New York: Vintage Books, 1993), p. 148.

3. "Sex O'Clock in America," *Current Opinion*, (1913), LV:113–114.
   The anonymous author of this essay borrowed the phrase from Reedy. See James R. McGovern, "The American Woman's Pre-World War I Freedom in Manner and Morals," *Journal of American History* 55 (1968): 315–333; and John C. Burnham, "The Progressive Era Revolution in American Attitudes Toward Sex," *Journal of American History* 53 (1973): 885–908, footnote 65.
4. William E. Leuchtenburg, *The Perils of Prosperity: 1914–32* (Chicago: University of Chicago Press, 1958), p. 167.
5. Frederick Lewis Allen, *Only Yesterday: An Informal History of the Nineteen Twenties,* (New York, 1931), pp. 88–122.
   For a discussion of the Flapper and her impact on American culture, see also McGovern, 1968, pp. 317, 318, 322; Kevin White, *The First Sexual Revolution: The Emergence of Male Heterosexuality in Modern America* (New York: New York University Press, 1993); Leuchtenburg, 1958, pp. 158–177.
6. McGovern, 1968, pp. 317, 322.
7. Leuchtenburg, 1958, p. 172.
8. White, 1993, p. 14.
9. Beth L. Bailey, *From Front Porch to Back Seat: Courtship in Twentieth-Century America* (Baltimore: The Johns Hopkins University Press, 1988), p. 17.
10. Martin King Whyte, *Dating, Mating, and Marriage* (New York: Aldine de Gruyter, 1990), p. 17.
11. Alfred Kinsey, Wardell B. Pomeroy, Clyde E. Martin, and Paul H Gebhard, *Sexual Behavior in the Human Female* (Philadelphia: W. B. Saunders Company, 1953), p. 298, see table 83.
12. Oswald Garrison Villard, "Sex, Art, Truth, and Magazines," *Atlantic Monthly* (March 1926), pp. 388–398.
13. White, 1993, p. 60.
14. White, 1993, p. 61; Villard, 1926, p, 391.
15. Villard, 1926, p. 392.
16. Villard, 1926, pp. 389, 392.
17. White, 1993, p. 62.
18. Villard, 1926, pp. 388–389.
19. Steven Seidman, *Romantic Longings: Love in America, 1830–1980* (New York: Routledge, Chapman and Hall, 1991), p. 74.
20. Alice Stockham, *Karezza* (Chicago: Leonidas, 1896), quoted in Seidman, 1991, p. 75.
21. Paul Popenoe, *Modern Marriage: A Handbook* (New York: Macmillan, 1925), p. 157.
22. Th. H. Van de Velde, *Ideal Marriage: Its Physiology and Technique* (New York: Random House, [1926], 1968), pp. xix, xx.
23. Van de Velde, 1926, 1968, p. 10.
24. Seidman, 1991, p. 121.
   It would be a serious shortcoming of any discussion on this early sexual revolution, which initiated the division between sexuality and marriage, not to mention two other foundational factors.
   First is the emergence and widespread acceptance of birth control. For a thoughtful discussion of this development, see Janet E. Smith, *Humanae Vitae: A Generation Later* (Washington, D. C.: Catholic University of America Press, 1992).
   Second is Henry Havelock Ellis's groundbreaking (and norm-breaking), multi-volume work *Studies in the Psychology of Sex.* The first six volumes were published between 1897 and 1910 with a seventh volume appearing in 1927, which consisted of various articles written since the original publication. It was Ellis, even more than Freud, who laid the intellectual foundation for broadening the spectrum for what was considered acceptable human sexual behavior. The first volume of his *Studies,* for instance, was *Sexual Inversion,* an effort to

show that homosexuality was not abnormal and could even be advantageous to society. A concise overview of Ellis's work is provided by Paul Robinson, *The Modernization of Sex* (New York: Harper & Row, 1976).

25. Pitirim A. Sorokin, *The American Sex Revolution* (Boston: Porter Sargent Publisher, 1956), p. 3.

26. Sorokin, 1956, p. 7.

27. Rustum and Della Roy, "Is Monogamy Outdated?" quoted in Lester A. Kirkendall and Robert N. Whitehurst, eds., *The New Sexual Revolution* (New York: Donald W. Brown, 1971), pp. 131–148.

28. Roy and Roy, 1971, p. 148.

29. Michael Anthony Waugh, "History of Clinical Developments in Sexually Transmitted Disease," quoted in King K. Holmes and others., eds., *Sexually Transmitted Disease* 2d ed., (New York: McGraw-Hill, 1990), pp. 3–16.

30. Burnham, 1973, p. 891.

31. Waugh, 1990, p. 12.

32. Burnham, 1973, p. 891.

33. Burnham, 1973, pp. 894, 895.

34. *Centers for Disease Control Division of STD/HIV Prevention 1991 Annual Report*, Centers for Disease Control, 1992, p. 3; "Sexually Transmitted Diseases in the U.S.: Risks, Consequences, and Costs," *Issues in Brief*, The Alan Guttmacher Institute, April 1994, p. 1.

35. "Sexually Transmitted Diseases in the United States," *Facts in Brief*, Alan Guttmacher Institute, September 1993, p. 1.

36. Alan Guttmacher Institute, 1993, pp. 1–2.

37. Alan Guttmacher Institute, 1994, p. 4.

38. "Sex in America," *U.S. News & World Report* (17 October 1994), pp. 74–81.

39. For a discussion of these early studies and their shortcomings, see Robert T. Michael, John H. Gagnon, Edward O. Laumann, and Gina Kolata, *Sex in America: A Definitive Survey* (Boston: Little, Brown, and Company, 1994), pp. 15–41.

40. "Now for the Truth About Americans and Sex," *Time* 17 October 1994, p. 64.

41. *Sex in America: A Definitive Survey*, see note 39; Edward O. Laumann, John H. Gagnon, Robert T. Michael, and Stuart Michaels, *The Social Organization of Sexuality: Sexual Practices in the United States* (Chicago: University of Chicago Press, 1994).

42. Michael and others., 1994, p. 1.

43. Michael and others., 1994, p. 131.

44. Laumann and others., 1994, p. 364, table 10.5.

45. Laumann and others., 1994, p. 368, table 10.7.

46. Michael and others., 1994, p. 225, figure 21. The remaining 4% are those women forced to perform a sexual act by a stranger.

47. Laumann and others., 1994, p. 370, table 10.8.

48. Laumann and others., p. 121.

49. Kari Jenson Gold, "Getting Real," *First Things* (January 1994), p. 6.

50. Winnifred B. Cutler, *Love Cycles: The Science of Intimacy* (New York: Villard Books, 1991), p. 4.

51. Cutler, 1991, p. 5.

52. Cutler, 1991, pp. 5, 21.

53. Cutler, 1991, p. 35.

54. Cutler, 1991, pp. 108–109.

55. Cutler, 1991, p. 244.

56. Andrew M. Greeley, *Faithful Attraction: Discovering Intimacy, Love, and Fidelity in American Marriage* (New York: Tom Doherty Associates, 1991).

See Chapter Six for Greeley's informative discussion of increased sexual pleasure in marriage. Greeley, a Catholic priest, adds an interesting nugget to the body of knowledge here. He reports that being married and Catholic correlates with higher sexual satisfaction than the average married person, but that being Irish, Catholic and married lifts that level higher even still (p. 71). While the NHSLS study confirms this for men, it found that Protestant married women were more sexually satisfied than Catholic women and those with no religious affiliation. However, conservative Protestant married women were the most sexually satisfied of any group. See Michael and others, 1994, p. 129, panel B.

57. Greeley, 1991, p. 201.
58. Joan R. Kahn and Kathryn A. London, "Premarital Sex and the Risk of Divorce," *Journal of Marriage and the Family* 53 (1991): 845–855.
59. Kahn and London, 1991, p. 846.
60. Diane N. Lye and Timothy J. Biblarz, "The Effects of Attitudes Toward Family Life and Gender Roles on Marital Satisfaction," Paper presented at the annual meeting of the Population Association of America, Toronto, 1990. Cited in Kahn and London, 1991, p. 847.
61. John D. Williams and Arthur P. Jacoby, "The Effects of Premarital Heterosexual and Homosexual Experience on Dating and Marriage Desirability," *Journal of Marriage and the Family* 51 (1989): 489–497.
62. Koray Tanfer and Jeanette J. Schoorl, "Premarital Sexual Careers and Partner Change," *Archives of Sexual Behavior* 21 (1992): 45–68.
63. Sorokin, 1956, pp. 106, 107.
64. Joseph Daniel Unwin, *Sex and Culture* (London: Oxford University Press, 1934). Unwin explains that while this work was completed in 1932, he didn't publish it immediately. Instead he wrote an abstract of the work, a 108-page volume titled: *Sexual Regulation and Human Behavior* (London: Williams & Norgate, 1933). For the nontechnician, this abstract is more appealing than the larger work because it is highly readable and gets right to the point. Given that, we will use the text of the abstract as our source for studying Unwin's work.
65. Unwin, 1933, pp. ix, x.
66. Unwin, 1933, pp. 1, 4.
67. Unwin's conclusion is supported by more recent anthropological research. Monogamous societies constructed more sophisticated socioeconomic systems than non-monogamous ones. See Marie W. Osmond, "Toward Monogamy: A Cross-Cultural Study of Correlates of Type of Marriage," *Social Forces* 44 (1965): 8–16.
68. Unwin, 1933, p. 71.
69. Unwin, 1933, p. 71.
70. Joseph Daniel Unwin, *Hopousia or The Sexual and Economic Foundations of a New Society* (New York: Oskar Piest, 1940).
71. Unwin, 1940, p. 348.
72. Unwin, 1933, p. 74.
73. Unwin, 1933, p. 77.
   Tendance is interaction with the spirit of the dead with the end of appeasement so the departed soul will not bring harm to the remaining relatives. *Cult* is interaction with the dead under the recognition that the dead have greater power than the living and can exercise that power on behalf of the living if approached in the right way by the right person in the proper place (see p. 2).
74. Unwin, 1933, p. 85.
75. Unwin, 1933, p. 80.
76. Quoted by Dennis Prager in *The Prager Perspective* (1 December 1996), p. 3.
77. Sorokin, 1956, p. 88.

Chapter Two: Troubled and Costly: The Hidden Consequences of Cohabitation
   1. Larry L. Bumpass, *The Declining Significance of Marriage: Changing Values in the United States*, National Survey of Families and Households Working Paper No. 66 (University of Wisconsin-Madison: Center for Demography and Ecology, 1995), p. 8.

2. Arlene F. Saluter, *Marital Status and Living Arrangements: March 1994*, U.S. Bureau of the Census, March 1996; Series P20–484, table A-9.
3. John D. Cunningham and John K. Antill, "Cohabitation and Marriage: Retrospective and Predictive Comparisons," *Journal of Social and Personal Relationships* 11 (1994): 77–93.
4. William G. Axinn and Arland Thornton, "The Relationship Between Cohabitation and Divorce: Selectivity or Casual Influence?" *Demography* 29 (1992): 357–374.
5. Elizabeth Thomson and Ugo Colella, "Cohabitation and Marital Stability: Quality or Commitment?" *Journal of Marriage and the Family* 54 (1992): 259–267.
6. Zheng Wu, "Premarital Cohabitation and Postmarital Cohabiting Union Formation," *Journal of Family Issues* 16 (1995): 212–232.
7. Thomson and Colella, 1992, p. 263.
8. Thomson and Colella, 1992, p. 266.
9. Cunningham and Antill, 1994, p. 90.
10. Alan Booth and David Johnson, "Premarital Cohabitation and Marital Success" *Journal of Family Issues* 9 (1988): 255–272.
11. Booth and Johnson, 1988, p. 261.
   Steven Nock also found significantly lower levels of happiness for cohabitors than for married couples. See Steven L. Nock, "A Comparison of Marriages and Cohabiting Relationships," *Journal of Family Issues* 16 (1995): 53–76.
12. Booth and Johnson, 1988, p. 263.
13. Jan E. Stets, "The Link Between Past and Present Intimate Relationships," *Journal of Family Issues* 14 (1993): 236–260.
14. Larry L. Bumpass, James A. Sweet, and Andrew Cherlin, "The Role of Cohabitation in Declining Rates of Marriage," *Journal of Marriage and the Family* 53 (1991): 913–927.
15. T. R. Balakrishnan, K. Vaninadha Rao, Evelyne Lapierre-Adamcyk, and Karol J. Krotki, "A Hazard Model of the Co-variaters of Marriage Dissolution in Canada," *Demography* 24 (1987): 395–406.
16. Neil G. Bennett, Ann Klimas Blanc, and David E. Bloom, "Commitment and the Modern Union: Assessing the Link Between Premarital Cohabitation and Subsequent Marital Stability," *American Sociological Review* 53 (1988): 127–138.
17. Wu, 1995, p. 227.
18. Michael D. Newcomb and P. M. Bentler, "Assessment of Personality and Demographic Aspects of Cohabitation and Marital Success," *Journal of Personality Assessment* 44 (1980): 11–24.
19. Frances Goldscheider, Arland Thornton, and Linda Young-DeMarco, "A Portrait of the Nest-Leaving Process in Early Adulthood," *Demography* 30 (1993): 683–699.
20. Goldscheider, Thornton, and Young-DeMarco, 1993, p. 695.
21. Stets, 1993, p. 251.
22. Margaret A. Segrest and M. O'Neal Weeks, "Comparison of the Role Expectations of Married and Cohabiting Subjects," *International Journal of Sociology of the Family* 6 (1976): 275–281.
23. See Gilder's *Sexual Suicide* (New York: Bantam Books, 1973); "In Defense of Monogamy," *Commentary* Nov. 1974, pp. 31–36; *Men and Marriage* (Gretna, La.: Pelican Books, 1992).
24. Kersti Yllo and Murray A. Straus, "Interpersonal Violence Among Married and Cohabiting Couples," *Family Relations* 30 (1981): 339–347.
25. Yllo and Straus, 1981, p. 343.
26. Jan E. Stets and Murray A. Straus, "The Marriage License as a Hitting License: A Comparison of Assaults in Dating, Cohabiting, and Married Couples," *Journal of Family Violence* 4 (1989): 161–180.
27. Stets and Straus, 1989, p.176; see also Nock, 1995, pp. 57, 67.

28. Stets and Straus, 1989, pp. 176–177.
29. See Bennett, Blanc, and Bloom, 1988, p. 137; Newcomb and Bentler, 1980, p. 21; Thomson and Colella, 1992, p. 266.
30. Stets and Straus, 1989, pp. 176–177.
31. Nock, 1995, p. 56.
32. Murray A. Straus, "Physical Assaults by Wives: A Major Social Problem," in Richard J. Gelles and Donileen R. Loseke, eds., *Current Controversies on Family Violence* (Newbury Park, Calif.: Sage Publications, 1993), pp. 67–87; see also Murray A. Straus and Richard J. Gelles, "Societal Changes and Change in Family Violence from 1975 to 1985 as Revealed by Two National Surveys," *Journal of Marriage and the Family* 48 (1986): 465–479; and Murray A. Straus and Richard J. Gelles, eds., *Physical Violence in American Families: Risk Factors and Adaptations to Violence in 8,145 Families* (New Brunswick, N.J.: Transaction Press, 1990), pp. 95–105.
33. Margo I. Wilson and Martin Daly, "Who Kills Whom in Spouse Killings? On the Exceptional Sex Ratio of Spousal Homicides in the United States," *Criminology* 30 (1992): 189–215.
34. Jan E. Stets, "Cohabiting and Marital Aggression: The Role of Social Isolation," *Journal of Marriage and the Family* 53 (1991): 669–680.
35. Stets, 1991, p. 674.
36. Stets, 1991, p. 674; Newcomb and Bentler, 1980, pp. 15, 21.
37. Albert R. Roberts, "Psychosocial Characteristics of Batterers: A Study of 234 Men Charged with Domestic Violence Offenses," *Journal of Family Violence* 2 (1987): 81–93.
38. Carolyn Wolf Harlow, *Female Victims of Violent Crime* (Washington, D. C.: U.S. Department of Justice, 1991), pp. 1–2.
39. "Criminal Victimization in the United States, 1992," U.S. Department of Justice, Office of Justice Programs, Bureau of Justice Statistics, (March 1994), p. 31, NCJ-145125.
40. U.S. Bureau of Justice Statistics, *Highlights from 20 Years of Surveying Crime Victims: The National Crime Victimization Survey, 1973–92* (Washington, D.C.: U.S. Department of Justice, 1993), p. 18.
41. Data on domestic violence is usually reported this way where the victim is either beaten by "husbands or boyfriends." This format is especially present in reports by the popular media. This needlessly indicts husbands when they are perpetrators of domestic violence at much lower rates than boyfriends are.
42. Centers for Disease Control, *Morbidity and Mortality Weekly Report (1994),* 43:8, pp. 132–133.
43. David Blankenhorn, *Fatherless America: Confronting Our Most Urgent Social Problem* (New York: Basic Books, 1995), p. 33.
44. Bumpass, Sweet, and Cherlin, 1991, p. 926; Saluter, 1996, table A-9.
45. Bumpass, Sweet, and Cherlin, 1991, p. 919.
46. Cohabiting relationships including children belonging to only one partner, rather than both, account for 27 percent of all cohabiting relationships. See Bumpass, Sweet, and Cherlin, 1991, p. 919.
47. Bumpass, Sweet, and Cherlin, 1991, p. 923.
48. For a larger discussion of the difference between how biological and nonbiological parents' care for children, see David Popenoe's essay on the biosocial aspect of parenting, "The Evolution of Marriage and the Problem of Stepfamilies: A Biosocial Perspective," in *Stepfamilies: Who Benefits? Who Does Not?* Alan Booth and Judy Dunn, eds., (Hillsdale, N.J.: Lawrence Erlbaum Associates, 1994), pp. 3–27.
49. Catherine Malkin and Michael Lamb, "Child Maltreatment: A Test of Sociobiological Theory," *Journal of Comparative Family Studies* 25 (1994): 121–133.
50. Leslie Margolin, "Child Abuse and Mother's Boyfriends: Why the Overrepresentation?" *Child Abuse and Neglect* 16 (1992): 541–551.

51. Michael Gordon and Susan J. Creighton, "Natal and Nonnatal Fathers as Sexual Abusers in the United Kingdom: A Comparative Analysis," *Journal of Marriage and the Family* 50 (1988): 99.
52. Bumpass, Sweet, and Cherlin, 1991, p. 921.
53. Lee Robins and Darrel Regier, *Psychiatric Disorders in America: The Epidemiologic Catchment Area Study* (New York: Free Press, 1991), p. 64.
54. Bumpass, Sweet, and Cherlin, 1991, p. 923.
55. Bumpass, Sweet, and Cherlin, 1991, p. 923.
56. Cunningham and Antill, 1994, p. 88; see also Lucy Jen Huang, "Some Patterns of Nonexclusive Sexual Relations Among Unmarried Cohabiting Couples," *International Journal of Sociology of the Family* 6 (1976): 265–274.
57. Cunningham and Antill, 1994, p. 89; see also Renata Forste and Koray Tanfer, "Sexual Exclusivity Among Dating, Cohabiting, and Married Women," *Journal of Marriage and the Family* 58 (1996): 33–47.
    Forste and Tanfer conclude from their work that cohabiting women approximate the sexual behavior of dating women rather than the behavior of married women (p. 45). This is true even for marriage preceded by cohabitation.
58. Bennett, Blanc, and Bloom, 1988, p. 137; Newcomb and Bentler, 1980, p. 21; and Thomson and Colella, 1992, p. 266.
59. It is noteworthy that these are the same character qualities essential in a good neighbor, coworker, citizen, and human being, which is why those who are good marital mates are more likely good members of society.
60. Cunningham and Antill, 1994, pp. 88–89, Thomson and Colella, 1992, p. 266.
61. Axinn and Thornton, 1992, p. 366.
62. Linda J. Waite, Frances Goldscheider, and C. Witsberger, "Nonfamily Living and the Erosion of Traditional Family Orientations Among Adults," *American Sociological Review* 51 (1986): 541–554.
63. Axinn and Thornton, 1992, p. 357.
64. Axinn and Thornton, 1992, p. 372.
65. Thomson and Colella, 1992, p. 264.
66. Booth and Johnson, 1988, p. 270; Stets, 1993, p. 257. David R. Hall and John Z. Zhao, "Cohabitation and Divorce in Canada: Testing the Selectivity Hypothesis," *Journal of Marriage and the Family* 57 (1995): 421–427.
67. Roy E. L. Watson and Peter W. DeMeo, "Premarital Cohabitation vs. Traditional Courtship and Subsequent Marital Adjustment: A Replication and Follow-up," *Family Relations* 36 (1987): 193–197.
68. William G. Axinn and Arland Thornton, "Mothers, Children, and Cohabitation: The Intergenerational Effects of Attitudes and Behaviors," *American Sociological Review* 58 (1993): 233–246.
69. Axinn and Thornton, 1993, p. 243.
70. Arland Thornton, William G. Axinn, and Daniel Hill, "Reciprocal Effects of Religiosity, Cohabitation, and Marriage," *American Journal of Sociology* 98 (1992): 628–651.
71. Thornton, Axinn, and Hill, 1992, p. 648.

Chapter Three: Only a Piece of Paper? The Benefits of Marriage for Adults
1. Quoted in Frances K. Goldscheider, and Linda J. Waite, *No Families, New Families* (Berkeley: University of California Press, 1991), p. 63.
2. Judith Wallerstein and Sandra Blakeslee, *The Good Marriage: How and Why Love Lasts* (Boston: Houghton Mifflin Company, 1995), p. 3.
3. The cover of the third edition boasts that the book spent over forty weeks on national bestseller lists, sold more than 200,000 hardcover copies and was selected by every major book club, (New York: Avon Books, 1973).
4. Nena and George O'Neill, *Open Marriage: A New Lifestyle for Couples* (New York: Avon Books, 1973), pp. 13–15.

5. Quoted in Bertrand Russell's *Marriage and Morals* (New York: Bantam Books, 1968), p. 95.
6. Robert H. Coombs, "Marital Status and Personal Well-Being: A Literature Review," *Family Relations* 40 (1991): 97–102.
7. Coombs, 1991, p. 97.
8. Catherine K. Riessman and Naomi Gerstel, "Marital Dissolution and Health: Do Males or Females Have Greater Risk?" *Social Science and Medicine* 20 (1985): 627–635.
9. Ecclesiastes 4:9–10.
10. Leonard I. Pearlin and Joyce S. Johnson, "Marital Status, Life Strains, and Depression," *American Sociological Review* 42 (1977): 704–15.
11. A similar explanation for the decreased well–being of unmarried individuals posits that since marriage is the cultural norm for adults, those who remain single find themselves going against the prescribed societal grain. Therefore, the unmarried are treated as people who are either unwilling or unable to conform to accepted practices and consequently face varied degrees of discrimination, leading to a lesser degree of well-being. However, Pearlin and Johnson argued in 1977 that this argument is "less convincing now than in earlier years" because of the degeneration of the idea of marriage (Pearlin and Johnson, 1977).
12. Coombs, 1991, p. 97.
13. Coombs, 1991, p. 97.
14. S. M. Rosenblatt, M. M. Gross, and S. Chartoff, "Marital Status and Multiple Psychiatric Admissions for Alcoholism," *Quarterly Journal of Studies on Alcoholism* 30 (1969): 445–447.
15. Coombs, 1991, p. 97.
16. Milton Terris, "Epidemiology of Cirrhosis of the Liver," *Journal of Health and Social Behavior* 57 (1967): 2076–2088.
17. Lee N. Robins and Darrel A. Regier, *Psychiatric Disorders in America: The Epidemiologic Catchment Area Study* (New York: The Free Press, 1991) pp. 1, 9.
18. Robins and Regier, 1991, p. 102.
19. Robins and Regier, 1991, p. 103.
20. Evelyn Bromet and Rudolf Moos, "Sex and Marital Status in Relation to the Characteristics of Alcoholics," *Journal of Studies on Alcohol* 37 (1976): 1302–1312; see also E. M. Coorigan, *Alcoholic Women in Treatment* (New York: Oxford University Press, 1980).
21. Coombs, 1991, p. 97.
22. Emile Durkheim, *Suicide: A Study in Sociology* (New York: Free Press, 1951), pp. 180–216.
23. For evidence on the increased social integration marriage brings to individuals, see James S. Goodwin, William C. Hunt, Charles R. Key, and Jonathan M. Samet, "The Effect of Marital Status on Stage, Treatment, and Survival of Cancer Patients, *Journal of the American Medical Association* 258 (1987): 3125–3130; Walter R. Gove, "Sex, Marital Status, and Mortality," *American Journal of Sociology* 79 (1973): 45–67; Frances E. Kobrin and Gerry E. Hendershot, "Do Family Ties Reduce Mortality? Evidence From the United States, 1966–1968," *Journal of Marriage and the Family* 39 (1977): 737–745; Richard G. Rogers, "Marriage, Sex, and Mortality," *Journal of Marriage and the Family* 57 (1995): 515–526; Holly Ann Williams, "A Comparison of Social Support and Social Networks of Black Parents and White Parents with Chronically Ill Children," *Social Science Medicine* 37 (1993): 1509–1520.
24. Jeffery A. Burr, Patricia L. McCall, and Eve Powell-Griner, "Catholic Religion and Suicide: The Mediating Effect of Divorce," *Social Science Quarterly* 75 (1994): 300–318.
    The variables analyzed in this study were church membership, marital status, employment status, family income, growth in new housing construction

(as a measure of "economic vitality and population stability"), female labor force participation, population density, and ethnic background.

25. Jack C. Smith, James A. Mercy, and Judith M. Conn, "Marital Status and the Risk of Suicide," *American Journal of Public Health* 78 (1988): 78–80.

Gove, in his previously mentioned study (1973) found even larger disparities in the suicide rates of the married and unmarried. He found the single are nearly twice as likely to take their own lives and the divorced almost five times as likely.

26. The contradictory study was by J. Rico–Velasco and L. Mynko, "Suicide and Marital Status: A Changing Relationship?" *Journal of Marriage and the Family* 35 (1973): 239–244. It was refuted in the next issue by D. Herr and D. MacKinnon, Letters to the Editor, "Suicide and Marital Status: A Rejoinder to Rico-Velasco and Mynko," *Journal of Marriage and the Family* 36 (1974): 6–10.

27. W. Farr, "Influence of Marriage on the Mortality of French People" in *Transactions of the National Association for the Promotion of Social Science*. G. W. Hastings, ed. (London: John W. Parker and Sons, 1858), pp. 504-513.

28. I. M. Joung, H. Van De Mheen, K. Stronks, F. W. A Van Poppel, and J. P. Mackenbach, "Difference in Self-Reported Morbidity by Marital Status and by Living Arrangement," *International Journal of Epidemiology* 23 (1994): 91–97.

29. Lee A. Lillard and Linda J. Waite, " 'Til Death Do Us Part: Marital Disruption and Mortality," *American Journal of Sociology* 100 (1995): 1131–1156.

30. Linda J. Waite, "Does Marriage Matter?" Presidential Address to the Population Association of America, April 8, 1995.

The study she cites for this data is Bernard L. Cohen and I-Sing Lee, "Catalog of Risks," *Health Physics* 36:707–722. Dr. Waite's address was later published as Linda J. Waite, "Does Marriage Matter?" *Demography* 32 (1995): 483–507.

31. Coombs, 1991, p. 98.

32. James S. Goodwin, William C. Hunt, Charles R. Key, and Jonathan M. Samet, "The Effect of Marital Status on Stage, Treatment, and Survival of Cancer Patients," *Journal of the American Medical Association* 258 (1987): 3152–3130.

33. Goodwin, Hunt, Key, and Samet, 1987, p. 3129.

34. Goodwin, Hunt, Key, and Samet, 1987, p. 3129

35. Lois M. Verbrugge and Donald J. Balaban, "Patterns of Change, Disability and Well-Being," *Medical Care* 27 (1989): S128–S147.

36. Coombs, 1991, p. 98.

37. Harold J. Morowitz, "Hiding in the Hammond Report," *Hospital Practice* (August 1975), p. 39.

38. James J. Lynch, *The Broken Heart: The Medical Consequences of Loneliness* (New York: Basic Books, 1977).

39. Frances E. Kobrin and Gerry E. Hendershot, "Do Family Ties Reduce Mortality? Evidence From the United States, 1966–1968," *Journal of Marriage and the Family* 39 (1977): 737–745.

40. Rogers, 1995, p. 520.

41. Maradee A. Davis, John M. Neuhaus, Deborah J. Moritz, and Mark R. Segal, "Living Arrangements and Survival among Middle-Aged and Older Adults in the NHANES I Epidemiologic Follow-up Study," *American Journal of Public Health* 82 (1992): 401–406.

42. Walter Gove, "Sex, Marital Status and Mortality," *American Journal of Sociology* 79 (1973): 45–67.

43. Gove, 1973, p. 57.

44. Gove, 1973, p. 59.

45. Waite, 1995, pp. 497–498.

46. Lillard and Waite, 1991; See also Debra Umberson, "Family Status and Health Behaviors: Social Control as a Dimension of Social Integration," *Journal of Health and Social Behavior* 28 (1987): 306–319.

47. Benjamin Malzberg, "Marital Status in Relation to the Prevalence of Mental Disease," *Psychiatric Quarterly* 10 (1936): 45–261.
48. Malzberg, 1936, p. 259.
49. Coombs, 1991, p. 99.
50. Robins and Regier, 1991, p. 44.
51. Duncan Cramer, "Social Support and Psychological Distress in Women and Men," *British Journal of Medical Psychology* 64 (1991): 147–158.
52. Elizabeth Cady Stanton. Speech at the Tenth National Women's Rights Convention, New York City, May 10, 1860. Quoted in *The Harper Book of American Quotations* (New York: Harper & Row, 1988), p. 374.
53. Christina Hoff Sommers, *Who Stole Feminism? How Women Have Betrayed Women* (New York: Simon & Schuster, 1994), p. 251.
54. Naomi Wolf, "Radical Heterosexuality . . . or How to Love a Man and Save Your Feminist Soul," quoted in Emilie Buchwald and others., eds., *Transforming a Rape Culture* (Minneapolis: Milkweed Editions, 1993).
55. Larry L. Bumpass, James A. Sweet, and Andrew Cherlin, "The Role of Cohabitation in Declining Rates of Marriage," *Journal of Marriage and the Family* 53 (1991): 913–927.
56. Robins and Regier, 1991, p. 72.
57. Pearlin and Johnson, 1977, p. 706.
58. Robins and Regier, 1991, p. 73.
59. Robins and Regier, 1991, p. 334.
60. David R. Williams, David T. Takeuchi, and Russell K. Adair, "Marital Status and Psychiatric Disorders Among Black and Whites," *Journal of Health and Social Behavior* 33 (1992): 140–157.
61. Coombs, 1991, p. 100.
62. Ellison explains these two dimensions of subjective well-being are *cognitive* and *affective*. "Affective" dimensions are those such as personal happiness, measuring mood-related assessments that fluctuate over time. "Cognitive" dimensions are those such as life satisfaction, which involve more reflective responses and are stable over time.
63. Christopher G. Ellison, "Family Ties, Friendships, and Subjective Well-Being Among Black Americans," *Journal of Marriage and the Family* 52 (1990): 298–310.
64. Karyn A. Loscocco and Glenna Spitz, "Working Conditions, Social Support, and the Well-Being of Female and Male Factory Workers," *Journal of Health and Social Behavior* 31 (1990): 313–327.
65. Kirby Hsu and Victor Marshall, "Prevalence of Depression and Distress in a Large Sample of Canadian Residents, Interns, and Fellows," *American Journal of Psychiatry* 144 (1987): 1561–1566.
66. Hsu and Marshall, 1987, p. 1565.
67. Hsu and Marshall, 1987, p. 1564.
68. Robert H. Coombs and Fawzy I. Fawzy, "The Effect of Marital Status on Stress in Medical School," *American Journal of Psychiatry* 139 (1982): 1490–1493.
69. Coombs and Fawzy, 1987, p. 1492.
70. I can attest to this in my own life. Being married and a student, I completed my undergraduate and graduate work in about four-and-a-half years, each time graduating with honors. These were also some of the best years of my life. Many of my very bright, but single fellow-students went through at a much slower pace. In short, my motivation was that I had someone to succeed for— my wife and family.
71. Coombs and Fawzy, 1987, p. 1492.
72. Wendy Wood, Nancy Rhodes, and Melanie Whelan, "Sex Differences in Positive Well-Being: A Consideration of Emotional Style and Marital Status," *Psychological Bulletin* 2 (1989): 249–264.
73. Woods, Rhodes and Whelan, 1989, p. 251.

74. Robert W. Levenson, Laura L. Carstensen, and John M. Gottman, "Long-Term Marriage: Age, Gender, and Satisfaction," *Psychology and Aging* (1993): 301–313.
75. Rogers, 1995, pp. 515, 516.
76. Randy M. Page and Galen E. Cole, "Demographic Predictors of Self-Reported Loneliness in Adults," *Psychological Reports* 68 (1991): 939–945.
77. Page and Cole, 1991, p. 939.
78. Page and Cole, 1991, p. 939.
79. Page and Cole, 1991, p. 943.
80. Catherine E. Ross, "Reconceptualizing Marital Status as a Continuum of Social Attachment," *Journal of Marriage and the Family* 57 (1995): 129–140.
81. Pearlin and Johnson, 1977, pp. 709–710.
82. Jan E. Mutchler and Jeffery A. Burr, "Racial Differences in Health and Health Care Service Utilization in Later Life: The Effect of Socioeconomic Status," *Journal of Health and Social Behavior* 32 (1991): 342–356.
83. W. Alex McIntosh, Peggy A. Shifflett, and J. Steven Picou, "Social Support, Stressful Events, Strain, Dietary Intake, and the Elderly," *Medical Care* 27 (1989): 140–153.
84. Ronald J. Angel and Jacqueline L. Angel, *Painful Inheritance: Health and the New Generation of Fatherless Families* (Madison: The University of Wisconsin Press, 1993), p. 7.
85. Angel and Angel, 1993, p. 127.
86. Angel and Angel, 1993, p. 132.
    The study is by Sara McLanahan, "Single Mothers and Psychological Well-Being: A Test of the Stress and Vulnerability Hypothesis," *Research in Community and Mental Health* 5 (1985): 253–266.
87. Angel and Angel, 1993, p. 138. This study is P. L. Berkman, "Spouseless Motherhood, Psychological Distress and Physical Morbidity," *Journal of Health and Social Behavior* 10 (1969): 323–334.
88. Angel and Angel, 1993, p. 139.
89. Angel and Angel, 1993, p. 148.
90. Yuareng Hu and Noreen Goldman, "Mortality Differentials by Marital Status: An International Comparison," *Demography* 27:233–250.
    Hu and Goldman looked at figures from the *National Demographic Yearbooks* for sixteen countries: Austria, Canada, Denmark, England and Wales, Finland, France, Hungary, Japan, Netherlands, Norway, Portugal, Scotland, Sweden, Taiwan, U.S.A., West Germany.
91. Arne Mastekaasa, "Marital Status, Distress, and Well-Being: An International Comparison," *Journal of Comparative Family Studies* 25 (1994): 189–204.
92. Mastekaasa, 1995, p. 201.
93. Mastekaasa, 1995, p. 201.
    Additionally, Rogers, "Marriage, Sex, and Mortality," *Journal of Marriage and the Family* 57 (1995): 525, found stronger marital health outcomes for males.
94. The studies that address the two hypotheses and favor the protection/support hypothesis are numerous. See Bromet and Moos, 1976; Coombs, 1991; Coombs and Fawzy, 1982; Durkheim, 1897; Goodwin, Hunt, Key, and Samet, 1987; Gove, 1973; Kobrin and Hendershot, 1977; Lillard and Waite, 1995; Lynch, 1977; McIntosh, Shifflett, and Picou, 1989; Mutchler and Burr, 1991; Robins and Regier, 1991; Rogers, 1995; Ross, 1995; Smith, Mercy, and Conn, 1988; and Williams, 1993. One work to make special note of is Linda J. Waite, "Does Marriage Matter?" presidential address to the Population Association of America, April 8, 1995, and the published version in *Demography* 32 (1995): 483–507.
95. Ross, 1995, p. 129.

Chapter Four: A Mom and a Dad: What Every Child Needs

1. One of the brightest and most entertaining writers on the hopes, fears and attitudes of Generation X is novelist Doug Coupland. His books are *Generation X: Tales for An Accelerated Culture*, (New York: St. Martin's Press, 1991); *Shampoo Planet* (New York: Pocket Books, 1992); *Life After God*, (New York: Pocket Books, 1994); *Microserfs* (New York: Regan Books/HarperCollins, 1995); *Polaroids from the Dead* (New York: Regan Books/HarperCollins, 1996).

2. William R. Mattox, Jr., "Split Personality: Why Aren't Conservatives Talking About Divorce?" *Policy Review* (Summer 1995), p. 50.

3. Sarah Ferguson, "The Comfort of Being Sad," *Utne Reader* (July/August 1994), p. 61.

4. Neil Howe and William Strauss, *13th Gen* (New York: Vintage, 1993), p. 53.

5. David Popenoe, "Fostering the New Familism," *The Responsive Community* 2 (1992): 31–39.

6. Popenoe, 1992, pp. 33–34.

7. Pamela Krueger, "Superwoman's Daughters," *Working Woman* (May 1994), p. 62.

8. Krueger, 1994, p. 61.

9. Krueger, 1994, p. 62.

10. Krueger, 1994, p. 62.

   This same sentiment is conveyed by Christine Thelmo, a twenty-seven-year-old communications director. She says, "Both of my parents were so busy. I will definitely be more involved and around when I have a family."

11. Maggie Mahar, "A Change of Place," *Barron's* (2 March 1994), pp. 33–38.

12. Mahar, 1994, p. 36.

   Barron's surveyed a mainstream and geographically representative sample of college-educated women in their twenties on their views of work and family. They report, "What was striking was how the respondents' answers overlapped with each other's—and with Hokenson's prophecy." Interestingly, only *one* of the women interviewed plans to pick up her old career full-time and only then if she doesn't have a second child.

   The *Wall Street Journal* has also recognized this trend, reporting that "when young women have good marriage possibilities . . . joining the workforce holds less appeal," and this has caused the first dip in the number of women presently in the workforce in twenty years. See Amanda Bennett, "Young Women May Trade Jobs for Marriage," *Wall Street Journal* (29 June 1994), p. B-1.

13. Personal communication between the author and David Blankenhorn, April 21, 1995.

14. Karl Zinsmeister, "Raising Hiroko," *The American Enterprise* (March/April 1990), pp. 53–59.

15. Pitirim A. Sorokin, *Society, Culture, and Personality* (New York: Harper & Row, 1947), pp. 246–247.

16. Sorokin, *The American Sex Revolution* (Boston: Porter Sargent, 1956), p. 5.

17. Bronislaw Malinowski, *Sex, Culture, and Myth* (New York: Harcourt, Brace & World, 1962), p. 63.

18. Elizabeth Herzog and Cecilia E. Sudia, "Children in Fatherless Families," in B. Caldwell and H. N. Riccuiti, eds., *Review of Child Development Research* vol. 3, (Chicago: University of Chicago Press, 1973), pp. 141–232.

19. Daniel Patrick Moynihan, *The Negro Family: The Case for National Action* (Washington, D.C.: Office of Planning and Research, United States Department of Labor, March 1965).

20. Of course, this was not a racist document. Moynihan did not blame the black community for the breakdown of its families. He indicted the nation's history of slavery, Reconstruction, poor education for blacks, rapid urbanization, and high unemployment, which made it difficult for black men to support families. Likewise, black mothers didn't seek their support. The controversy over this report

is detailed in Lee Rainwater and William L. Yancey, *The Moynihan Report and the Politics of Controversy* (Cambridge: MIT Press, 1967). This book also contains the full text of the Moynihan report.

21. Judith S. Wallerstein and Joan B. Kelly, *Surviving the Breakup: How Children and Parents Cope with Divorce* (New York: Basic Books, 1980).

22. Kenneth Auletta, *The Underclass* (New York: Random House, 1982).

23. Barbara Dafoe Whitehead, "Dan Quayle Was Right," *Atlantic Monthly*, (April 1993), p. 61.

24. Irwin Garfinkel and Sara S. McLanahan, *Single Mothers and Their Children: A New American Dilemma* (Washington, D. C.: The Urban Institute Press, 1986).

25. Sara S. McLanahan and Gary Sandefur, *Growing Up with a Single-Parent: What Hurts, What Helps* (Cambridge: Harvard University Press, 1994), p. 19.

26. McLanahan and Sandefur, 1994, p. 20.

27. McLanahan and Sandefur, 1994, p. 21.

28. McLanahan and Sandefur, 1994, p. 22; see also David T. Ellwood, *Poor Support: Poverty in the American Family* (New York: Basic Books, 1988).

29. The four nationally representative data sets used by McLanahan and Sandefur are the *Panel Study of Income Dynamics* (PSID), the *National Longitudinal Survey of Young Men and Women* (NLSY), the *High School and Beyond Study* (HSB) and the *National Survey of Families and Households* (NSFH). The first three surveys are longitudinal, each following its population over time. The last one is a cross-sectional survey, which asks people to recall their past experiences.

The *Panel Study of Income Dynamics* followed approximately 5,000 American families since 1968 and re-interviewed them every year. The children from these original families are followed and tracked into adulthood, providing data on how they fare in childhood and adulthood. The *National Longitudinal Survey of Young Men and Women* followed nearly 14,000 men and women who were born between 1958 and 1965. Respondents were first interviewed in 1979 and have been re-interviewed every year since. The *High School and Beyond Study* followed approximately 50,000 high school sophomores and seniors for 1,000 high schools in the United States. The first interviews took place in 1980 and the sample was re-interviewed in 1982, 1984 and 1986. The *National Survey of Families and Households* was conducted in 1987. Respondents were asked about their family experiences while growing up and their achievements in adulthood.

The data sets and variables of these studies are explained in greater detail in Appendix A of McLanahan and Sandefur, 1994, pp. 157–164.

30. McLanahan and Sandefur, 1994, p. 41.

31. McLanahan and Sandefur, 1994, p. 41.

32. McLanahan and Sandefur, 1994, p. 47.

33. Darin R. Featherstone, Bert P. Cundick, and Larry C. Jensen, "Differences in School Behavior and Achievement Between Children From Intact, Reconstituted, and Single-Parent Families," *Adolescence* 27 (1992): 1–12.

34. Featherstone, Cundick, and Jensen, 1992, p. 10.

35. Lise M. C. Bisnaire, Philip Firestone, and David Rynard, "Factors Associated With Academic Achievement in Children Following Parental Separation," *American Journal of Orthopsychiatry* 60 (1990): 67–76.

36. Deborah A. Dawson, "Family Structure and Children's Health and Well-Being: Data from the 1988 National Health Interview Survey on Child Health," *Journal of Marriage and the Family* 53 (1991): 573–584.

37. Greg J. Duncan, Jeanne Brooks-Gunn, and Pamela Kato Klebanov, "Economic Deprivation and Early Childhood Development," *Child Development* 65 (1994): 296–318.

38. Dawson, 1991, pp. 578–579.

39. The *National Longitudinal Survey of Youth* (NLSY) observed 12,686 men and

women age 14 through 21 and interviewed them every year beginning in 1979, extending at least through 1993 when Wojtkiewicz published. The study boasts a culturally and economically diverse population and an extremely high response rate over the length of the study.

40. Roger A. Wojtkiewicz, "Simplicity and Complexity in the Effects of Parental Structure on High School Graduation," *Demography* 30 (1993): 701–717.
41. Doris Goldberg, Margaret McLaughlin, Margaret Grossi, Alex Tytun, and Steve Blum, "Which Newborns in New York City Are at Risk for Special Education Placement?" *American Journal of Public Health* 82 (1992): 438–440.
42. Kay Donahue Jennings, Sylvia Mendelsohn, Kathleen May, and Gwyn M. Brown, "Elementary Students in Classes For the Emotionally Disturbed: Characteristics and Classroom Behavior," *American Journal of Orthopsychiatry* 58 (1988): 65–76.
43. Nan Marie Astone and Sara S. McLanahan, "Family Structure, Parental Practices, and High School Completion," *American Sociological Review* 56 (1991): 309–320.
44. Ralph B. McNeal, Jr., "Extracurricular Activities and High School Dropouts," *Sociology of Education* 68 (1995): 62–81.
45. Sheila Fitzgerald Krein and Andrea H. Beller, "Educational Attainment of Children From Single-Parent Families: Differences by Exposure, Gender, and Race," *Demography* 25 (1988): 221–233.
46. McLanahan and Sandefur, 1994, pp. 48–49.
47. McLanahan and Sandefur, 1994, p. 50.
48. McLanahan and Sandefur, 1994, p. 51.
49. Erik Erikson, *Childhood and Society* (New York: Norton, 1963), p. 259.
50. David Popenoe, "The Family Condition in America," in Henry J. Aaron, Thomas E. Mann, Timothy Taylor, eds., *Values and Public Policy* (Washington, D. C.: Brookings Institute, 1994), p. 95.
51. James Q. Wilson, "Culture Incentives and the Underclass" in *Values and Public Policy* Henry J. Aaron and others., eds. (Washington D. C.: Brookings Institute, 1994), pp. 70–71.
52. Jeanne Brooks-Gunn, Greg Duncan, Pamela Kato Klebanov, and Naomi Sealand, "Do Neighborhoods Influence Child and Adolescent Development?" *American Journal of Sociology* 99 (1993): 353–395.
53. Michael R. Gottfredson and Travis Hirschi, *A General Theory of Crime* (Stanford: Stanford University Press, 1990), p. 103.
54. Elaine Kamarck and William A. Galston, "Putting Children First: A Progressive Family Policy for the 1990s," whitepaper from the *Progressive Policy Institute* (27 September 1990), pp. 14–15.
55. Travis Hirschi, *Causes of Delinquency* (Berkeley: University of California Press, 1969), p. 299.
56. M. Anne Hill and June O'Neill, "Underclass Behaviors in the United States: Measurement and Analysis of Determinants," (Center for the Study of Business and Government, Baruch College/The City University of New York, August 1993), p. 73.
57. M. Eileen Matlack, M. S. Mac McGreevy, Robert Rouse, Charles Flatter, and Robert Marcus, "Family Correlates of Social Skill Deficits in Incarcerated and Nonincarcerated Adolescents," *Adolescence* 29 (1994): 117–132.
58. L. Edward Wells and Joseph H. Rankin, "Families and Delinquency: A Meta-Analysis of the Impact of Broken Homes," *Social Problems* 38 (1991): 71–89.
59. Douglas A. Smith and G. Roger Jarjoura, "Social Structure and Criminal Victimization," *Journal of Research in Crime and Delinquency* 25 (1988: 27–52.
60. David Blankenhorn, *Fatherless America: Confronting our Most Urgent Social Problem* (New York: Basic Books, 1995), p. 31.
61. McLanahan and Sandefur, 1994, p. 52.

These are women who earned either a regular high school diploma or a

GED. Only 55 percent of young mothers complete their high school diplomas on time, excluding GEDs. Regarding earning potential, there are indications that the General Equivalency Diploma (GED) is *not* equivalent to a regular high school diploma. See Stephen V. Cameron and James J. Heckman, "The Nonequivalence of High School Equivalents," *Journal of Labor Economics* 11 (1993): 1–47.

62. Wade F. Horn, "The Importance of Being Father," *American Civilization* (July 1995), p. 4.

63. Judith S. Musick, *Young, Poor, and Pregnant: The Psychology of Teenage Motherhood* (New Haven: Yale University Press, 1993), p. 60.

64. E. Mavis Hetherington, "Effects of Father Absence on Personality Development in Adolescent Daughters," *Developmental Psychology* 7 (1972): 313–326.

   Roland Fleck, of the Rosemead Graduate School of Professional Psychology, also found that when fathers were absent, adolescent girls were more likely to be sexually aggressive and engage in more premarital sexual intercourse than their counterparts in intact families. See J. Ronald Fleck, Cheryl C. Fuller, Sharon Malin, Dixon H. Miller, and Kenneth R. Acheson, "Father Psychological Absence and Heterosexual Behavior, Personal Adjustment, and Sex–Typing in Adolescent Girls," *Adolescence* 15 (1980): 847–860.

65. McLanahan and Sandefur, 1994, p. 53.

66. Irwin Garfinkel and Sara S. McLanahan, *Single Mothers and Their Children: A New American Dilemma* (Washington D. C.: The Urban Institute Press, 1986), pp. 30–31.

   McLanahan and Bumpass's study was "Intergenerational Consequences of Family Disruption," a paper presented at the annual meeting of the Population Association of America, San Francisco, California, April 3–5, 1986.

67. Hill and O'Neill, 1993, p. 90.

68. Emily Rosenbaum and Denise B. Kandel, "Early Onset of Adolescent Sexual Behavior and Drug Involvement," *Journal of Marriage and the Family* 52 (1990): 783–798.

69. Dennis P. Hogan, and Evelyn M. Kitagawa, "The Impact of Social Status, Family Structure, and Neighborhood on the Fertility of Black Adolescents," *American Journal of Sociology* 90 (1985): 825–855.

70. Stephen A. Small and Tom Luster, "Adolescent Sexual Activity: An Ecological Risk Factor Approach," *Journal of Marriage and the Family* 56 (1994): 181–192; Sharon D. White and Richard R. DeBlassie, "Adolescent Sexual Behavior," *Adolescence* 27 (1992): 183–191.

71. McLanahan and Sandefur, 1994, p. 37.

72. Arland Thornton and Donald Camburn, "The Influence of the Family on Premarital Sexual Attitudes and Behaviors," *Demography* 24 (1987): 323–340.

73. Lawrence L. Wu and Brian C. Martinson, "Family Structure and the Risk of a Premarital Birth," *American Sociological Review* 58 (1993): 210–232.

74. David T. Ellwood, *Poor Support: Poverty in the American Family* (New York: Basic Books, 1988), p. 46.

75. Garfinkel and McLanahan, 1986, p. 11.

76. U.S. Bureau of the Census, *Statistical Abstract of the United States: 1994* 114th ed. (Washington, D. C.), p. 387.

77. Dennis P. Hogan and Daniel T. Lichter, "Children and Youth: Living Arrangements and Welfare," in Reynolds Farley, ed., *State of the Union: America in the 1990s, Vol II Social Trends* (New York: Russell Sage Foundation, 1995) pp. 101–102.

78. *Families First*, Report of the National Commission on America's Urban Families, John Ashcroft, Chairman, (Washington, D.C., 1993), p. 25.

79. David J. Eggebeen and Daniel T. Lichter, "Race, Family Structure and Changing Poverty Among American Children," *American Sociological Review* 56 (1991): 801–817.

Eggebeen and Lichter measure *"deep poverty"* as a family income less than 50 percent of the official poverty threshold for a same-size family. *"Relative poverty"* is a level compared with the changing consumption level of a society. *"Official poverty"* is based on whether a family's income from all sources (i.e., earnings and public assistance, etc.) is below general poverty income thresholds. See p. 804.

80. Eggebeen and Lichter, 1991, p. 802.

81. U.S. Bureau of the Census, *Statistical Abstract of the United States: 1992* 112th ed. (Washington, D. C.); Victor R. Fuchs and Diane M. Reklis, "America's Children: Economic Perspectives and Policy Options," *Science,* (3 January 1992), p. 42.

82. "Are Families Our Biggest Asset?" *Investor's Business Daily* (19 August 1993), p. A-1.

83. Kamarck and Galston, 1990, p. 12.

84. Daniel Yankelovich, "Foreign Policy After the Election," *Foreign Affairs* (Fall 1992), pp. 3–4.

85. Ronald J. Angel and Jacqueline Lowe Worobey, "Single Motherhood and Children's Health," *Journal of Health and Social Behavior* 29 (1988): 38–52.

86. Dawson, 1991, pp. 573–574.

87. Dawson, 1991, pp. 578–579.

88. De-Kun Ling and Janet R. Daling, "Maternal Smoking, Low Birth Weight, and Ethnicity in Relation to Sudden Infant Death Syndrome," *American Journal of Epidemiology* 134 (1991): 958–964.

89. Ronald J. Angel and Jacqueline L. Angel, *Painful Inheritance: Health and the New Generation of Fatherless Families* (Madison: The University of Wisconsin Press, 1993), pp. 91–93.

90. Thomas M. Achenbach, Catherine T. Howell, Stephanie H. McConaughy, and Catherine Stanger, "Six-Year Predictor of Problems in a National Sample of Children and Youth: I. Cross Informant Syndromes," *Journal of American Academy Child and Adolescent Psychiatry* 34 (1995): 336–347.

91. Robert J. Haggerty, Klaus J. Roghmann, and Ivan B. Pless, *Child Health and the Community* (New York: John Wiley and Sons, 1975).

92. Theodore L. Dorpat, Joan K. Jackson, and Herbert S. Ripley, "Broken Homes and Attempted and Completed Suicide," *Archives of General Psychiatry* 12 (1965): 213–216; cited in Angel and Angel, 1993, p. 100.

93. James Peterson and Nicholas Zill, "Marital Disruption, Parent-Child Relationships and Behavioral Problems in Children," *Journal of Marriage and the Family* 48 (1986): 295–307.

94. John Guidubaldi and Helene Cleminshaw, "Divorce, Family Health, and Child Adjustment," *Family Relations* 34 (1985): 35–41; Jane D. McLeod and Michael J. Shanahan, "Poverty, Parenting, and Children's Mental Health," *American Sociological Review* 58 (1993): 351–366; Susan Gore, Robert Aseltine, and Mary Ellen Colton, "Social Structure, Life Stress and Depressive Symptoms in a High-School Aged Population," *Journal of Health and Social Behavior* 33 (1992): 97–113.

95. Angel and Angel, 1993, p. 101.

96. Terry E. Duncan, Susan Duncan, and Hyman Hops, "The Effects of Family Cohesiveness and Peer Encouragement on the Development of Adolescent Alcohol Use: A Cohort-Sequential Approach to the Analysis of Longitudinal Data," *Journal of Studies on Alcohol* 55 (1994): 588–599; Jeannine Studer, "A Comparison of the Self-Concepts of Adolescent from Intact, Maternal Custodial, and Paternal Custodial Families," *Journal of Divorce and Remarriage* 19 (1993): 219–227.

97. McLanahan and Sandefur, 1994, p. 38.

Chapter Five: Shattering the Myth: The Broken Promises of Divorce and Remarriage
1. Ailsa Burns and Cath Scott, *Mother-Headed Families and Why They Have Increased* (Hillsdale, N.J.: Lawrence Erlbaum Associates Publishers, 1994), pp. 5, 9.
2. Marilyn Ihinger-Tallman and Kay Pasley, "Divorce and Remarriage in the American Family: A Historical Review," in Kay Pasley and Marilyn Ihinger-Tallman, eds., *Remarriage and Stepparenting: Current Research and Theory* (New York: Guilford Press, 1987), pp. 3–18.
3. David Popenoe, *Life Without Father: Compelling New Evidence that Fatherhood and Marriage Are Indispensable for the Good of Children and Society* (New York: The Free Press, 1996), p. 21; Andrew Cherlin, *Marriage, Divorce, and Remarriage* (Cambridge: Harvard University Press, 1992), p. 25.
4. Cherlin, 1992, p. 126.
5. Barbara Dafoe Whitehead, *The Divorce Culture* (New York: Knopf, 1997), p. 143.
6. Norval D. Glenn, "The Recent Trend in Marital Success in the United States," *Journal of Marriage and the Family* 53 (1991), pp. 261–270.
7. Glenn, 1991, pp. 268–269.
8. Judith S. Wallerstein and Sandra Blakeslee, *Second Chances: Men, Women, and Children a Decade After Divorce* (New York: Ticknor & Fields, 1990), p. xxi.
9. "Marriage in America: A Report to the Nation," a report issued by the Council on Families in America; Institute for American Values, 1995, p. 3.
   The report has also been reprinted in David Popenoe, Jean Bethke Elshtain and David Blankenhorn, eds., *Promises to Keep: Decline and Renewal of Marriage in America* (Lanham, Md.: Rowman & Littlefield Publishers, 1996), pp. 293–318.
10. Wallerstein and Blakeslee, 1990, p. x.
11. Wallerstein and Blakeslee, 1990, p. xv.
12. Judith S. Wallerstein and Joan B. Kelly, *Surviving the Breakup: How Children and Parents Cope with Divorce* (New York, Basic Books, 1980).
13. Wallerstein and Blakeslee, 1990, p. xvii.
14. Wallerstein and Blakeslee, 1990, p. xviii.
15. Wallerstein and Kelly, 1980, p. 11.
16. Judith S. Wallerstein, "The Long-Term Effects of Divorce on Children: A Review," *Journal of the American Academy of Child and Adolescent Psychiatry* 30 (1991): 349–360.
17. Wallerstein, 1991, p. 358.
18. Wallerstein and Blakeslee, 1990, p. xix.
19. Wallerstein's work has been widely acclaimed. However, it is not without its critics. Some of the most serious criticism comes from Frank Furstenberg and Andrew Cherlin, who do not necessarily disagree with Wallerstein's final conclusion, however, they question the significance of her study population. See Frank F. Furstenberg and Andrew J. Cherlin, *Divided Families: What Happens to Children When Parents Part* (Cambridge: Harvard University Press, 1991), p. 68.
   It should be noted that Wallerstein's original study has been vindicated, not only by the large body of data which is presented in this chapter, but also by a meta-analysis she conducted and published in 1991. In this analysis she considered the work of nine separate longitudinal studies regarding divorce's impact on children. The collective findings are very similar to the conclusion reached by her original study. See Wallerstein, 1991, cited above.
20. E. Mavis Hetherington, "Family Relations Six Years after Divorce," in Kay Pasley and Marilyn Ihinger-Tallman, eds., *Remarriage and Stepparenting: Current Research and Theory* (New York: Guilford Press, 1987), pp. 185–205.
21. E. Mavis Hetherington, Margaret Stanely-Hagan, and Edward R. Anderson, "Marital Transitions: A Child's Perspective," *American Psychologist* 44 (1989): 303–312.
22. Catherine Kohler Riessman and Naomi Gerstel, "Martial Dissolution and

Health: Do Males or Females Have Greater Risk?" *Social Science and Medicine* 20 (1985): 627–635.

23. Hetherington, 1987, p. 192.
24. James J. Lynch, *The Broken Heart: The Medical Consequences of Loneliness* (New York: Basic Books, 1977).
25. Vicki Garvin, Neil Kalter, and James Hansell, "Divorced Women: Individual Differences in Stressors, Mediating Factors, and Adjustment Outcomes," *American Journal of Orthopsychiatry* 62 (1993): 232–240.
26. Debra Umberson and Christine L. Williams, "Divorced Fathers: Parental Role Strain and Psychological Distress," *Journal of Family Issues* 14 (1993): 378–400.
27. Robin W. Simon, "Parental Role Strain, Salience of Parental Identity and Gender Differences in Psychological Distress," *Journal of Health and Social Behavior* 33 (1992):2 5–35; E. Mavis Hetherington, M. Cox, and R. Cox, "Effects of Divorce on Parents and Children," in Michael Lamb, ed., *Nontraditional Families* (Hillsdale, N.J.: Lawrence Erlbaum and Associates, Publishers, 1982), pp. 233–288; Wallerstein and Kelly, 1980, pp. 36–41.
28. Hetherington, Stanely-Hagan, and Anderson, 1989, p. 308.
29. Sylvie Drapeau and Camil Bouchard, "Support Networks and Adjustment Among 6- to 11-Year-Olds From Maritally Disrupted and Intact Families," *Journal of Divorce and Remarriage* 19 (1993): 75–97.
30. Hetherington, 1987, p. 193.
31. Hetherington, 1987, p. 193.
32. Hetherington, Stanely-Hagan, and Anderson, 1989, p. 308.
33. Hetherington, Cox, and Cox, 1982, pp. 233–288.
34. E. Mavis Hetherington, "Stress and Coping in Children and Families," in Anna-Beth Doyle, Dolores Gold, and Debbie S. Moskowitz, eds., *Children in Families Under Stress* (San Francisco: Jossey-Bass, 1984), pp. 7–33.
35. Hetherington, 1984, p. 12.
36. Hetherington, 1984, p. 24; see also Wallerstein and Kelly, 1980.
37. Michael Gurian, *The Wonder of Boys: What Parents, Mentors and Educators Can Do to Shape Boys into Exceptional Men* (New York: Jeremy P. Tarcher/Putnam Books, 1996), p. 44.
38. Ann Goetting, "Divorce Outcome Research: Issues and Perspectives," in Arlene S. Skolnick and Jerome H. Skolnick, eds., *The Family in Transition* (Boston: Little, Brown, and Co., 1983), pp. 367–386.
39. Hetherington, Stanley-Hagan, and Anderson, 1989, p. 308.
40. Hetherington, Cox, and Cox, 1982, pp. 233–288; Hetherington, 1987, p. 193.
41. Hetherington, 1987, p. 194.
42. Hetherington, 1987, p. 194.
43. L. Edward Wells and Joseph H. Rankin, "Families and Delinquency: A Meta-Analysis of the Impact of Broken Homes," *Social Problems* 38 (1991): 71–89.
44. Drapeau and Bouchard, 1993, p. 78.
45. The *National Survey of Children* comprises two waves of longitudinal studies on children in the United States. The first wave was conducted in the fall and winter of 1976–1977 and was based on a national probability sample of children from seven to eleven years old. The second wave of the study was conducted in the spring and summer of 1981, when the children were twelve to sixteen years old. The follow-up data was gathered on a total of 1,423 children.
46. James L. Peterson and Nicholas Zill, "Marital Disruption, Parent-Child Relationships, and Behavior Problems in Children," *Journal of Marriage and the Family* 1986, 48:295–307.
47. Peterson and Zill, 1986, p. 298.
48. Peterson and Zill, 1986, pp. 301–305.
49. Nicholas Zill, Donna Morrison, and Mary Jo Coiro, "Long-Term Effects of Parental Divorce on Parent-Child Relationships, Adjustment, and Achievement

in Young Adulthood," *Journal of Family Psychology* 7 1993: 91–103.
50. Zill, Morrison, and Coiro, 1993, pp. 99–100.
51. Teresa M. Cooney, "Young Adults' Relations With Parents: The Influence of Recent Parental Divorce," *Journal of Marriage and the Family* 56 (1994): 45–56.
52. Cooney, 1994, p. 53.
53. Paul R. Amato, "Children's Adjustment to Divorce: Theories, Hypotheses, and Empirical Support," *Journal of Marriage and the Family* 55 (1993): 23–38.
54. Paul R. Amato and Bruce Keith (a), "Parental Divorce and the Well-Being of Children: A Meta-Analysis," *Psychological Bulletin* 110 (1991): 26–46.
55. Those domains were (1) *school achievement* (taken from standardized achievement tests, grades, teachers ratings, or intelligence); (2) *conduct* (misbehavior, aggression, or delinquency); (3) *psychological adjustment* (depression, anxiety, happiness); (4) *self-concept* (self-esteem, perceived competence, or internal locus of control); (5) *social adjustment* (popularity, loneliness, or cooperativeness); (6) *mother-child relationships* (affection, help, or quality of interaction); (7) *father-child relationships* and (8) other. See Amato and Keith, 1991 (a), p. 28.
56. Paul R. Amato, "Life-Span Adjustment of Children to Their Parents' Divorce," *The Future of Children* 4 (1994): 43–164. Published by The Center for the Future of Children, Los Altos, California.
57. Amato and Keith, 1991 (a), p. 30.
58. Drapeau and Bouchard, 1993, pp. 82, 88.
59. Donna Ruane Morrison and Andrew J. Cherlin, "The Divorce Process and Young Children's Well-Being: A Prospective Analysis," *Journal of Marriage and the Family* 57 (1995): 800–812
60. Michael Workman and John Beer, "Depression, Suicide Ideation, and Aggression Among High School Students Whose Parents Are Divorced and Use Alcohol At Home," *Psychological Reports* 70 (1992): 503–511.
61. John Guidubaldi and Helen Cleminshaw, "Divorce, Family Health, and Child Adjustment," *Family Relations* 34 (1985): 35–41.
62. Beverly Raphael, Jeff Cubis, Michael Dunne, Terry Lewin, and Brian Kelly, "The Impact of Parental Loss on Adolescent's Psychological Characteristics," *Adolescence* 25 (1990): 689–700.
63. Jeannine Studer, "A Comparison of Adolescents from Intact, Maternal Custodial, and Paternal Custodial Families," *Journal of Divorce and Remarriage* 19 (1993): 219–227.
64. David M. Ferguson, John Horwood, and Michael Lynskey, "Parental Separation, Adolescent Psychopathology and Problem Behaviors," *Journal of the American Academy of Child and Adolescent Psychiatry* 33 (1994): 1122–1131.
65. Paul R. Amato and Bruce Keith (b), "Parental Divorce and Adult Well-Being: A Meta-Analysis, *Journal of Marriage and the Family* 53 (1991): 43–48.
66. These categories are very comprehensive, consisting of: (1) *psychological* well-being (emotional adjustment, depression, anxiety, and life satisfaction); (2) *behavior/conduct* (criminal behavior, drug use, alcoholism, suicide, teenage pregnancy, and teenage marriage); (3) *use of mental health services;* (4) *self-concept* (self-esteem, self-efficacy, sense of power, and internal locus of control); (5) *social well-being* (number of friends, social participation, social support, and contact with parents and extended family); (6) *marital quality* (marital satisfaction, marital disagreements, and marital instability); (7) *separation or divorce;* (8) *one-parent family status;* (9) *quality of relations with one's children;* (10) *quality of general family relations* (overall ratings of family life); (11) *educational attainment* (high school graduation, years of education); (12) *occupational quality* (occupational prestige, job autonomy, and job satisfaction); (13) *material quality of life* (income, assets held, housing quality, welfare dependency, and perceived economic strain); (14) *physical health* (chronic problems and disability); and (15) other. See Amato and Keith, 1991 (b), p. 46.

67. Amato, 1994, p. 146.
68. Amato and Keith, 1991 (a), p. 40.
69. Frank F. Furstenberg and Julien Teitler, "Reconsidering the Effects of Marital Disruption: What Happens to Children of Divorce in Early Adulthood?" *Journal of Family Issues* 15 (1994): 173–190; Elizabeth Mazur, "Development Differences in Children's Understanding of Marriage, Divorce, and Remarriage," *Journal of Applied Developmental Psychology* 14 (1993): 191–212; Hilevi M. Aro and Ulla K. Palossaari, "Parental Divorce, Adolescence, and Transition to Young Adulthood: A Follow-Up Study," *American Journal of Orthopsychiatry* 62 (1992): 421–429; Bryan Rodgers, "Pathways Between Parental Divorce and Adult Depression," *Journal of Child Psychology and Psychiatry* 35 (1994): 1289–1308.
70. Anders Romelsjo, George Kaplan, Richard Cohen, Peter Allebeck, and Sven Andreasson, "Protective Factors and Social Risk Factors for Hospitalization and Mortality Among Young Men," *American Journal of Epidemiology* 135 (1992): 649–658.
71. Allan Bloom, *The Closing of the American Mind: How Higher Education Has Failed Democracy and Impoverished the Souls of Today's Students* (New York: Simon & Schuster, 1987), p. 120.
72. Amato, 1994, pp. 150–152.
73. See also Frank Furstenberg and C. W. Nord, "Parenting Apart: Patterns of Childrearing After Marital Disruption," *Journal of Marriage and the Family* 47 (1985): 893–904; and J. A. Setzer, "Relationships Between Fathers and Children Who Live Apart: The Father's Role After Separation," *Journal of Marriage and the Family* 53 (1991): 79–101.
74. Hetherington, Cox, and Cox, 1982, p. 233.
75. Lenore J. Weitzman, *The Divorce Revolution: The Unexpected Social and Economic Consequences for Women and Children in America* (New York: The Free Press, 1987), p. 323.
76. Richard R. Peterson, "A Re-evaluation of the Economic Consequences of Divorce," *American Sociological Review* 61 (1996) :528–536. Weitzman's response to Peterson follows this article on page 537.
77. Atlee L. Stroup and Gene E. Pollock, "Economic Consequences of Marital Dissolution," *Journal of Divorce & Remarriage* 22 (1994): 7–54.
78. William J. Goode, *World Changes in Divorce Patterns* (New Haven: Yale University Press, 1993), p. 166.
79. Furstenberg and Cherlin, 1991, p. 56; see also Glen H. Elder, Jr., *Children of the Great Depression* (Chicago: University of Chicago Press, 1974).
80. J. D. McLeod and M. J. Shanahan, "Poverty, Parenting and Children's Mental Health," *American Sociological Review* 58 (1993): 351–366; D. R. Williams, "Socioeconomic Differentials in Health: A Review and Redirection," *Social Psychology Quarterly* 52 (1990): 81–99; Sara S. McLanahan and Karen Booth, "Mother-only Families: Problems, Prospects, and Politics," *Journal of Marriage and the Family* 51 (1989): 557–580; John Guidubaldi, Helen Cleminshaw, J. D. Perry, and C. S. McLoughlin, "The Impact of Parental Divorce on Children: Report of the Nationwide NASP Study," *School Psychology Review* 12 (1983): 300–323.
81. Furstenberg and Cherlin, 1991, p. 65.
82. See Eleanor E. Maccoby and John A. Martin, "Socialization in the Context of the Family: Parent-Child Interactions," in E. Mavis Hetherington, ed., *Handbook of Child Psychology* vol. 4 (New York: John Wiley, 1983), pp. 1–101.
83. Sara S. McLanahan, "Family Structure and Stress: A Longitudinal Comparison of Two-Parent and Female-Headed Families," *Journal of Marriage and the Family* 45 (1984): 347–357.
84. Furstenberg and Cherlin, 1991, p. 67.

85. Andrew Cherlin, "Remarriage as an Incomplete Institution," *The American Journal of Sociology* 84 (1978): 634–650.

86. Charles Hobart, "Conflict in Remarriages," *Journal of Divorce and Remarriage* 15 (1991): 69–86.

87. Cherlin, 1978, p. 639.

88. David Popenoe (a), "The Evolution of Marriage and the Problems of Stepfamilies: A Biosocial Perspective," in Alan Booth and Judy Dunn, eds., *Stepfamilies: Who Benefits? Who Does Not?* (Hillsdale, N.J.: Lawrence Erlbaum Associates, 1994), pp. 3–27.

89. James H. Bray, "Children's Development in Early Remarriage," in E. Mavis Hetherington and J. D. Arasteh eds., *Impact of Divorce, Single-Parenting, and Stepparenting on Children* (Hillsdale, N.J.: Erlbaum, 1988), pp. 279–298.

90. E. Mavis Hetherington and Kathleen M. Jodl, "Stepfamilies as Settings for Child Development," in Alan Booth and Judy Dunn, eds., *Stepfamilies: Who Benefits? Who Does Not?* (Hillsdale, N.J.: Lawrence Erlbaum Associates, 1994), pp. 55–79.

91. Frank F. Furstenberg, Jr., "Divorce and the American Family," *Annual Review of Sociology* 16 (1990): 379–403.

92. Stith Thompson, *Motif-Index of Folk Literature: A Classification of Narrative Element in Folktales, Ballads, Myths, Fables, Mediaeval Romances, Exempla, Fabliaux, Jest-books, and Local Legend* rev. ed. in 6 volumes (Bloomington: Indiana University Press, 1955).

93. Popenoe, 1994 (a), p. 5.
    Some researchers and family commentators appraise such statements regarding stepfamilies as dangerous because they can serve to stigmatize people who find themselves in these nontraditional families. This stigmatization can serve only to contribute to the problems these families face, it is argued, so it is best not to make them at all. Norval Glenn questions the veracity of this concern. He explains that "any stigma attached to stepfamilies has declined appreciably in recent years, and it is unlikely that stigma now ranks high among the causes of stress and discomfort of persons in those families, or that the content of scholarly publications has much effect on the amount of stigma." See Norval D. Glenn, "Biology, Evolutionary Theory, and Family Social Science," in Alan Booth and Judy Dunn eds., *Stepfamilies: Who Benefits? Who Does Not?* (Hillsdale, N.J.: Lawrence Erlbaum Associates, 1994), pp. 45–51.

94. Andrew Greeley, *Faithful Attraction: Discovering Intimacy, Love, and Fidelity in American Marriage* (New York: A Tor Book, 1991), p. 200.

95. David R. Hall and John Z. Zhao, "Cohabitation and Divorce in Canada: Testing the Selectivity Hypothesis," *Journal of Marriage and the Family* 57: 421–427.

96. Lynn K. White and Alan Booth, "The Quality and Stability of Remarriages: The Role of Stepchildren," *American Sociological Review* 50 (1985): 689–698.

97. White and Booth, 1985, p. 697.

98. Elizabeth Thomson, Sara S. McLanahan, and Roberta Braun Curtin, "Family Structure, Gender, and Parental Socialization," *Journal of Marriage and the Family* 54 (1992): 368–378.

99. Thomson, McLanahan, and Curtin, 1992, p. 375.

100. Furstenberg and Cherlin, 1991, pp. 81–82.

101. Frank F. Furstenberg, "The New Extended Family: The Experience of Parents and Children After Remarriage," in Kay Pasley and Marilyn Ihinger-Tallman eds., *Remarriage and Stepparenting: Current Research and Theory* (New York: Guilford Press, 1987), pp. 42–61.

102. Hetherington and Jodl, 1994, p. 66.

103. Furstenberg, 1987, p. 54.

104. Furstenberg, 1987, p. 50.

105. "Shuttle Diplomacy," *Psychology Today* (July/August 1993), pp. 15–16.

106. Cheryl L. Pruett, Robert J. Calsyn, and Fred M. Jensen, "Social Support Received by Children in Stepmother, Stepfather, and Intact Families," *Journal of Divorce and Remarriage* 19 (1993): 165–179.

107. Douglas B. Downey, "Understanding Academic Achievement Among Children in Stephouseholds: The Role of Parental Resources, Sex of Stepparent, and Sex of Child," *Social Forces* 73 (1995): 875–894. See also Hetherington, 1987; Hetherington, 1989; Peterson and Zill, 1986; Pruett, Calsyn, and Jensen, 1993.

108. This figure is for mother-stepfather families. Children from father-stepmother families are *five* times as likely to need or receive this type of help than those living with mother and father. There were five times as many mother-stepfather families than father-stepmother families in this 1981 study conducted by the National Center for Health Statistics (NCHS).

109. Nicholas Zill, "Behavior, Achievement, and Health Problems Among Children in Stepfamilies: Findings from a National Survey of Child Health," in E. Mavis Hetherington and J. D. Arasteh eds., *Impact of Divorce, Single-Parenting, and Stepparenting on Children* (Hillsdale, N.J.: Erlbaum, 1988), pp. 325–367.

110. Nicholas Zill, "Understanding Why Children in Stepfamilies Have More Learning and Behavior Problems Than Children in Nuclear Families," in Alan Booth and Judy Dunn eds., *Stepfamilies: Who Benefits? Who Does Not?* (Hillsdale, N.J.: Lawrence Erlbaum Associates, 1994), p. 99.

111. Zill, 1994, p. 100.

112. Zill, 1994, pp. 103–105.

113. Zill, 1994, p. 102.
However, Zill warns that "high-involvement [by stepfamilies] does not totally ameliorate the negative effects of marital conflict, divorce, and remarriage" (p. 105). He explains that while all children from high to moderate involvement families showed lower incidence of grade repetition, the difference here was less pronounced in stepfamilies.

114. Zill, Morrison, and Coiro, 1993, pp. 99, 101.
Regarding the income benefit of stepfamilies over single-parent families, Zill reports that the average incomes of mother-stepfather families are somewhat lower than in biological, two-parent families. See Zill, 1994, p. 98.

115. M. Eileen Matlack, M. S. Mac McGreevy, Robert Rouse, Charles Flatter, and Robert Marcus, "Family Correlates of Social Skill Deficits in Incarcerated and Nonincarcerated Adolescents," *Adolescence* 29 (1994): 117–132; Randal D. Day, "The Transition to First Intercourse Among Racially and Culturally Diverse Youth," *Journal of Marriage and the Family* 54 (1992): 749–762. See also Furstenberg, 1991, pp. 394, 396.

116. Barbara A. Mitchell, "Family Structure and Leaving the Nest: A Social Resource Perspective," *Sociological Perspectives* 37 (1994): 651–671.

117. Deborah A. Dawson, "Family Structure and Children's Health and Well-being: Data from the National Health Interview Survey on Child Health, *Journal of Marriage and the Family* 53 (1991): 573–584.

118. David Popenoe (b), "The Family Condition in America," in Henry J. Aaron and others., eds., *Values and Public Policy* (Washington D.C.: Brookings Institute, 1994), pp. 81–112.

119. Sara S. McLanahan, Nan Marie Astone, and Nadine F. Marks, "The Role of Mother-only Families in Reproducing Poverty," in Aleth C. Huston, ed., *Children in Poverty: Child Development and Public Policy* (Cambridge: Cambridge University Press, 1991), pp. 51–78.

120. Nan Marie Astone and Sara S. McLanahan, "Family Structure, Parental Practices, and High School Completion," *American Sociological Review* 56 (1991): 309–320. See also Downey, 1995, and Furstenberg, 1987.

121. Frank F. Furstenberg, "History and Current Status of Divorce in the United States," *The Future of Children: Children and Divorce* 4 (1994): 29–43.

122. Hetherington and Jodl, 1994, pp. 57–58.
123. Popenoe, 1994 (a), p. 19.
    Hetherington and Jodl find credence for this sociobiological theory in their essay (same volume, p. 67) explaining that even in long-established blended families, biological parents and children tended to show more warmth and affection for each other regardless of the type of family they were in as compared with parent and child in a steprelationship.
124. Popenoe, 1994 (a), p. 20.
125. Margo Wilson and Martin Daly, "Risk of Maltreatment of Children Living With Stepparents," in Richard J. Gelles and Jane B. Lancaster, eds., *Child Abuse and Neglect: Biosocial Dimensions* (Hawthorne, N.Y.: Aldine De Gruyter, 1987), pp. 215–232.
126. Glenn, 1994, p. 49.
127. James A. Sweet and Larry L. Bumpass, *American Families and Households* (New York: Russell Sage Foundation, 1987), table 5.12.
128. Martin Daly and Margo Wilson, "Child Abuse and Other Risks of Not Living with Both Parents," *Ethology and Sociobiology* 6 (1985): 197–210.
129. Wilson and Daly, 1987, p. 227.
130. Wilson and Daly, 1987, p. 230.
131. Daly and Wilson, 1985, pp. 205–206.
132. Daly and Wilson, 1985, p. 206.
133. Michael Gordon, "The Family Environment of Sexual Abuse: A Comparison of Natal and Stepfather Abuse," *Child Abuse and Neglect* 13 (1989): 121–130.
134. Stephanie Coontz, *The Way We Never Were* (New York: Basic Books, 1992); E. L. Kain, *The Myth of Family Decline* (Lexington: D. C. Heath, 1990); Judith Stacey, *Brave New Families: Stories of Democratic Upheaval in Late Twentieth-Century America* (New York: Basic Books, 1990).
135. Marilyn Ihinger-Tallman and Kay Pasley, "Divorce and Remarriage in the American Family: A Historical Review," in Kay Pasley and Marilyn Ihinger-Tallman eds., *Remarriage and Stepparenting: Current Research and Theory* (New York: Guilford Press, 1987), pp. 3–18.
136. Steven Mintz and Susan Kellogg, *Domestic Revolutions: A Social History of American Family Life* (New York: The Free Press, 1988), p. 38.
137. Cherlin, 1978, p. 637.
138. Ihinger-Tallman and Pasley, 1987, p. 10.
139. Cherlin, 1978, p. 637.
140. Cherlin, 1978, p. 638.
141. Amato, 1994, pp. 143–144.
142. Ihinger-Tallman and Pasley, 1987, p. 14.
143. David R. Hall and John Z. Zhao, "Cohabitation and Divorce in Canada: Testing the Selectivity Hypothesis," *Journal of Marriage and the Family* 57 (1995): 421–427.
144. Ihinger-Tallman and Pasley, 1987, p. 14.
    The studies they reference are J. Burgoyne and D. Clark, *Making a Go of It: A Study of Stepfamilies in Sheffield* (London: Routledge and Kegan Paul, 1984); L. Duberman, "Stepkin Relationships," *Journal of Marriage and the Family* 35 (1973,): 283–292; L. Duberman, *The Reconstituted Family: A Study of Remarried Couples and Their Children* (Chicago: Nelson-Hall, 1975); E. Ferri, *Stepchildren: A National Study* (Windsor: NFER-Nelson, 1984).
145. I. M. Joung, H. Van De Mheen, K. Stronk, F. W. Van Poppel, and J. P. Mackenbach, "Differences in Self-Reported Morbidity by Marital Status and by Living Arrangement," *International Journal of Epidemiology* 23 (1994): 91–97.
146. Bryan Rodgers, "Pathways Between Parental Divorce and Adult Depression," *Journal of Child Psychology and Psychiatry* 35 (1994): 1289–1308.
147. Kathleen E. Kiernan, "The Impact of Family Disruption in Childhood on Transitions Made in Young Adult Life," *Populations Studies* 46 (1992): 213–234.

148. Wells and Rankin, 1991, p. 84.
149. Mitchell, 1994, p. 653.
150. James Egan, "When Fathers are Absent," address given at the National Summit on Fatherhood, sponsored by the National Fatherhood Initiative; Dallas, Texas, October 27, 1994.

Epilogue: The Future of Marriage

1. Quoted in Steven Mintz and Susan Kellogg, *Domestic Revolutions: A Social History of American Family Life* (New York, The Free Press, 1988), p. 210.
2. *The Negro Family: The Case for National Action* (Washington, D. C.: Office of Policy Planning and Research, U.S. Department of Labor, March 1965), p. 8.
3. Mintz and Kellogg, 1988, p. 213.
4. Mintz and Kellogg, 1988, p. 211.
5. Daniel Patrick Moynihan, "Defining Deviancy Down," *The American Scholar* 62 (1993): 17–30.
6. Moynihan, 1993, p. 19.
7. Moynihan, 1993, p. 27.
8. Moynihan, 1993, p. 26.
9. Norval D. Glenn, "Values, Attitudes and the State of American Marriage," in David Popenoe, Jean Bethke Elshtain and David Blankenhorn, eds., *Promises to Keep: Decline and Renewal of Marriage in America* (Lanham, Md: Rowman & Littlefield Publishers, 1996), pp. 15-33.
10. Robert Bellah, Richard Marsden, William Sullivan, Ann Swidler, and Steven Tipton, *Habits of the Heart: Individualism in American Life* (New York: Harper & Row, 1985), pp. 85–112.
11. C. S. Lewis, *The Four Loves* (New York: Harcourt Brace Jovanovich, 1960), pp. 134–135.
12. Eric Fromm, *The Art of Loving* (New York: Harper & Row, 1956, 1962), pp. 55–56.
13. G. K. Chesterton, *What's Wrong With the World* (San Francisco: Ignatius Press, 1910, 1994), p. 46.

   Another stimulating discussion of the virtue of family is found in Chesterton's "On Certain Modern Writers and the Institution of the Family," where he turns our understanding of family upside down. He explains that many modern writers denounce the family because it is "not always very congenial." Of course it is not, says Chesterton, and this is not a fault of the family, but its defining virtue. Chesterton says the family is like the world: It bothers us and demands that we change. It asks something of us. It asks that we be considerate, temperate, and patient—someone other than who we are now. Marriage and family prunes us and that is not pleasant, but necessary. A much-needed message for our time. This essay can be found in Chesterton's *Collected Works* vol. 1 (San Francisco: Ignatius Press, 1986), pp. 136–145.
14. See Barbara Dafoe Whitehead, "The Failure of Sex Education," *Atlantic Monthly* (October 1994), pp. 55–74.
15. For a detailed survey of twenty leading family education textbooks and how they treat the issue of marriage, see Norval Glenn's working paper, "The Textbook Story of American Marriages and Families," prepared for the Council on Families in America, publication forthcoming from the Institute for American Values.
16. A survey of the AAMFT's annual conference manuals for the past few years indicates that the overwhelming majority of seminar workshops and plenary sessions are on topics that deal with various types of family pathology rather than on how to build strong first-time marriages.
17. Alexis de Tocqueville, *Democracy in America* (New York: Anchor Books, 1969), p. 291.
18. Bellah and others., 1985, p. 85.

Index

-M-

Madonna, 29, 190n26
Malinowski, Bronislaw, 101, 201n17
Malkin, Catherine, 186, 195n49
Malzberg, Benjamin, 84-85, 183, 199n47,48
Margolin, Leslie, 66, 186, 195n50
Marriage and adults, 71-95
  benefits for women, 80, 81-83, 85-86, 88-90, 93-94
  general well-being and physical health, 76-93
  international consistency of findings, 93-94
  and mental health, 84-87
  rates of people entering, 21-22
  rates of never-marrieds, 21-22
marriage manuals, 37-38
Martinson, Brian, 116, 204n73
Mastekaasa, Arne, 93-94, 200n91-93
masturbation, 46
Mattox, William, 201n2
McGovern, James R., 35, 191n3,5,6
McLanahan, Sara, 93, 102-105, 107-110, 113, 115-117, 122, 142, 151, 184, 200n86, 202n24-32, 203n43,46-48,61 204n65,66,71,75, 205n97, 209n80,83, 210n98,99 211n119,120
McNeal, Ralph, 108, 203n44
medical training, residency and marriage, 88-90
Mencken, H. L., 35
mental health, 84-87
Michael, Robert T. and others, Sex in America, 41-43, 192n39,41,42,43,46
Mintz, Steven (and Susan Kellogg), Domestic Revolutions, 26, 154, 161, 181, 190n1, 212n136, 213n1,3,4
Mitchell, Barbara, 151, 157, 211n116, 213n149
morbidity and mortality, adults, 79-84, 93
  compared to living w/ non-spouse, 82, 93
Morowitz, Harold, 81, 198n37

Morrow, Prince A., 40
Moynihan, Daniel Patrick, 102, 160-162, 201n19,20, 213n5-8
Musick, Judith, Young, Poor and Pregnant, 114, 204n63

-N-

National Opinion Research Center, 41
nest-leaving process, 60, 151, 157
Never-married parents
  rates of children living with, 23, 25
Newcomb, Michael, 59, 63, 67, 182, 194n18, 195n29, 196n58
Newsweek, 29, 190n26
Nock, Steven, 62, 182, 194n11, 195n31
non-marital births, rates of, 23-25

-O-

O'Neill, June, 112, 115, 203n56, 204n67
O'Neill, Nena and George, Open Marriage, 72, 196n4

-P-

Pasley, Kay, 155, 185-186, 206n2, 20, 210n101, 212n135,138,142
Pearlin, Leonard, 75, 91-92, 197n10, 199n57
Péguy, Charles, 13, 189n3
Peterson, James, 121, 205n93, 207n46-48, 211n107
Peterson, Richard, 142, 184, 209n76, polis, 31
Pollock, Gene, 142, 209n77
Popenoe, David, 14, 24, 31, 98-99, 111, 126, 144-145, 151-152, 181, 184, 189n5, 195n48, 201n5,6, 203n50, 206n3,9, 210n88,93, 211n118, 212n123,124, 213n9
Popenoe, Paul, Modern Marriage, 37, 191n21
Prager, Dennis, 193n76
Progressive Policy Institute, 111, 118
Psychology Today, 147, 210n105

Author

GLENN STANTON is the research analyst for marriage and family studies and the Director of Seminars and Research at Focus on the Family. His research has been translated into many foreign languages and he has published articles in a variety of magazines and newspapers around the country, including *Christianity Today*, *The American Enterprise*, *The World and I*, and the *Atlanta Journal-Constitution*. Glenn is also a contributor to *The Fatherhood Movement: A Call To Action*.

A graduate of the University of West Florida, Glenn earned a Masters degree in interdisciplinary humanities with an emphasis in philosophy, history, and religion. He also taught in each of these disciplines.

Glenn lives in Colorado Springs with his wife Jackie, a former elementary school teacher, and their three children, Olivia, and twins, Schaeffer and Sophie. Glenn enjoys reading, foraging in used book stores, listening to obscure music, and most of all, spending time with his wife and playing with his children.

Practical ideas to make your marriage last

Tightening the Knot

Here's tried-and-true advice from the real experts. *Tightening the Knot* collects wisdom, encouragement, and humor about marriage from real couples who have experienced first-hand what it means to invest in marriage and make it last.

Tightening the Knot
Susan Alexander Yates and Allison Yates Gaskins
$6/Paperback

How to Be Your Husband's Best Friend
How to Be Your Wife's Best Friend

Part of making your marriage last is not just telling your spouse you care—it's *showing* you care. Each of these books offers 365 simple and creative ideas to express your love in tangible and exciting ways. You'll be amazed at how such small investments can pay such big dividends.

How to be Your Husband's Best Friend
Cay Bolin and Cindy Trent
$6/Paperback

How to Be Your Wife's Best Friend
Dan Bolin and John Trent
$6/Paperback

Available at your local bookstore, or call (800) 366-7788.